The Complete Book of Fashion Illustration

The Complete Book of Fashion Illustration THIRD EDITION

SHARON LEE TATE
The Fashion Center, Los Angeles
Trade-Technical College

MONA SHAFER EDWARDS
The Fashion Center, Los Angeles
Trade-Technical College

Prentice Hall
Englewood Cliffs, New Jersey 07632

Library of Congress Cataloging-in-Publication Data

Tate, Sharon Lee.
  The complete book of fashion illustration / Sharon Lee Tate, Mona
Shafer Edwards. — 3rd ed.
    p. cm.
  Includes index.
  ISBN 0-13-059222-6
  1. Fashion drawing. I. Edwards, Mona Shafer, [date].
II. Title.
  TT509.T37   1996   95-1946
  741.6'72—dc 20   CIP

Acquisitions editor: Elizabeth Sugg
Director of Production and Manufacturing: Bruce Johnson
Managing Editor: Mary Carnis
Editorial/production supervision: Inkwell Publishing Services
Cover design: Mona Shafer Edwards
Manufacturing buyer: Edward O'Dougherty

©1996 by Prentice-Hall, Inc.
A Simon & Schuster Company
Englewood Cliffs, New Jersey 07632

Printed in the United States of America

10 9 8 7 6 5 4 3 2 1

ISBN 0-13-059222-6

Prentice-Hall International (UK) Limited, *London*
Prentice-Hall of Australia Pty. Limited, *Sydney*
Prentice-Hall Canada Inc., *Toronto*
Prentice-Hall Hispanoamericana, S.A., *Mexico*
Prentice-Hall of India Private Limited, *New Delhi*
Prentice-Hall of Japan, Inc., *Tokyo*
Simon & Schuster Asia Pte. Ltd., *Singapore*
Editors Prentice-Hall do Brasil, Ltda., *Rio de janeiro*

To Allison, Kevin, Marisa, and Marc

C O N T E N T S

CHAPTER 9
SOURCES OF INSPIRATION   **253**

CHAPTER 10
DRAWING MEN   **301**

PREFACE

This book is designed for anyone who is planning a career in fashion. The ability to draw a fashion figure may be one of the skills you will need. Professional fashion illustrators, of course, need the most developed graphic skills to earn a livelihood by illustrating apparel for a wide variety of clients. Fashion sketching is also a necessary skill for designers and pattern makers. Even buyers can use sketches to record the merchandise they see at markets. Whatever students' career goals and drawing abilities might be, they can use *The Complete Book of Fashion Illustration*, Third Edition, to learn to draw the fashion figure. Novice sketchers will learn the basics, and sketchers with intermediate skills will learn to improve and refine their drawings. This third edition has been updated in several ways. Because styles in illustrating change almost as rapidly as fashion does, many illustrations in the book have been redrawn. Also, technology, especially in the area of computer graphics, has added new tools to delight illustrators and designers. Finally, Mona and I have used the first and second editions in the classroom, and the feedback from our students has been used to improve our sketches and teaching techniques. One

of the pleasures of drawing is changing and improving your techniques, and we have experienced this satisfaction as we evaluated past editions and prepared this revision.

In addition to being used in the classroom, *The Complete Book of Fashion Illustration* may be used as a self-teaching manual because the demonstration pages break sketching skills down into simple steps. Each step builds students' confidence and ability as they work through an exercise to master a specific skill so that they can produce competent fashion sketches.

Chapters 1 through 7 stress basic drawing and rendering skills. These chapters complement a beginning sketching class, in which models can animate the lessons presented and the instructor can guide and critique the students' work. After completing these chapters, students understand how to communicate a design or illustration concept graphically. Chapters 8 and 9 introduce intermediate graphic skills. These chapters concentrate on layout design and development of a unique style. Chapter 9, Sources of Inspiration, guides students to contemporary and period art that can enhance their conceptual skills.

Chapters 10 through 12 deal with specialized illustration categories. Men's and children's fashions are covered in detail, as are drawing and rendering accessories. The last two sections (Chapters 8 through 12) could easily be the basis for an advanced illustration course.

The Complete Book of Fashion Illustration can be used by a person who is sketching for the first time or by an experienced illustrator who wants to specialize in fashion. The only prerequisite is that the reader desire to develop good drawing skills. If the readers apply themselves consistently and thoroughly to the exercises and demonstrations presented in this book, they should be able to communicate fashion concepts graphically.

ACKNOWLEDGMENTS

This book could not have been written without the contributions of many outstanding artists and others in the fashion industry. Special thanks go to the following people, publications, and institutions:

To Mia Carpenter, Gregory Weir-Quiton, Steve Biek, David Horri, Paul Lowe, Marie Shafer, Robert Passantino, Steve Stipelman, Catherine Clayton Purnell, Antonio, John C. Jay, and the artists whose period illustrations were gleaned from the pages of twentieth-century fashion publications. To Charles Bush, photographer extraordinaire, for his fashion photographs.

To *Vogue* and *Harper's Bazaar*, who kindly allowed me to research their back issues for outstanding artists.

To Edward Mader of the Los Angeles County Museum of Art, Textile and Costume Department for the permission to use the Erté drawing.

To the University of California at Los Angeles, which allowed me to have access to the fine graphics in the Grunwald Graphic Art Collection. To the fashion reporting services *Pat Tunskey, Inc.*, *Report West*, and *The Fashion Service*. These fine professional publications are continuing to influence illustration styles because of the excellence of their artists and editors.

And last, but not least, to Mona Edwards, who persevered as the major illustrator of this text. She continues to grow as an illustrator and instructor, and we remain good friends after eight books and look forward to the next project.

Sharon Lee Tate

CHAPTER 1

Beginning to Draw

WHO CAN DRAW?

Look at the objects that surround you. Every piece of furniture, every building, every household tool, every garment—in fact, every manufactured object—began as a designer's sketch. This sketch first captured the physical reality of an idea. It was the plan from which the object was constructed, the symbol of the designer's thought. Without the skill of drawing, the idea could not have been communicated and translated into a three-dimensional object. And that skill—the ability to draw—can be learned. Of course, not everyone can be an artist. But with training and practice, most people can develop their graphic ability to the point at which they can use drawing to communicate their ideas.

To understand why this is true, try to remember your experiences as a child. Children have an innate ability to draw. They relish capturing an image. They find it thrilling to draw with a bright crayon, to splash paint on a clean piece of paper. Children enjoy creating a drawing more than evaluating the final product. To them, the creative act is fun in itself. Unfortunately, many adults impose product-oriented goals on the spontaneous creativity of children. "Johnny, leaves aren't blue." "Sally, the people in your picture shouldn't be larger than the houses." Such value judgments often discourage children from continuing their graphic experiments.

In addition, verbalizing and writing are the important building blocks of a traditional education, so those skills, rather than creative, artistic pursuits, are stressed in the early school years.

Imagine how different your drawing ability would be if you had spent years of early education practicing figure drawing or pencil-shading techniques instead of the ABCs.

To counteract disappointing experiences and recover spontaneity, many people have to begin with very simple approaches to drawing. They must overcome their negative feelings of being unable to draw before they can enjoy and develop their native drawing ability. If this is true for you, begin to draw, develop simple graphic skills, and do not worry about producing a professional image. The product will improve as you relax and begin to enjoy sketching.

The first human figure a beginner draws usually reflects his or her own physical and mental image. A man tends to draw figures with large shoulders and slim hips. A beginner with low self-esteem will tend to draw a figure with a small, pointed head or a tiny, cramped, thin figure. One of the first steps in drawing a fashion figure is to neutralize your self-image and study the typical fashion figure. As your sketching skill develops, you may start to incorporate desirable personal traits into your drawings.

Children draw with a natural, bold line and an eager enthusiasm that provide the basis for developing drawing into a skill.

WHAT IS FASHION DRAWING?

Unlike regular descriptive drawing, fashion drawing does not aim for realism. Rather, current ideals of beauty are emphasized to create a stylized, exaggerated version of reality. To create good fashion drawings, the illustrator must understand the current ideal of beauty and how clothing is used to enhance the human body.

Developing drawing skills is the important first step for drawing the fashion figure. There is no substitute for drawing to build skills. Begin with simple shapes and subjects and practice whenever possible. Take general drawing courses in addition to courses on the fashion figure. If you have a serious mental block, read the book *Drawing on the Right Side of the Brain* by Betty Edwards (Boston: Houghton Mifflin Co., 1969) and do the exercises.

A companion book to this text, *The Snap Fashion Handbook: Sketching and Design the Fast and Easy Way,* by Sharon Tate and Bill Glazer (Englewood Cliffs, NJ: Prentice Hall, 1995), starts the beginner drawing basic fashion sketches using figure templates and tracing garment details. This method is especially appropriate for the person who wants to master the basics quickly and does not want to develop sophisticated illustration skills. *The Snap Fashion Handbook* is based on SnapFashun® software that allows a person to design by combining a vast library of current garments, silhouettes, and details. The style components are updated monthly. SnapFashun.® is widely used in commercial fashion design.

Developing a sense of what is currently fashionable is also critical to developing good fashion drawing skills. In addition, you must develop a taste level—your own personal point of view about the way an object or design should look. Today this means being aware of lifestyle trends as well as trends in apparel. Reading newspapers, books, and magazines that reflect trends in home furnishings, sports, literature, graphics, and fine arts—as well as apparel—will broaden your taste level. Creativity is the ability to combine several ideas into something new—to synthesize and organize elements in a unique way. Being sensitive to the way other art forms relate to apparel design and fashion illustration will help you develop your creativity.

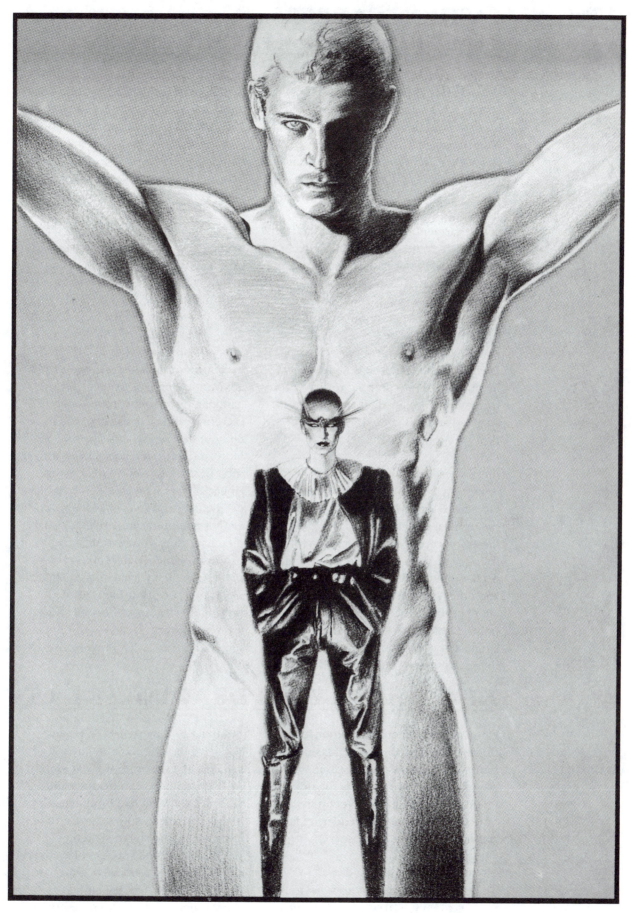

Courtesy of Paul Lowe.

FASHION CAREERS THAT REQUIRE SKETCHING

Many careers in fashion use drawing skills. For example, fashion and theatrical costume designers sketch their ideas so they can be interpreted by a pattern maker. This working sketch, also called a *croquis* (cro-key) or flat, must accurately show the silhouette and style details. The collar, cuffs, and trims must be drawn to scale so the actual garment can be constructed in fabric. Often, notes will indicate technical details to the pattern maker and sample maker. This sketch does not have to be exciting. It should have a minimum of exaggeration and should relate directly to the product to be created. The only purpose of the croquis is to transform the designer's mental image into graphic reality from which the product can be constructed and evaluated by other people.

Illustrators have a different purpose in drawing a garment; they want to emphasize the style details to enhance the original design concept. Fashion illustrators are creating the *image* of a fashionable product—not the garment itself—so they will often omit wrinkles and other imperfections, and exaggerate the silhouette to make a fashion point. Illustrations are intended to stimulate customers into projecting themselves into the garment. The kind of garment and how the illustration will be used influences how the drawing will be done. A product advertisement drawn to sell a garment is usually more realistically rendered than a sketch used to emphasize the fashion image of a garment, designer, or store. Photographs are more realistic than illustrations, and many art directors feel photos sell a product more effectively. Today an illustrator must compete against other illustrators and photography as well. Thus, illustrators must be innovative and creative to be hired to create fashion advertisements.

Buyers who can sketch will often make picture notes of garments they are purchasing. For instance, most handbag buyers must have rough sketching ability because of the difficulty in describing similar products. More and more retailers are creating their own merchandise under store labels. Buyers who can sketch have a decided advantage over those who cannot communicate visually. Visual merchandisers draw layout sketches of proposed window and interior displays. Commercial artists who specialize in figure work often train with fashion illustrators to become more aware of current trends in fashion illustration.

DEVELOPING YOUR DRAWING SKILLS

Drawing skills begin with knowledge of the body, interpreted as a fashion figure, which today is tall, slim, and athletic. Drawing clothes is the next technical skill to master. Techniques of drawing apparel and rendering fabrics can be learned by observation and practice.

The most important way to learn to draw is to do it. Carry a small sketchbook and doodle. Draw in the margins of books and magazines. Whenever you have to wait, look around for an interesting face or object and sketch it. Collect *scrap,* photographs and sketches that you like from magazines and newspapers, so you have a reference when you start a sketch or design. Next time you visualize something you want to make or purchase, try to sketch it first. Substitute a drawn image for a written description of an object.

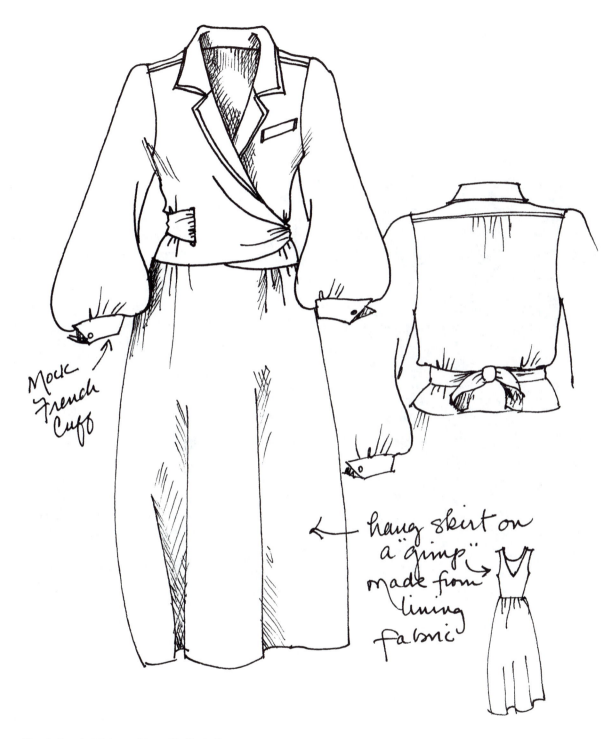

Mock
French
Cuff

hang skirt on
a "gimp"
made from
lining
fabric

*The design sketch is used to guide the pattern
maker and sample sewer in constructing the
garment exactly as the designer envisioned it.
Many technical details and a realistic
proportion are necessary.*

The store advertisement presents garments so that a consumer can identify with the illustration and be motivated to buy the outfit. The style is enhanced but not overly exaggerated.

As your drawing skills develop, you can use more complicated *media* (paint, felt pens, pencils, and so forth) to achieve different effects. Learn the techniques of other illustrators by imitating their work, then adapt those techniques to your own style. Experimenting with different media and techniques will increase your design repertoire and enable you to more quickly and accurately render a concept. As drawing the image becomes easier for you, you can begin to design the whole page. A figure floating on a blank page has a very amateurish look when compared to an illustration that is designed to relate to the whole page. Finally, you can expand to drawing related fashion figures. Children and men are specialties that are relatively easily drawn after you have developed a firm basis in female body proportion. The differences are ones of emphasis: You do not have to learn a totally new structure.

Drawing is a skill that can be mastered by constant practice. Your early products are less important than the process of doing the sketch. Do not be critical of your early work. Instead, appreciate the successful parts of your drawing. Work on repeating those good elements and improving the weaker aspects in your next sketch. When you have mastered one style or technique, try another. Do not be afraid of copying a drawing you like. Trace or copy it, trying to analyze how and why the artist created the image. Then use these techniques to illustrate a different garment in another pose. Use what you see to enhance your own drawing ability and style. Do not limit yourself to one style. To have longevity, an artist should always be open to change.

*The editorial illustration is primarily intended
to present an exciting fashion concept in which
details are less important than impact.*

BEGINNING DRAWING SUPPLIES

Before you can begin drawing, you must have the proper materials. You will find a detailed discussion of supplies in Chapter 7. For now, though, the following list of materials should be adequate.

PAPERS

1. Overlay or vellum tablets are durable transparent paper to use for tracing and reworking sketches. A pad 14 by 17 inches is a handy size.

2. Bond paper is an inexpensive, semitranslucent, all-purpose paper for pencils and marking pens. Buy a pad that is 14 by 17 inches or larger.

3. A 6-by-8 inch sketchbook with a plain cover is easy to carry yet large enough for quick sketches.

MARKERS AND PENCILS

1. Buy a dozen #2 soft lead pencils and sharpen all of them. Change pencils as the points become blunt. In addition, buy several types of soft drawing pencils. The HB series will provide you with a variety of lead qualities.

2. Fine-line red markers are used for correcting and redrawing your sketch exercise.

3. A fine-line black marker ("razor point") or a Rapidograph with changeable points is used for detailed line drawings. Buy ink if you are using a Rapidograph.

4. Prismacolor pencils are available in a wide variety of colors. The beginner should buy two or three blacks, a white, and several shades of gray for basic work.

5. Purchase markers with blunt or chisel points in several shades of cool gray. The tones of gray are numbered, the lighter the tone, the lower the number. A #2, #4, #5, and #8 will make a good basic selection. Buy a pointed black marker for a heavier line than that given by the fine-point markers.

6. A portable pencil sharpener is handy and saves time.

OTHER EQUIPMENT

1. *Drawing board:* Buy a lightweight Masonite board with clips and a handhold for portability. The board should be at least 18 by 26 inches.

2. *Ruler:* An 18-by-2-inch plastic see-through ruler is best for doing the basic exercises.

3. *Masking tape:* A roll of ¾-inch-wide tape is a basic tool.

4. *Mat knives:* These are the basic tools for cutting paper, illustration board, and tape.

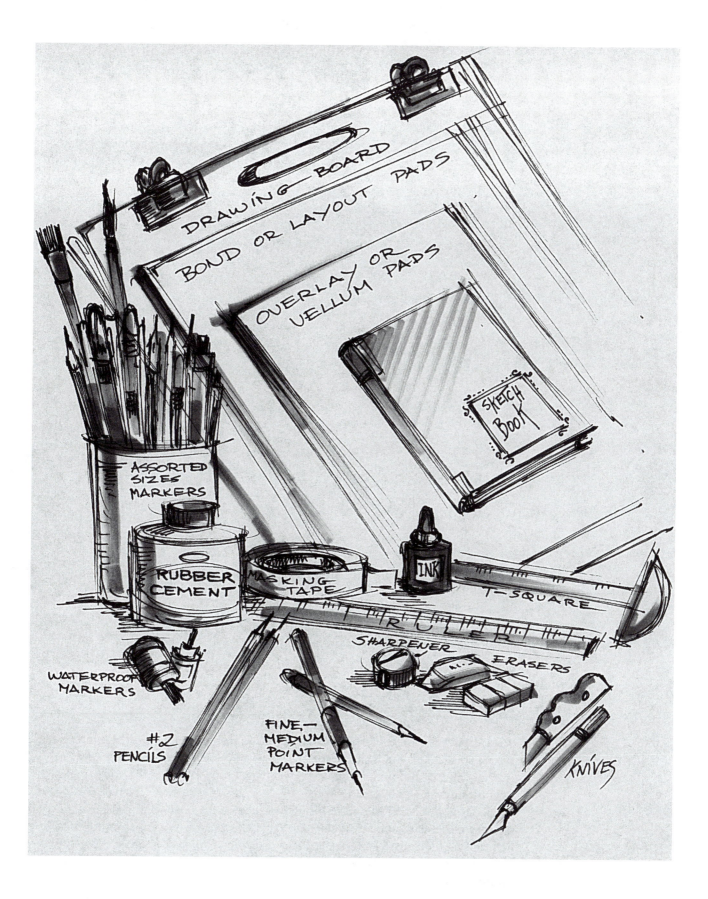

BASIC EXERCISES

A lead pencil is a friendly tool because we are so familiar with it as a writing instrument. It is also very versatile. Begin your exercises by toning in rectangles 1 by 1½ inches in a series of five steps from darkest black to the lightest lead tone possible. (Look at the illustration on the facing page.) Feel how much pressure you have to apply to the pencil point to create each step. Next, draw a circle and imagine that it is a ball. Imagine a light shining on the center of the ball. Tone the edges of the circle with the dark tone you perfected in your first rectangle. Gradually lighten the edges of the circle until you leave clean white paper in the very center. Notice how the shadow makes your circle look three dimensional. Experiment with the same techniques to make the other shapes at the right look like solid objects.

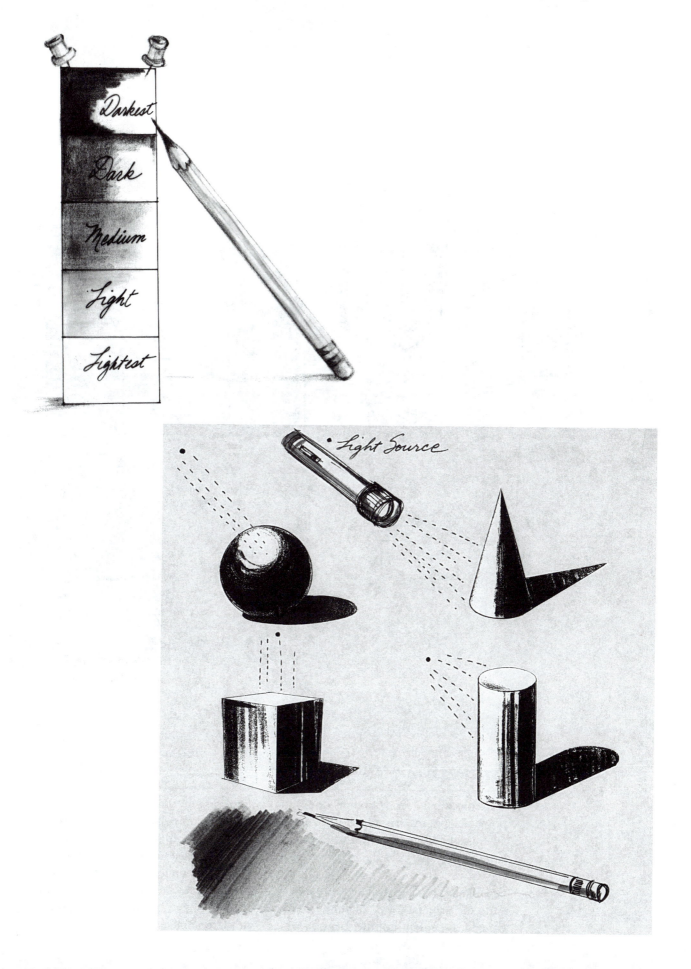

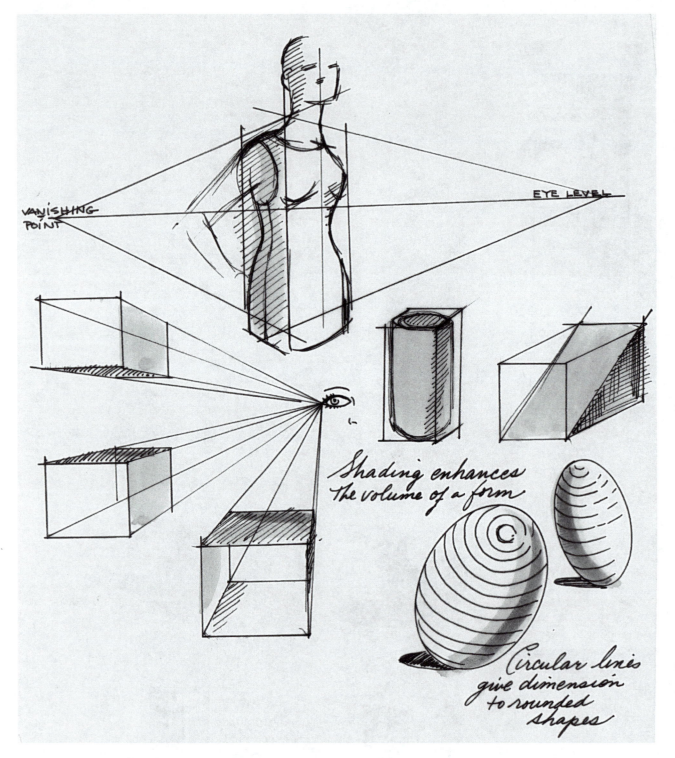

Shading enhances the volume of a form

Circular lines give dimension to rounded shapes

PERSPECTIVE

A simple way to see volume is one-point perspective, in which horizontal edges of a form converge at a vanishing point that is at the eye level of the viewer. The vertical elements in your sketch remain straight and parallel to the original form. Shading enhances the depth of the form.

Experiment with these basic shapes that are components of the body. Use vanishing points at various distances from the basic forms to alter the depth and angles of the form. It is important to hold the concept of the volume of an object as you begin to draw the figure.

C H A P T E R 2

Fashion Figure Proportion

THE CURRENT FASHION FIGURE

Fashion illustration of every period emphasizes the ideal of beauty for the age. Today's ideal figure for showing apparel is a tall (5 feet 7 inches to 5 feet 11 inches), slender, athletic young woman. She has a small bosom and broad shoulders so clothes hang easily over her lithe silhouette. She wears a size 6 to a size 10. Her face, hair, and body have a natural look when she is showing casual or active sportswear. The mood of her hairstyle and make-up is more stylized when she is wearing suits, evening wear, and more expensive apparel.

The fashion ideal is far from the proportions and appearance of most bodies. Today's American woman is taller than in past decades, but average height is still only about 5 feet 4 inches. Nor is the typical woman as slender as the fashion ideal.

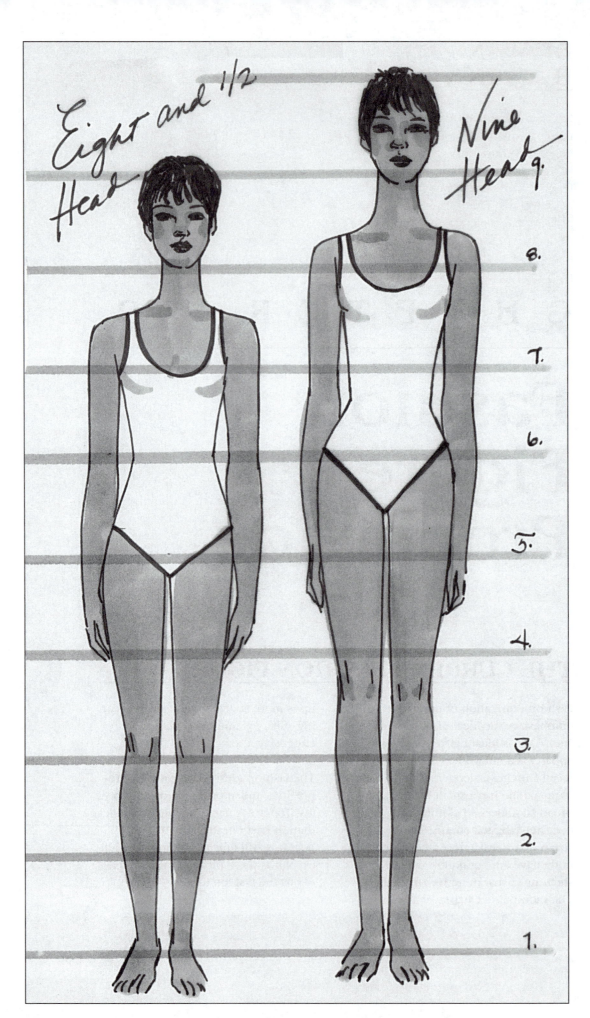

Eight and 1/2 Head

Nine Head 9.

8.

7.

6.

5.

4.

3.

2.

1.

DRAWING THE EIGHT-AND-ONE-HALF-HEAD FIGURE

Fashion drawing changes the average figure to the modern ideal by lengthening the body proportion from a realistic seven- and-one-half-head lengths figure to eight-and-one-half-head lengths. This means that the total body length is eight-and-one-half times the length of the head. The figure is lengthened at the neck and legs, the proportion of the torso remains fairly realistic. Fashion illustrators often attenuate the figure even more, making it as tall as nine-and-one-half-heads high for a very sophisticated look. Optical illusions are also used to heighten the figure. For example, designers might dress their mannequins in high-heeled or platform shoes that can be covered by long pants or skirts.

Notice that the main difference between the seven-and-one-half-head figure and the eight-and-one-half-head figure is the length of the leg. If the proportions of the torso are distorted too greatly, the clothes look matronly and awkward. Select one of the proportions to draw, depending on the kind of illustration you ultimately intend to do. A theatrical designer should concentrate on the more realistic proportions such as the seven-and-one-half-head figure. This is also true of an apparel designer when drawing a working sketch. An exaggerated working sketch will confuse a pattern maker.

High-fashion illustrators often use more exaggerated proportions. Once you have become comfortable drawing the figure, you will be able to adapt the proportion to the kind of illustration you are doing. The following guidelines will help you begin:

1. Study the geometric figures on the following pages. Notice that the body components can be broken down into relatively simple shapes. Draw a 9½ inch straight line on a piece of tracing paper and mark it off in 1-inch increments.

2. Draw an oval between the top line and the first inch mark. Next, divide the space below the oval in half. Draw the torso block between this line and slightly above line 3. Line 3 is the position of the true waistline and is also the point at which the elbow hits the body.

3. Now draw the pelvic block between lines 3 and 4. A figure in which the torso is longer than the legs will look very dumpy.

4. Locate the circular joints at the shoulders, elbows, wrists, knees, and ankles. These circles represent rotating joints that allow the body to move 90 degrees to 180 degrees. The flat ovals at the crotch line indicate the less flexible leg joints.

5. Connect the circles with simple shapes to represent the limbs in which muscles cover relatively long and inflexible bones that remain straight, bending only at the joints.

6. Realistically rendering the feet, with proper foreshortening, would create a visually disturbing absence of a supportive base for the figure. For this reason, the fashion artist exaggerates the foot, imagining that the viewer is looking down at the top of the foot. This illusion is further exaggerated if the figure is wearing high heels. It is necessary to exaggerate the foot even more for a taller figure so it will appear to have sufficient support.

Exaggerating the foot size of these eight-and-one-half head figures focuses attention on the leg fashion. Courtesy of Focus, published by Pat Tunskey, Inc.

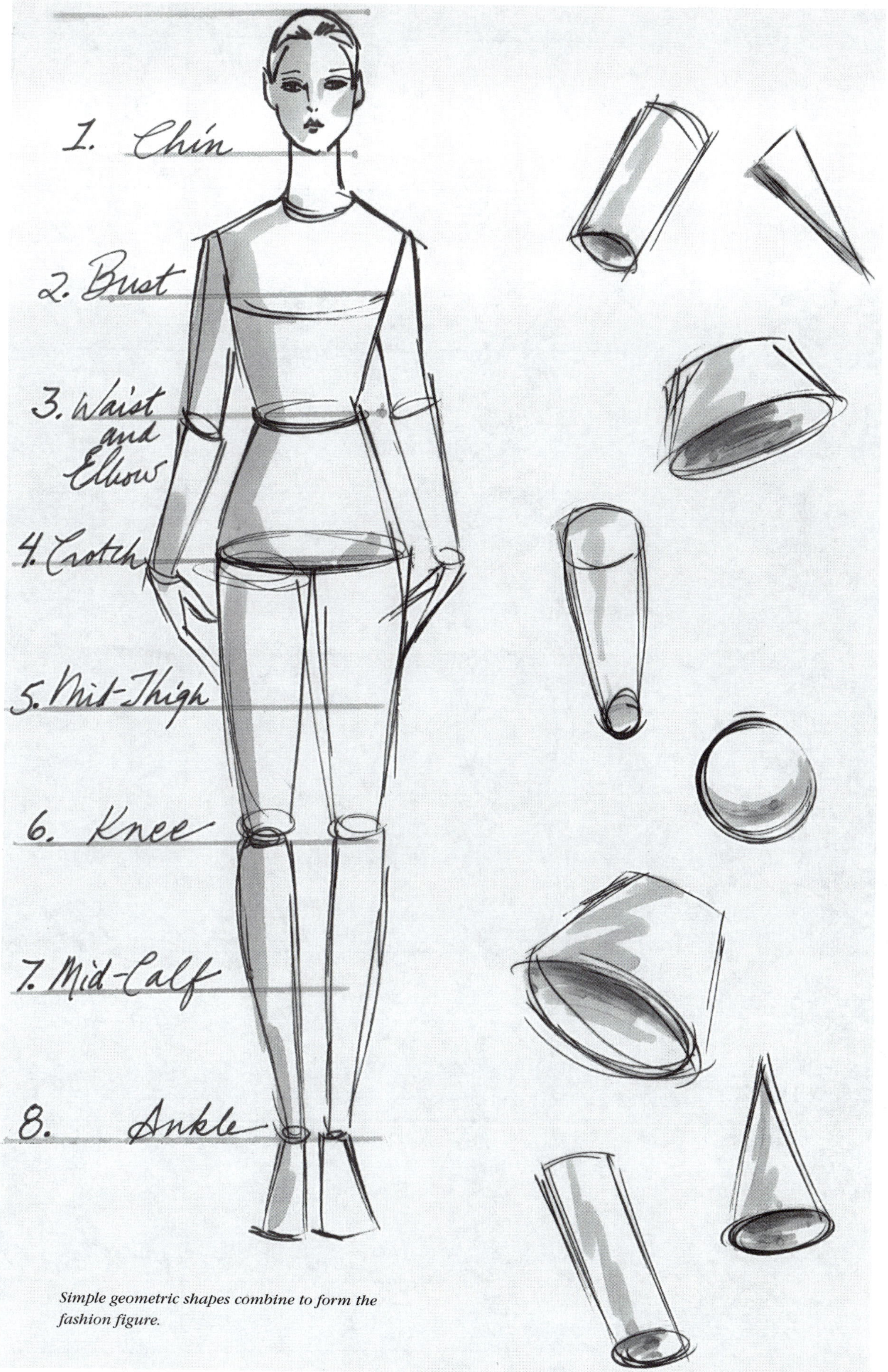

1. Chin

2. Bust

3. Waist
and
Elbow

4. Crotch

5. Mid-Thigh

6. Knee

7. Mid-Calf

8. Ankle

Simple geometric shapes combine to form the fashion figure.

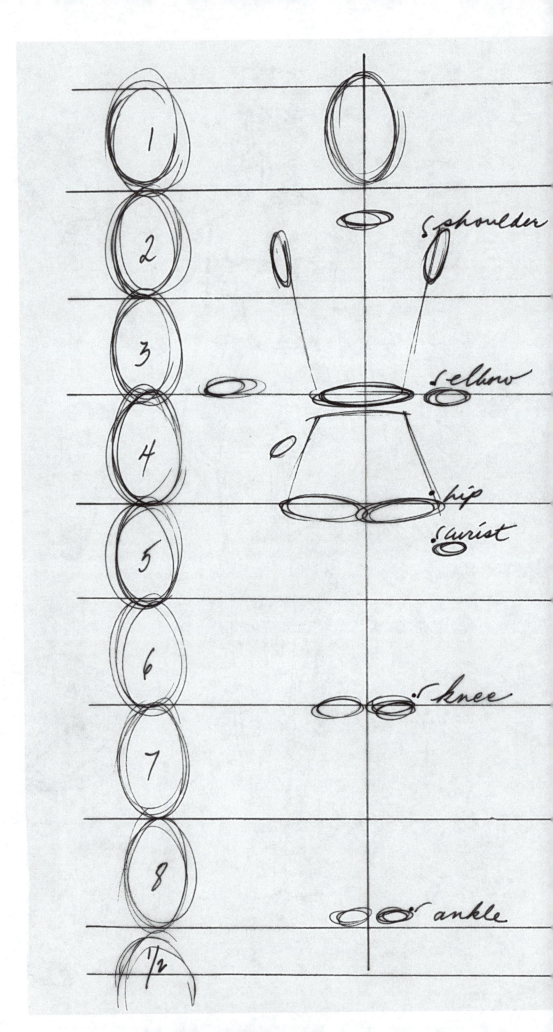

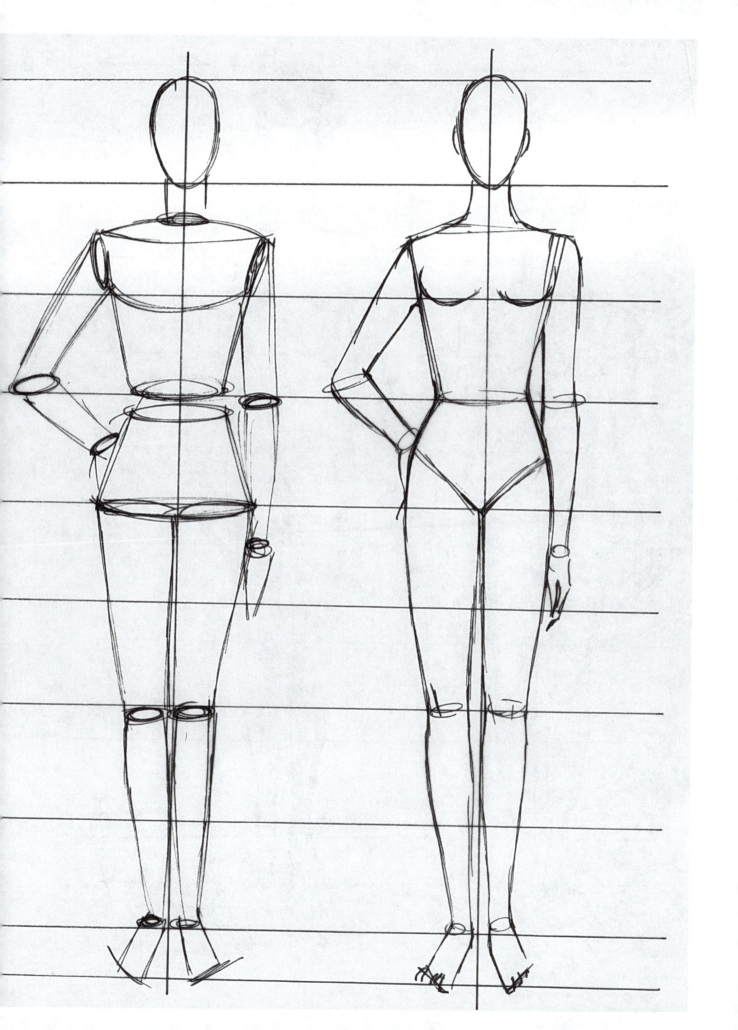

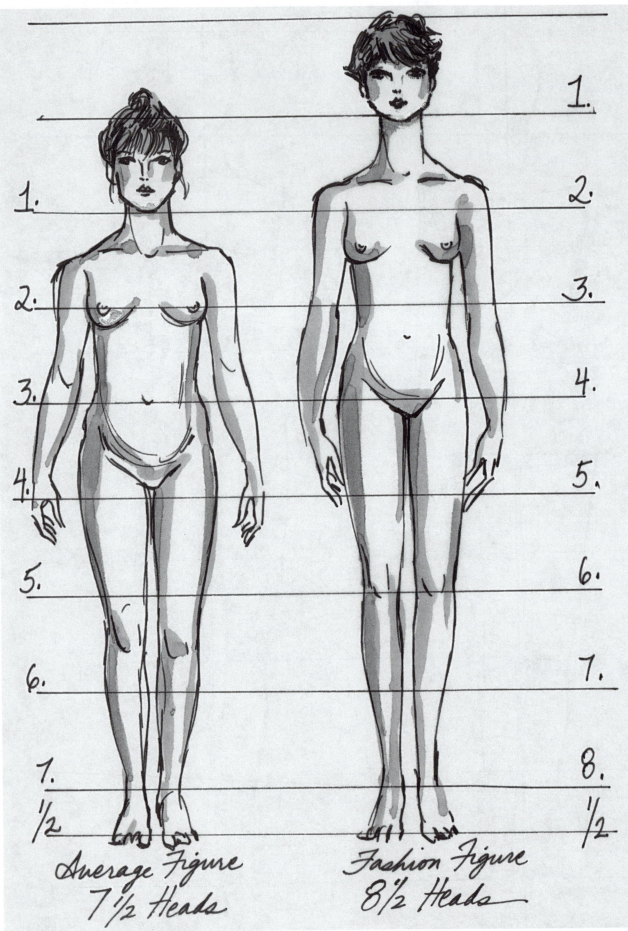

Average Figure
7½ Heads

Fashion Figure
8½ Heads

*Realistic proportion is compared to the more
exaggerated fashion figure.*

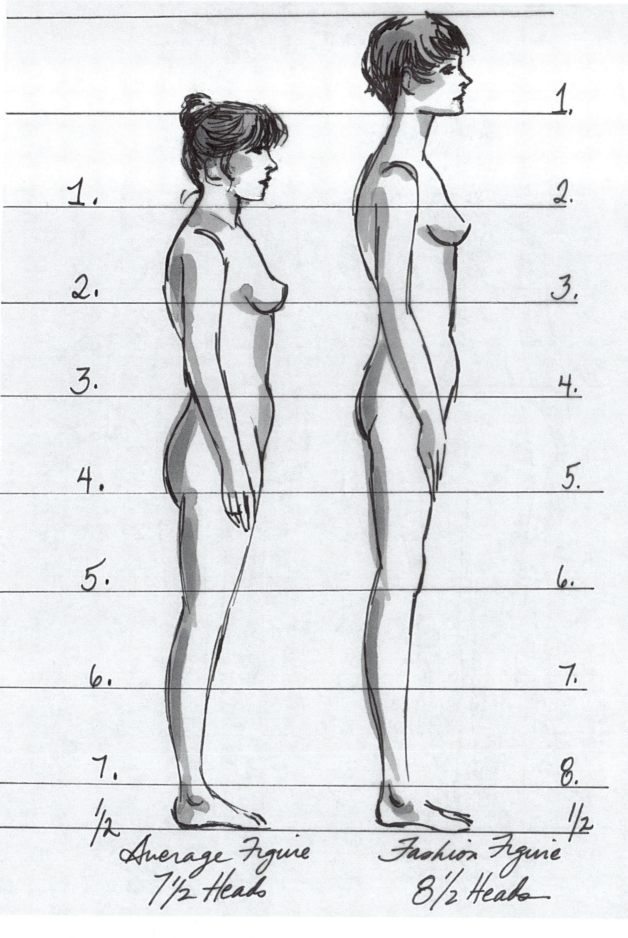

1.

2.

3.

4.

5.

6.

7.

1/2

Average Figure
7 1/2 Heads

1.

2.

3.

4.

5.

6.

7.

8.

1/2

Fashion Figure
8 1/2 Heads

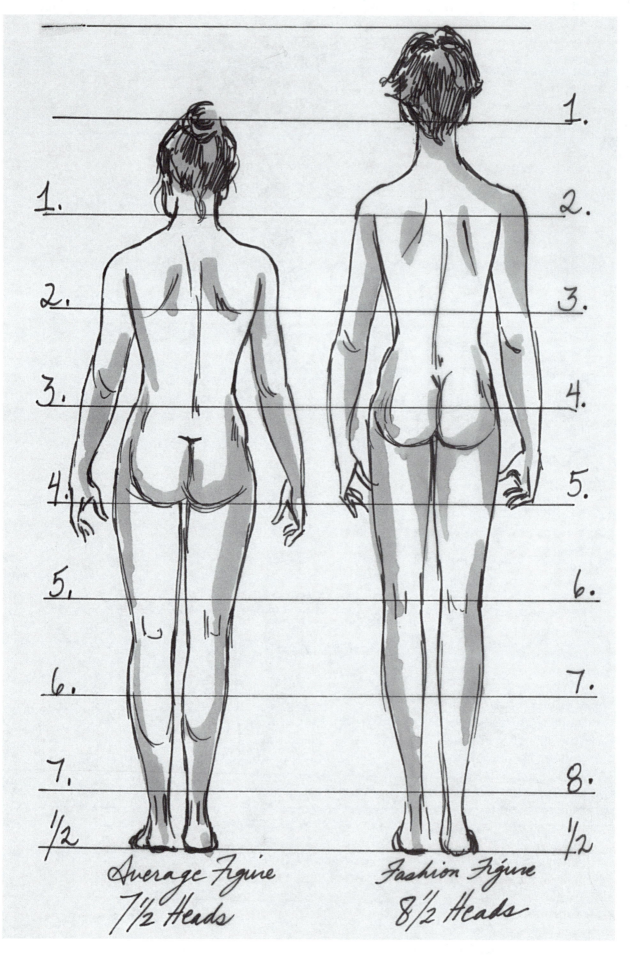

1.

1.

2.

2.

3.

3.

4.

4.

5.

5.

6.

6.

7.

7.

8.

½

½

Average Figure
7½ Heads

Fashion Figure
8½ Heads

*Exaggerated proportion is effective for bathing
suit illustrations because longer legs are desirable.*

Put your sketch over the figure on the
preceding page to see how closely
your drawing compares to the standard. With a colored felt pen, redraw
the areas that do not match the standard. Trace the figure several times,
fleshing out the geometric components so your drawing looks like a figure. Make an effort to draw the ideal
and not to impose your own body
image onto the sketch.

Hold your pencil with a relaxed, comfortable grip. A #2 soft lead pencil,
kept very sharp, is the best tool for
these basic exercises. Sharpen eight or
ten pencils and pick up a new one as
the one you are using becomes blunt
to save time and keep your drawing
from getting smudged. Attach your
practice piece of overlay paper to the
book with a small piece of masking
tape. (No damage will be done to the
book.) Draw this figure many times,
gradually eliminating the guidelines
until you can sketch it freehand.
Measure your drawings from the head
to the crotch and make sure the legs
are equal to or longer than this distance. The crotch line (line 4) is
always at least the halfway point of
any fashion sketch. The legs may be
longer than the head and torso, but
never shorter.

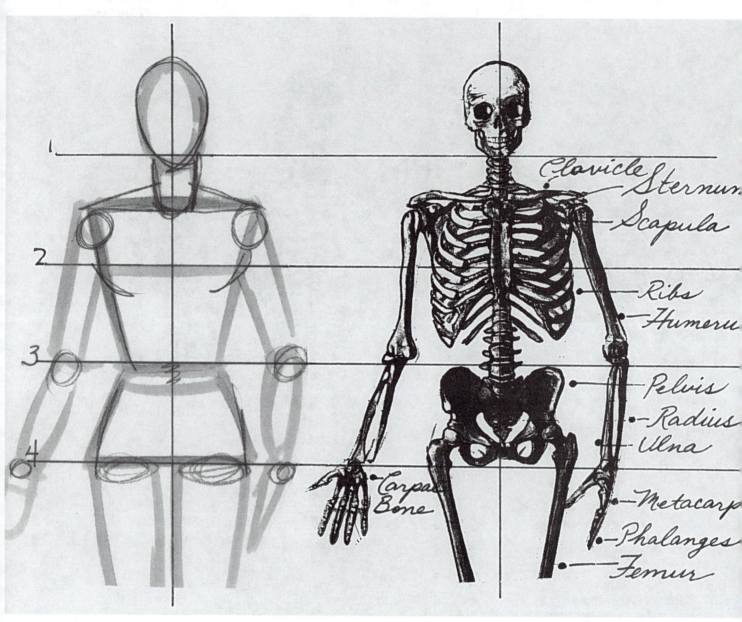

1

2

3

4

Clavicle Sternum
Scapula

Ribs
Humeru

Pelvis
Radius
Ulna

Carpa
Bone

Metacarp
Phalanges
Femur

Sternocleidomastoid

Trapezius

Pectoralis Minor

Serratus Anterior

Tendinous Inscription

Obliquus Internus

TORSO BONE STRUCTURE

The bone structure of a fashion model is important because she is very slender and her bones are visible at the joints, rib cage, and pelvic area. The anatomical drawings are seven-and-one-half-head lengths, or realistic proportions. Compare the skeleton drawings to the block figure. It is important to study skeletal structure to understand which parts of the body can bend. The arms can move at the shoulder, elbow, and wrist but not in between because of the straight, solid humerus (upper arm) and the radius and ulna (lower arm) bones. The leg moves from the hip, knee, and ankle joints only. Feel the joints of your own body to understand how they move. Look at yourself in the mirror and test where your arms and legs can bend.

Trace the front and profile skeleton, drawing it several times on overlay paper. Say the names of the major bones as you draw. On one sketch, draw all the straight bones with pencil and draw the movable joints with a fine-line red marker. Remember to include the spine and neck as flexible joints. The red areas will alert you to where the body can move.

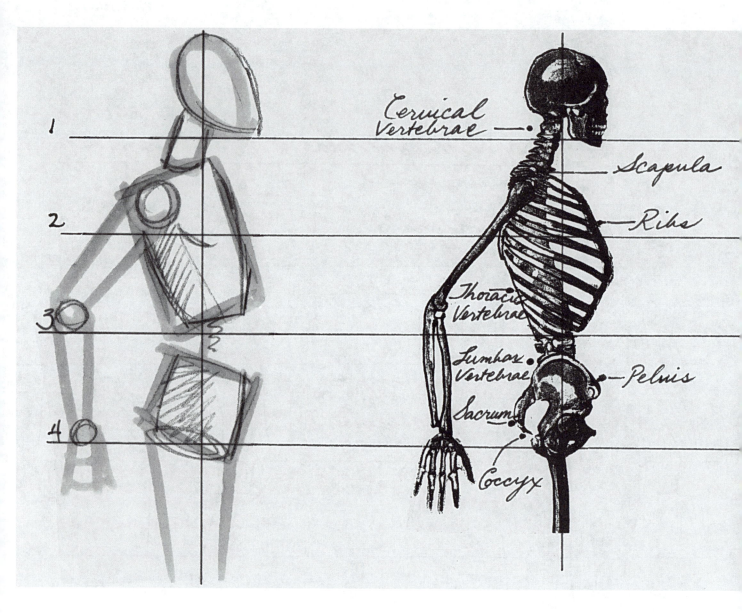

Cervical
Vertebrae —•

Scapula

Ribs

Thoracic
Vertebrae

Lumbar
Vertebrae•

Pelvis

Sacrum

Coccyx

TORSO MUSCLE STRUCTURE

The fashion model has long, lithe, healthy muscle structure, but her muscles are not as defined as a man's. She has very little extra fat on her body. When an arm moves, the muscle will contract slightly, making a smooth curve.

Place a drawing you have done of the bones over the drawing of the muscled body shown on the next page. Notice how the skeleton supports and relates

to the muscle structure of the body. Now move your tracing of the skeleton over the fleshed-out body and compare the supporting bones with the body.

Practice drawing the finished figure and muscles shown here and on page 27. Follow these steps:

1. Trace the muscled figure several times. Say the names of the major muscles as you draw them.

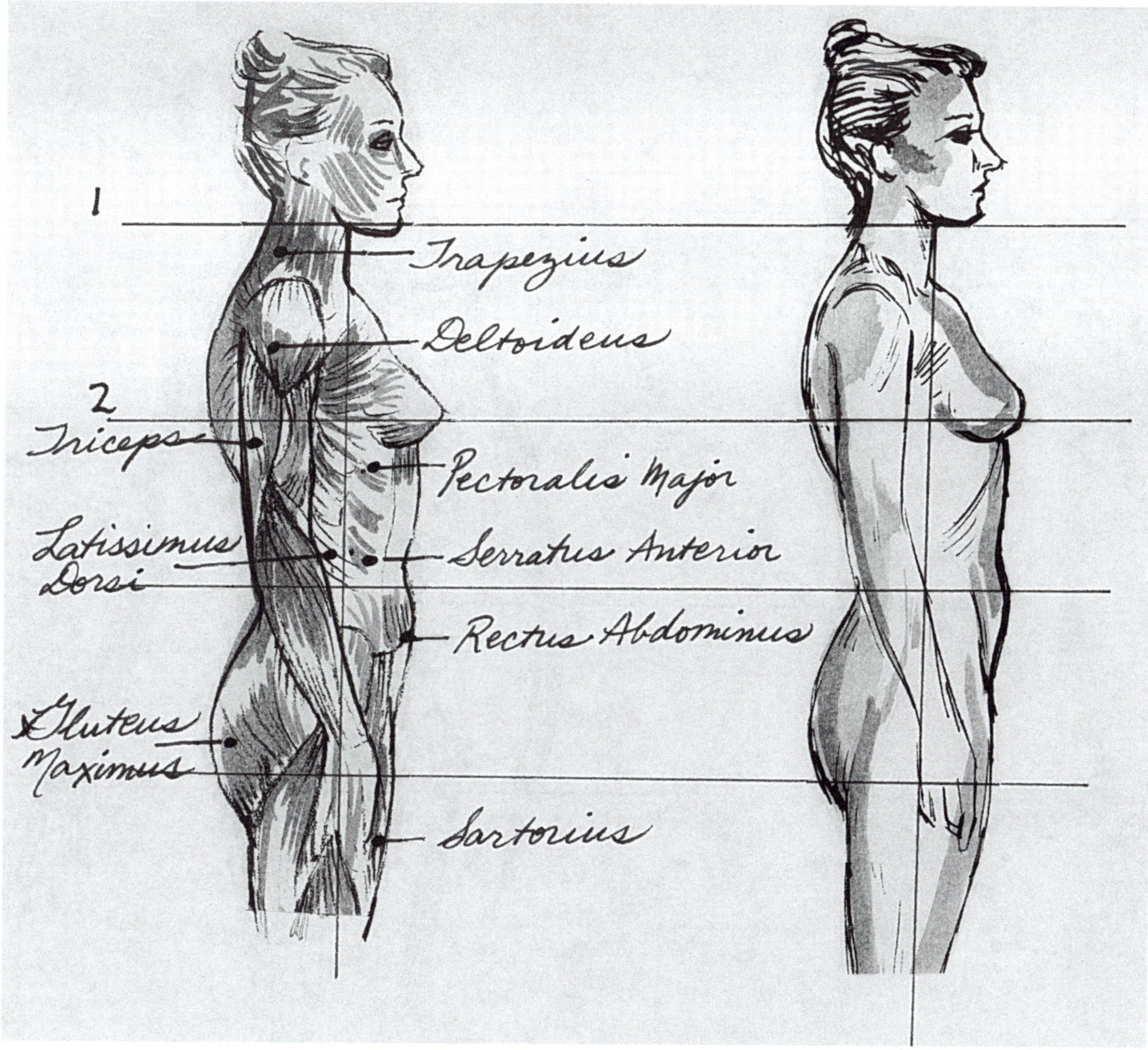

I

Trapezius

Deltoideus

2

Triceps

Pectoralis Major

Latissimus
Dorsi

Serratus Anterior

Rectus Abdominus

Gluteus
Maximus

Sartorius

2. Put a piece of overlay paper on one of your tracings of the muscles. Draw a fleshed-out figure over your drawing of the muscles. Take away the muscle drawing and compare your sketch to the figure in the book.

3. Draw over your sketch of the skeleton on a fresh sheet of over-

lay paper. Using the skeleton as a guide to proportion, draw a fleshed-out figure. Correct your drawing with a red marking pen by comparing it to the finished figure in the book.

4. Do these exercises until you find it easy to draw the shapes of the limbs in the correct proportion.

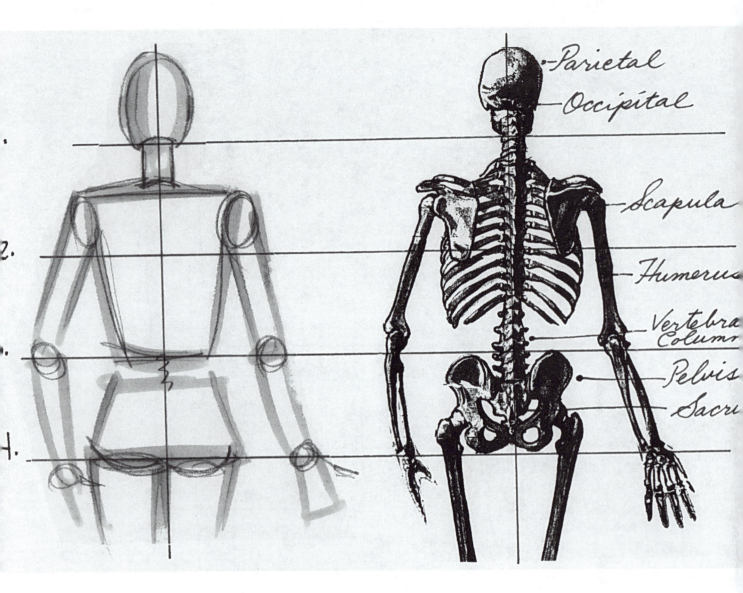

Parietal
Occipital
Scapula
Humerus
Vertebra Column
Pelvis
Sacru

THE BACK TORSO

The back view of a fashion figure has the same proportion as the front view, but the bones and muscle structure differ. It is important to show back views to illustrate garments with back interest.

Practice drawing the back view, following these steps:

1. Draw a line 5 inches long on a piece of overlay paper and mark the inches as you did in the first exercise on proportion. Sketch the geometric shapes of the figure freehand. Place your drawing over the block figure and correct your sketch with a red marking pen. Draw the block figure freehand until you do not have to make any corrections.

2. Trace the back view of the skeleton on the overlay paper. Say the names of the bones as you draw them.

3. Trace the back view of the muscles on overlay paper, saying the names of the muscles as you draw them. Line up your sketch of the muscles over the skeleton and compare the two sketches.

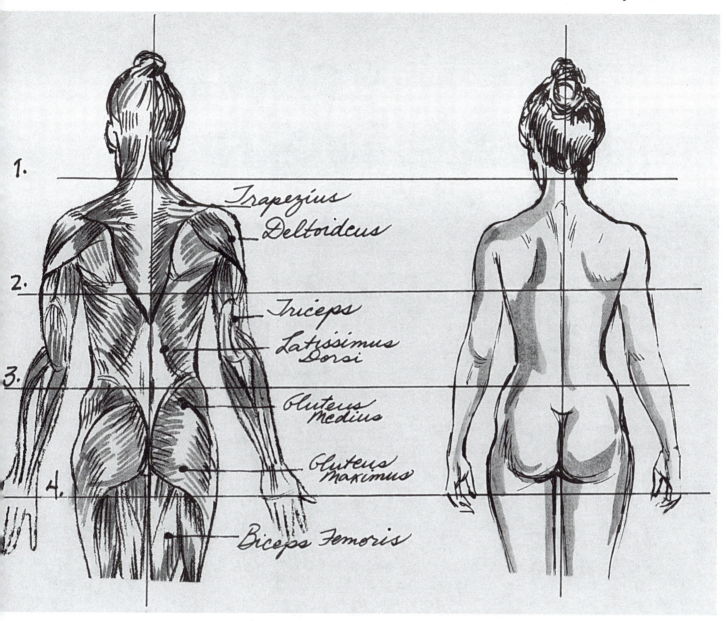

1.

Trapezius
Deltoideus

2.

Triceps
Latissimus
Dorsi

3.

Gluteus
Medius

Gluteus
Maximus

4.

Biceps Femoris

4. Put a fresh piece of overlay paper over the two sketches of the bones and muscles. Using these sketches as a guide, draw a fleshed-out figure. Compare this sketch to the fleshed-out figure in the book and make any corrections with red felt pen.

5. Repeat the last step until you are easily able to sketch a fleshed-out back-view figure.

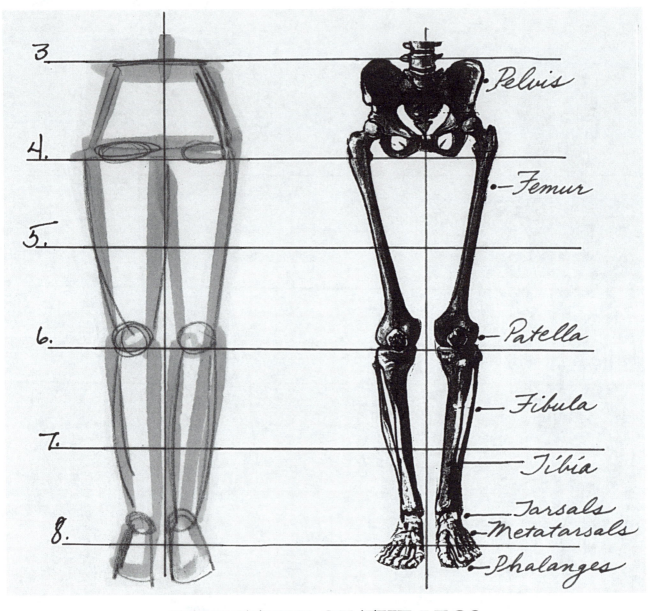

STRUCTURE OF THE LEGS AND FEET

The structure of the legs and feet is important to a fashion sketch because that structure supports the visual weight of the figure. Notice that the feet are sketched as if you were looking directly down on them. This gives the feet enough size to support the figure.

When the leg moves, the muscles controlling the movement contract and make the leg thicken slightly.

Use the following exercises to practice drawing legs:

1. Draw a line 5½ inches long on a piece of overlay paper and mark the inches as you did in the first exercise on proportion, starting with the top line as line 4. Using the first sketch as a guide, draw the geometric structure of the legs from the pelvis block to the feet. Compare your sketch to the

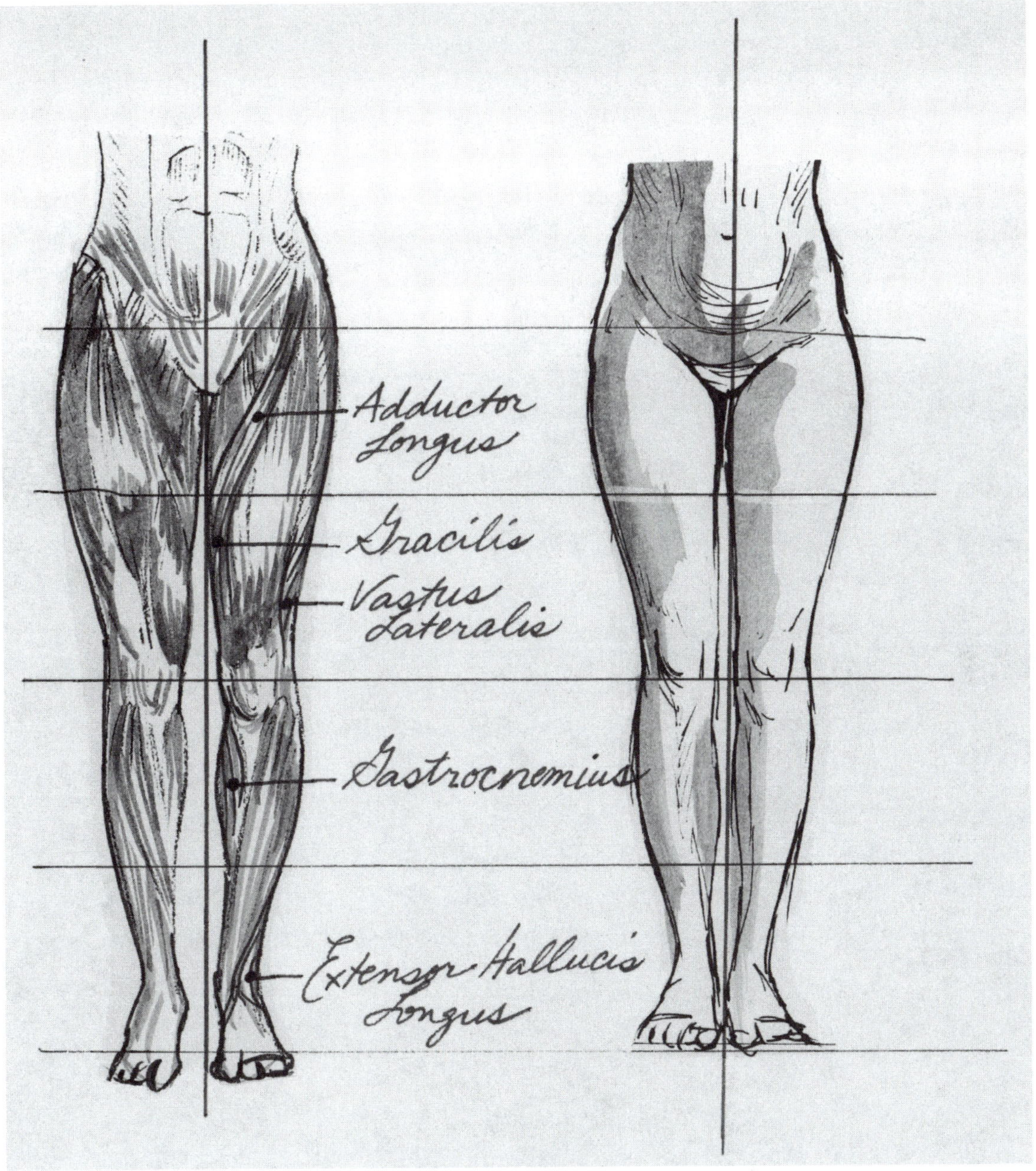

Adductor
Longus

Gracilis

Vastus
Lateralis

Gastrocnemius

Extensor Hallucis
Longus

block figure and make corrections in your sketch with a red
felt pen.

2. Trace the diagram of the bone
   structure of the legs on overlay
   paper. Say the names of the
   major bones as you draw them.

3. Trace the muscle diagrams on
   overlay paper. Compare them to
   your skeleton diagram.

4. Draw a finished, fleshed-out
   sketch of the legs on a fresh
   sheet of overlay paper, using
   your drawing of the muscles as
   a guide.

5. Practice drawing legs and feet
   freehand. Try to imagine the
   bone and muscle stucture of the
   fleshed-out legs as you draw
   them. Practice until you can
   draw a realistic leg and foot.

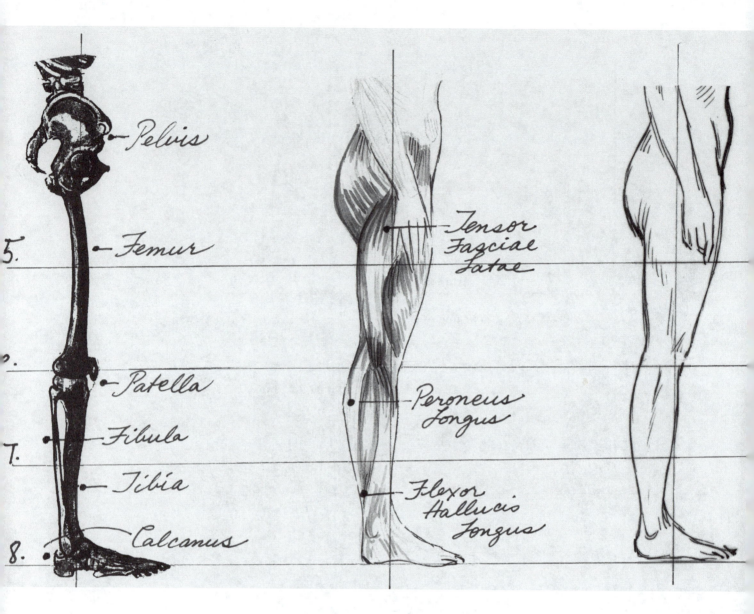

Pelvis

5.   Femur

Patella

Fibula

7.   Tibia

Calcanus

8.

Tensor
Fascial
Latae

Peroneus
Longus

Flexor
Hallucis
Longus

Abstract leg shapes exaggerate the anatomical body structure. Courtesy of The Fashion Service.

STRUCTURE OF THE HAND

The hand is a complicated area of the body to draw, but sketching becomes easier if you break the hand down into four major components: the wrist, the thumb, the fingers, and the hand proper (palm). Drawing the thumb in the correct position relative to the hand and fingers is of primary importance to a realistic sketch. The fashion hand should have a strong, poised look. The fingernails should be well groomed but not exaggerated. The folds of skin over the knuckles are usually simplified in a fashion drawing.

The hand is as large as the face from the chin to the eyebrows. Measure your own hand in relationship to your face.

Observation and trial-and-error sketching are the best ways to improve your ability to draw hands. Trace the block hand and bone diagrams, draw your own hand in a relaxed pose, and draw the other hand studies shown here. Do each exercise several times.

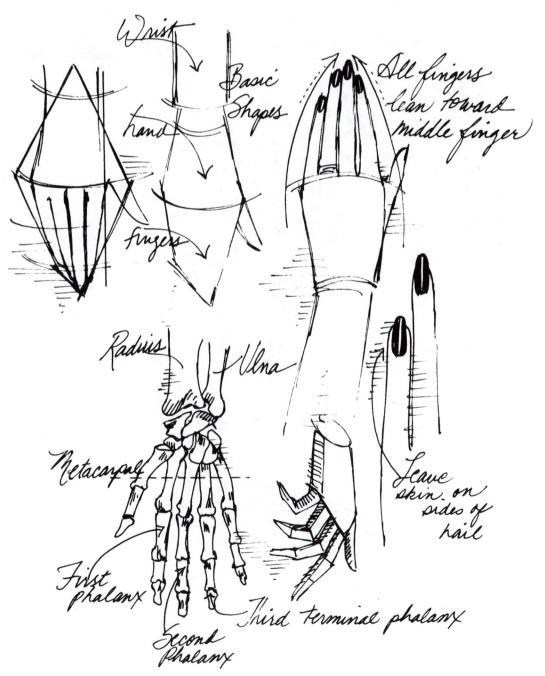

Wrist

Basic Shapes

hand

fingers

All fingers lean toward middle finger

Radius

Ulna

Metacarpal

Leave skin on sides of nail

First phalanx

Third Terminal phalanx

Second Phalanx

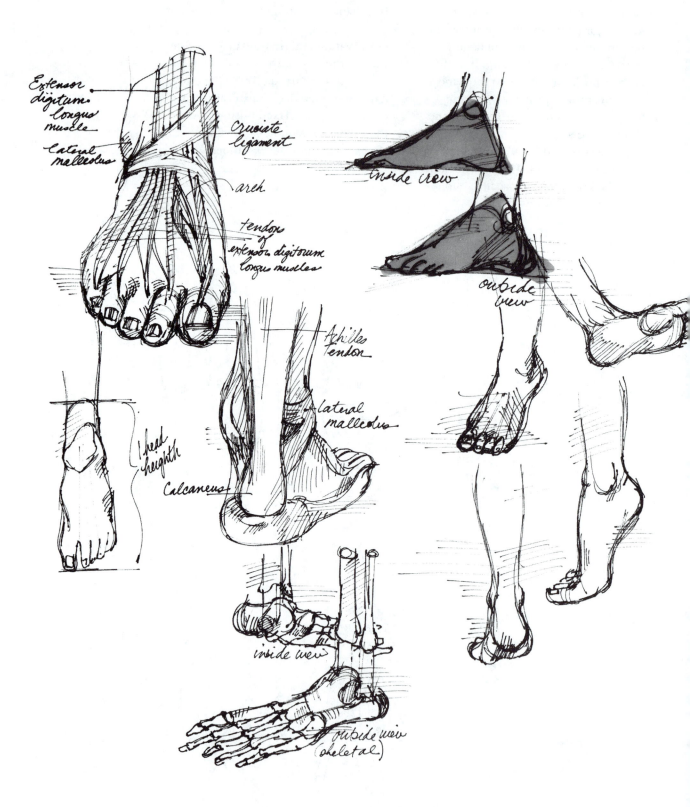

Extensor digitorum longus muscle

lateral malleolus

cruciate ligament

arch

tendon of extensor digitorum longus muscles

inside view

outside view

head height

Achilles tendon

lateral malleolus

Calcaneus

inside view

outside view (skeletal)

DRAWING THE FOOT

The shape of the foot can be simplified to a wedge, but a convincing
fashion sketch should have a well-
drawn foot that is large enough to
support the weight of the figure. The
basic shape of the foot is altered
when high heels are worn. The foot
appears slenderer and shorter and the
arch becomes more obvious.

Study these diagrams of the foot in a
flat position and in shoes with heels.
Trace the studies several times, then
try to draw them freehand. Finally,
draw your own foot by looking
straight down at it. Sketch shoes and
an imaginary foot in them.

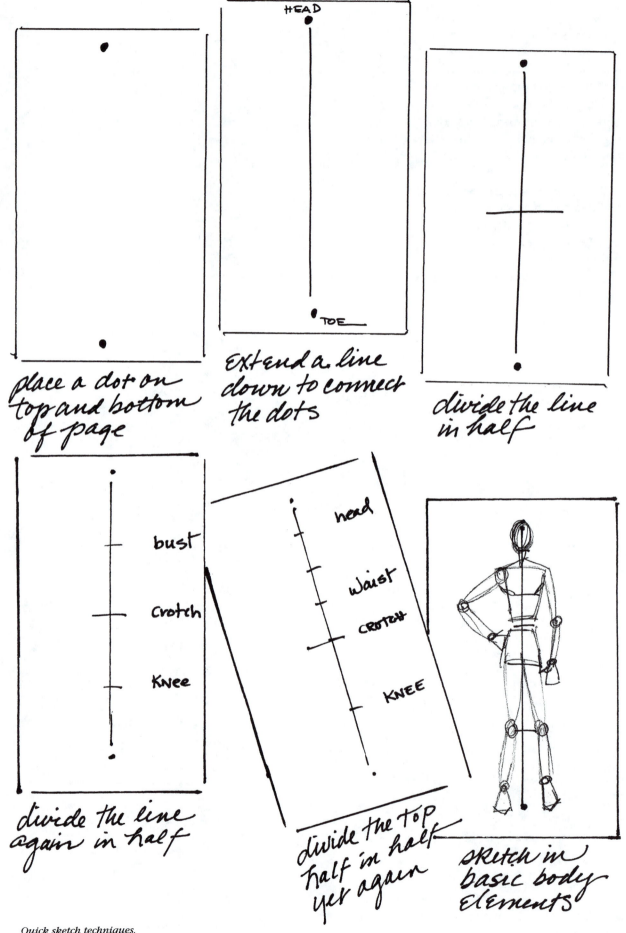

place a dot on top and bottom of page

HEAD

TOE

Extend a line down to connect the dots

divide the line in half

bust

Crotch

Knee

divide the line again in half

head

waist

CROTCH

KNEE

divide the top half in half yet again

sketch in basic body elements

Quick sketch techniques.

QUICK SKETCH TECHNIQUES

Now that you have mastered the concept of body shapes and proportion, practice this short-cut method for developing a figure croquis. Draw a straight line vertically at the center of a piece of paper. Leave a space at the top and bottom of the line. Divide the line in half with a small mark. This is the crotch line.

Divide both the upper and lower spaces in half again with a small mark. The top mark indicates the bust line. The bottom division indicates the knees. Divide the upper portion of the line in half again, which is the chin line, and divide the space between the first division and the bust in half. Now, let's "fill in the dots." Draw the head in the top space. Fill in the bodice block, drawing the bust at the second dot on the center line. The base of the neck falls exactly half way between the bust and chin line.

Add the hip block from the half-way mark up to the waist. Draw the long columnar upper leg to the bottom

half-way mark. Continue the lower leg columns to the bottom of your line. Add the foot wedges to complete the figure.

Add arms by quickly sketching in the circular ball joints at the shoulder. Draw two circles at the waistline and connect the two balls with long columns. Draw smaller balls indicating the wrist joints just at the crotch line, and add the hand shape.

This quick sketch formula creates an eight-and-one-half-head figure. To lengthen the figure, simply move the first mark up slightly above the half-way mark, and proceed as before, dividing the upper and lower space into successively smaller divisions.

Many designers develop figure croquis that they trace over as a guide when designing garments. Several front and back examples are sketched with median and princess lines indicated to guide the designer who does not have the time to draw a figure from scratch for each design.

Courtesy of Steve Bieck.

CHAPTER 3

Drawing the Fashion Face

The face is a focal point in a picture and the first thing the viewer looks at. A child's first drawing is usually an attempt to draw a face because a mother's face is the most important early human image a baby recognizes. The face gives a fashion illustration definition and character. A poorly drawn face will detract from an otherwise good illustration, just as a well-drawn face will enhance a poor drawing.

The face establishes the age of a fashion figure. A youthful face has a natural look with a slightly rounded nose and full mouth, a natural hairstyle, and little makeup. The sophisticated fashion face has sharper, more defined features, subtle but definite makeup, and a tailored hairstyle. Evening gowns are sketched on elegant models with stylized makeup and hairstyles.

Usually a simple hairstyle and makeup are more effective because the drawing of the face does not detract from the garment. Begin collecting *scrap* (photographs and sketches of faces and hairstyles) to inspire your drawing. Sketch from life and try to capture the personality of your models.

Hint: Sometimes all you need is a few brushstrokes to create a fashion face and attitude!

FACIAL PROPORTIONS

Study the face shown here. The head is oval shaped, with the fuller end representing the forehead. The features are balanced symmetrically on either side of the vertical *median* (central) line.

The eyes are placed on the horizontal median of the head. They are almond-shaped, with almost the length of a whole eye between them. Eyebrows begin at the inside corner of the eye, arch over the midpoint of the almond shape, and extend slightly beyond the outer edge.

The nose falls at the lower one-third division of the face and lines up with the inner corner of the eyes. The mouth is centered below the nose.

The chin is slender and well defined.

The oval shape of the face is accented with prominent cheekbones defined by shadows. The tops of the ears align with the eyes and end parallel to the mouth. The natural hairline curves around the skull above line 1. The neck lines up with the outer corner of the eyes, extending on the side lateral lines connecting to the head at the back of the neck.

Practice drawing smooth, even, oval shapes between two vertical lines with a #2 soft pencil. Hold your pencil with a light, firm grip as you draw the ovals.

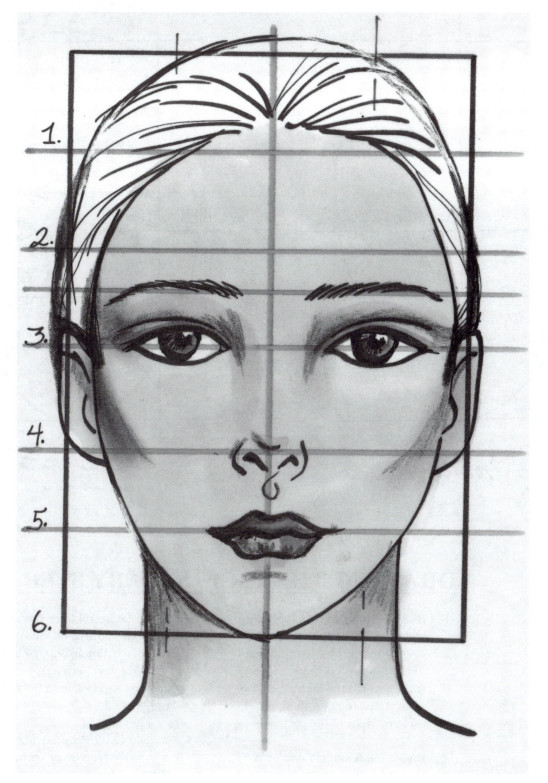

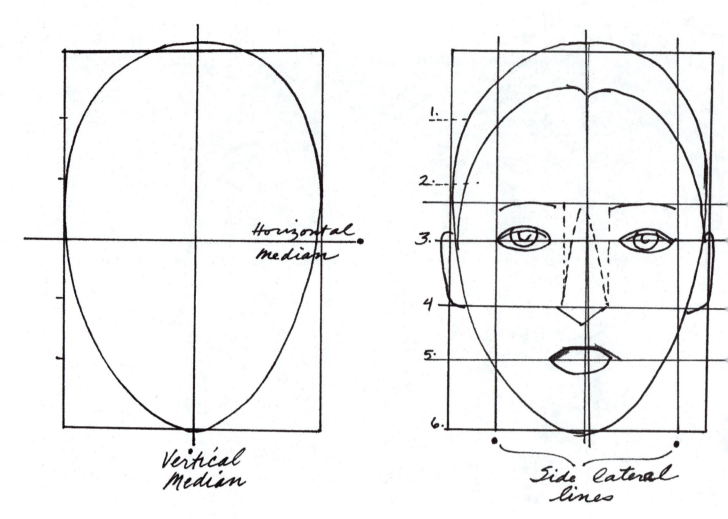

Horizontal median

Vertical Median

Side lateral lines

DRAWING THE FACE, STEP BY STEP

1. Draw a rectangle 6 inches long and 4 inches wide on a piece of overlay paper. Measure and mark the 6 inches on the sides of the rectangle. Fill the rectangle with an oval that touches the bottom, top, and sides of the rectangle.

2. Divide the rectangle into quarters—2 inches on either side of the vertical median, 3 inches on either side of the horizontal median.

3. Measure 1½ inches on either side of the vertical median and lightly draw the two side lateral lines.

4. From the lateral lines inward along the horizontal median, draw two 1-inch-long, almond-shaped eyes. Notice that there is approximately 1 inch between the eyes.

5. Extend two light guidelines down from the inner corners of the eyes. Indicate the nostrils, which are evenly balanced on either side of the vertical median (line 4).

6. Draw shallow ear shapes at the sides of the head between the eyes (line 3) and nose (slightly beyond line 4).

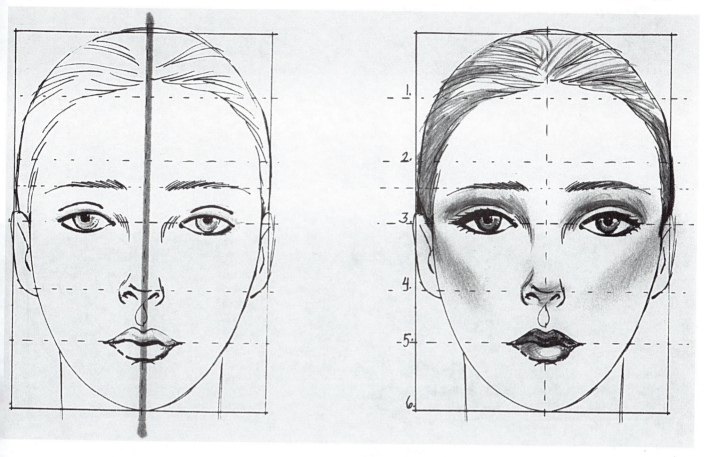

7. Draw the mouth, extending it slightly beyond the inner lateral lines above line 5.

8. Curve the side lateral lines slightly inward and draw the neck.

9. Add cheekbone contours inside the ears, and shade them.

10. Draw eyebrows beginning at the inner corners of the eyes. Arch the brows at the center and extend them slightly beyond the outer edges of the eyes. Use light, short lines to imitate the way eyebrow hairs grow. (Hard pencil lines are passé.)

11. Detail the eyes with lids and pupils.

12. Add the hairline above line 1, extending it to the sides of the ears.

13. Shade the eyes and bridge of the nose.

Put your finished exercise over the face on page 43 and compare the two. Make corrections in fine-line red felt pen. Practice the front face many times. Draw the eyes and mouths on the following pages. Draw faces from life, photographs, and other drawings. Develop personality and style for your illustrations.

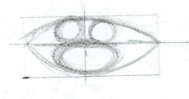

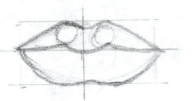

FEATURES

DRAWING THE MOUTH

1. Divide a small rectangle as shown. The top lip is usually smaller than the bottom lip.
2. Draw two circles in the top part of the rectangle and a larger oval below these.
3. Detail the shape of the mouth, using the ovals as a guide and carrying the lines to the edge of the rectangle.
4. Shade and shape the lips.

Notice the many ways the basic features can be drawn to create exciting, unique faces.

DRAWING THE EYE

1. Draw an almond shape.
2. Divide the top third of the almond with the curved lid line. Fill at least one-third of the eye with a round circle for the iris. Notice that the lid covers the top of the iris.
3. Add the pupil to the center of the iris and shape the inner corner of the eye.
4. Detail the eye with subtle lashes, highlights, and shadows.

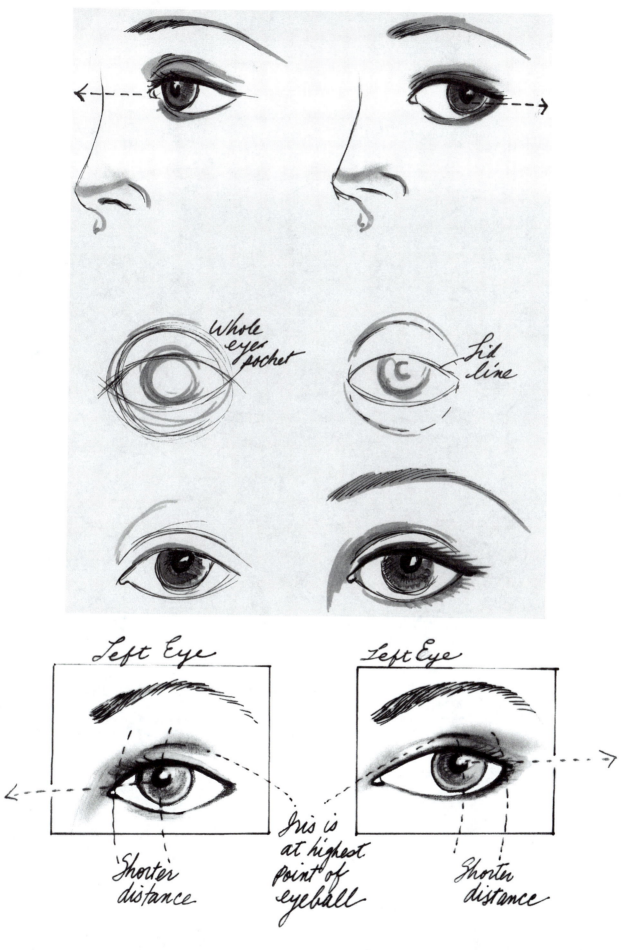

Whole eyes pocket

Lid line

Left Eye

Left Eye

Shorter distance

Iris is at highest point of eyeball

Shorter distance

The Black face has rounder forehead and high cheekbones. The bridge of the nose and nostrils are wider. Eyes are rounder, lips fuller

The Oriental face has heavy eyelids, flatter nose. Hair looks best when done as a graphic shape.

A smile should never be indi-cated by individual teeth

Hair makes a statement here, and completes the look of a High Fashion — bordering-on-Blasè-Style!

Make accessories complement the hair and fashion style

THE PROFILE FACE

The profile head fills an approximate square. The shape of the head is roughly an oval with a pointed lower corner representing the chin. The face fills the front diagonal half of the square. Notice how placement of the features relates to placement on the front face. The eyes fall on the horizontal median, and the nose falls at line 4. The lips are drawn in the same position, slightly above line 5, as on the front face. The placement of the ear is between the eyes and the nose.

The hairline conforms roughly to the diagonal line through the square. Do not emphasize the jawbone, which connects to the neck behind the ear, as it will look too masculine.

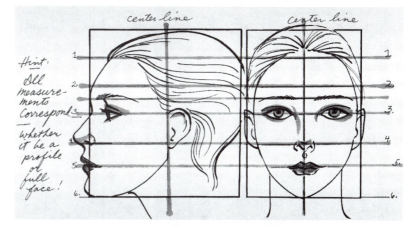

Placement of the features on the front and profile heads are aligned

Notice how the eye and mouth are drawn in profile (see pages 50 and 51). Practice drawing several of these features before you attempt the step-by-step profile drawing on the next pages.

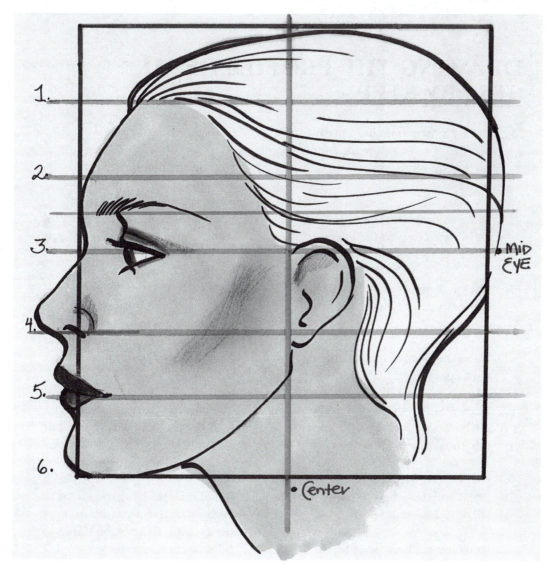

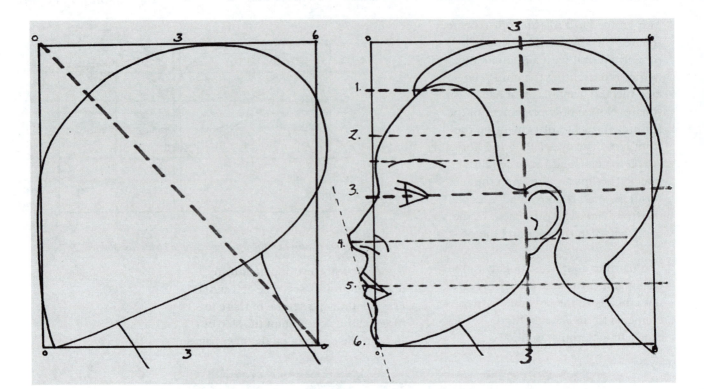

DRAWING THE PROFILE HEAD, STEP BY STEP

1. Draw a square 6 inches long by 5½ inches wide and mark 1-inch vertical divisions using overlay paper.

2. Draw an oval with the narrow end slanted toward the lower corner of the square.

3. Draw a diagonal guideline from corner to corner, bisecting the square.

4. Divide the square into quarters with light lines.

5. Draw a wedge shape centered on the horizontal median, line 3. Indicate the profile eye shape here.

6. Shape the nose, indenting it at line 3 and drawing the triangular shape ending at line 4.

7. Draw the ear between the eye and the nose on the vertical

   median of the square.

8. Outline the mouth and chin.

9. Draw the neck coming from behind the diagonal in a graceful curve.

10. Draw the mouth above line 5.

11. Curve the chin but do not make it weak or too exaggerated. Draw a line from the nose to the chin. The lips should just touch this line.

12. The hairline corresponds roughly to the diagonal. Curve the hair around the ears and at the nape of the neck.

13. Detail the eye. Notice how the eyebrow arches over the front of the eye as it follows the skull's ridge over the eye socket.

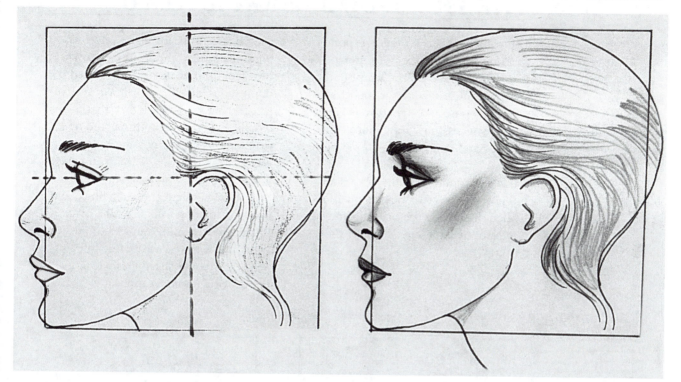

14. Add the nostril and the outer curve of the nose. Refine the profile of the nose.

15. Detail and shadow the mouth, and shadow the cheekbones.

Place your sketch over the first profile drawing on page 49. Compare your drawing to the standard, and correct errors with a fine-line red felt pen.

Sketch profiles from life, photographs, and other drawings. Notice the infinite variety of shapes of faces and noses. Draw the profiles facing left and right, so that you will be able to draw both. (Beginners tend to draw a profile facing in the direction of their weaker hand.)

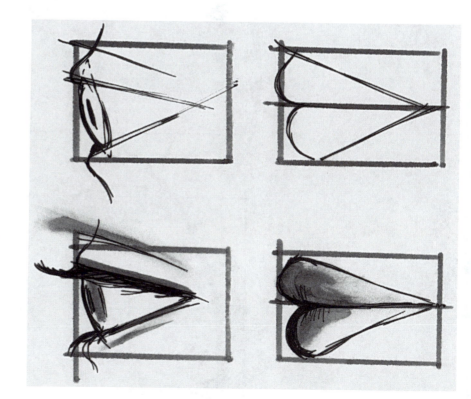

TURNING THE HEAD:
THE THREE-DIMENSIONAL HEAD

The volume of the head corresponds to a box drawn in one-point perspective. The features can be simplified to stylized indications, but a concrete idea of volume and structure is necessary to successfully draw more complicated and realistic faces.

Study the volume sketches that show the nose and eyes in various positions. Notice that tilting the head up and down subtly alters the shape of the features.

Sketch several heads using photographs as inspiration. Break down the structural elements of the head by outlining the shadowed areas. Always identify the part of the face that is closest to you because it has the truest proportions for the accurate placement of the features. When you have a good rough drawing in a square, trace over it, leaving out the guidelines, and use light shadows done with a black Prismacolor pencil to model the head. Draw the features with a fine-line black felt pen, a sharp Prismacolor pencil, or a Rapidograph.

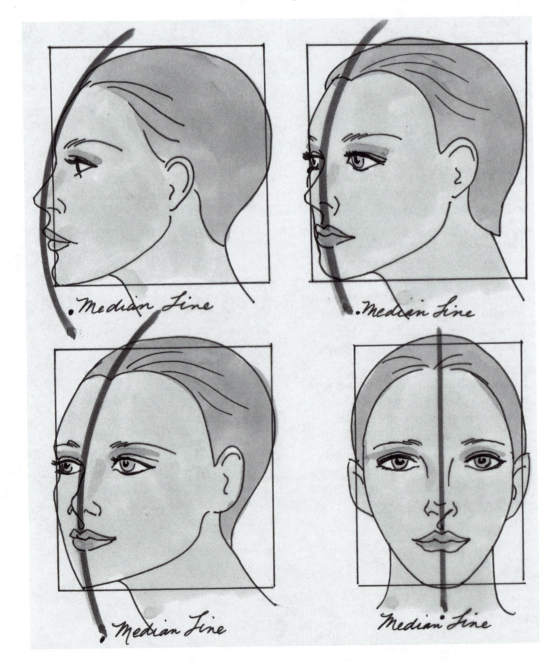

Median Line

Median Line

Median Line

Median Line

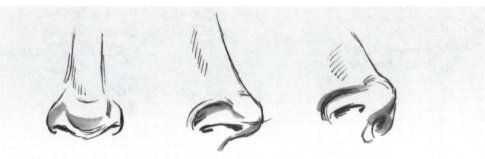

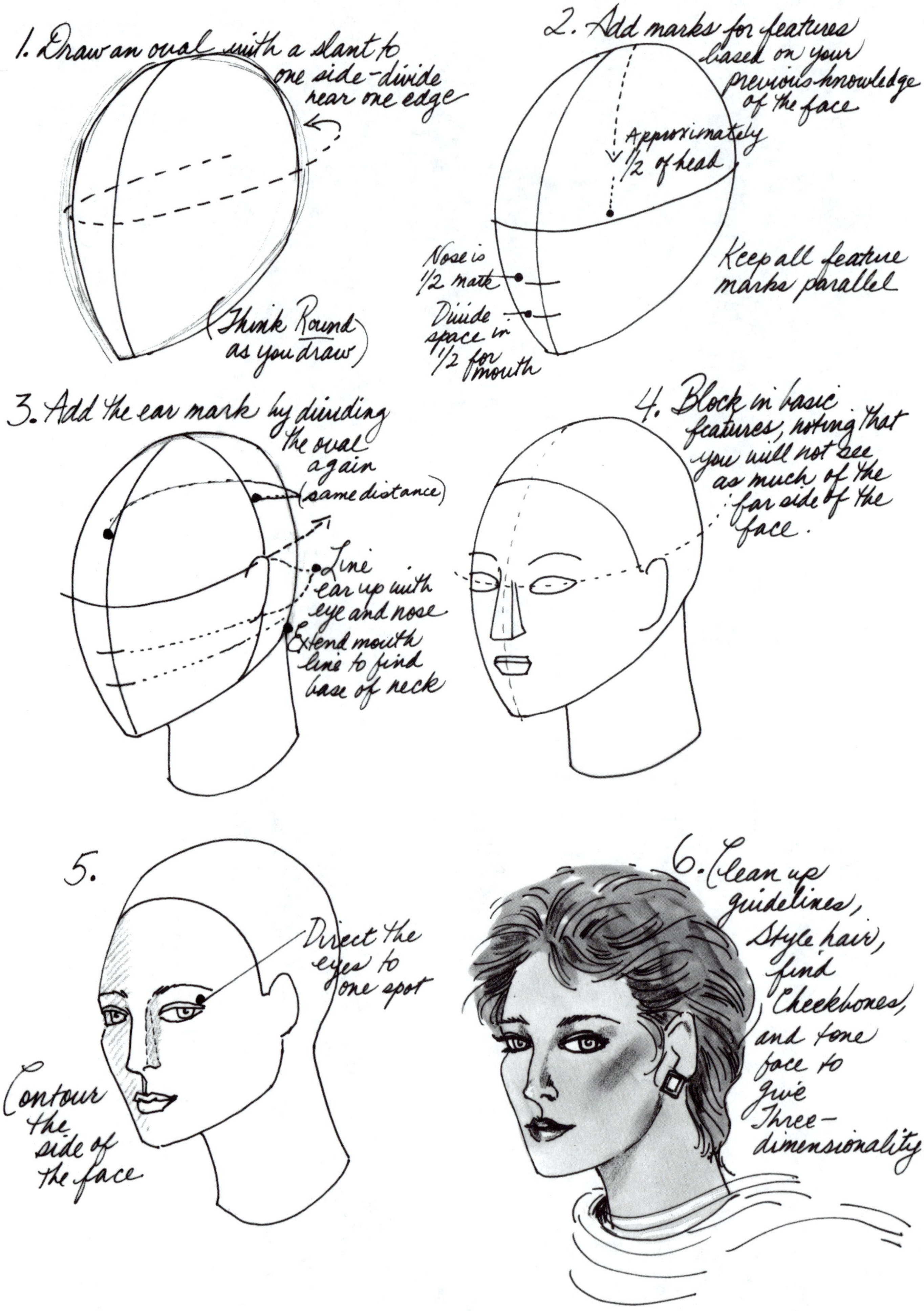

1. Draw an oval with a slant to one side - divide near one edge

(Think Round as you draw)

2. Add marks for features based on your previous knowledge of the face

↓ Approximately 1/2 of head

Nose is 1/2 mark

Divide space in 1/2 for mouth

Keep all feature marks parallel

3. Add the ear mark by dividing the oval again (same distance)

Line ear up with eye and nose

Extend mouth line to find base of neck

4. Block in basic features, noting that you will not see as much of the far side of the face.

5.

Direct the eyes to one spot

Contour the side of the face

6. Clean up guidelines, style hair, find cheekbones, and tone face to give three-dimensionality

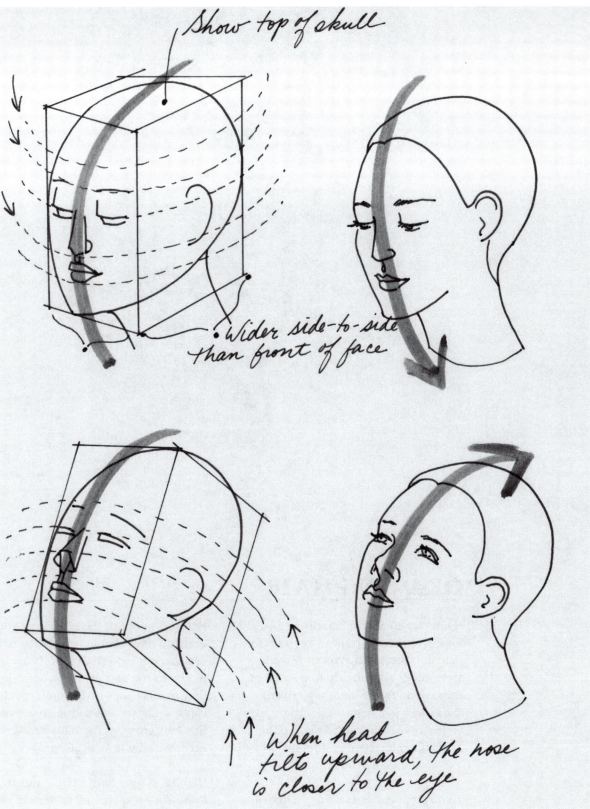

Show top of skull

Wider side-to-side
than front of face

When head
tilts upward, the nose
is closer to the eye

DRAWING HAIR

Hairstyles change as rapidly as fashions, so it is important to keep up to date. It is also important to use a hairstyle that is appropriate to the age of the fashion figure and the garment she is wearing. A stylized, ornate hairstyle would be as out of place on a fashion model wearing a tennis dress as it would be on the tennis court.

To inspire your selection of hairstyles, observe and collect photographs (scrap) from fashion magazines. Look at people and study the way well-groomed hair looks. Remember that the hairstyle you select should not detract from the garment.

Hair grows out of the scalp, and your drawing lines should imitate the natural growth pattern of hair. Draw the direction the hair grows with irregularly spaced lines that simplify and capture the volume of the style. Soft, fine hair grows at the hairline, so render it with light, delicate strokes.

Highlights give hair a sleek, healthy look. They are created by letting the white of the paper remain as the light accent, darkening in natural shadows, and then accenting the lines that indicate the direction the hair flows.

Block in face and features— Check proportions, create a mood

Add tone, refine face shape and features

DRAWING HAIR, STEP BY STEP

1. Draw a face with a light pencil line indicating the features and skull.

2. Block in the general silhouette of the hairstyle.

3. Erase the vague indication of the skull.

4. Draw directional lines starting at the hairline and flowing out to the edge of the silhouette. Make the lines irregularly spaced. Continue to detail the features as you work on the hairstyle.

5. Shadow and highlight the hair. Observe hairstyles in photographs, noticing how the highlights occur in various styles and hair colors. A darker area around the face is an effective contrast device.

6. Fully detail and shadow the features.

7. To render blond hair, use more highlight areas and fewer deep shadows. Do not eliminate all tone, however, or the hairstyle will lack definition.

More tone, refine linework, add highlights

8. An upswept hairstyle accented with a dressy hair ornament is appropriate for a more sophisticated outfit.

Sketch a series of ten hairstyles from magazine photographs. Experiment with felt pens and Prismacolor and lead pencil. Try using only line to illustrate some of the hairstyles. Illustrate a variety of ages. Try adding hair accessories such as combs and ribbons to vary the effect.

THE YOUTHFUL FACE
A young junior model should have a simple
hairstyle and natural makeup. The cheeks are
often shadowed on top of the cheekbone so the
face looks suntanned. A casual pose completes
the natural look.

Simple Hairdo

Light
Eyebrows

Less
Eye
Make Up

Less defined
cheekbones

Freckles

Softer, Fuller
Lips

Sunglasses:
an effective
prop

Casual hairstyle
with movement

Little makeup

Casual, easy
linework –
looking
quite
effortless

THE ACTIVE FACE
*Active clothes look best on a
sports figure with a bright, active
look. The hairstyle should be
very casual. Props appropriate to
the sport and sunglasses help set
the stage.*

THE DAYTIME HIGH-FASHION FACE
This model should have the look of polished
sophistication. A simple but elegant hairstyle
and makeup will not detract from the clothes
being illustrated.

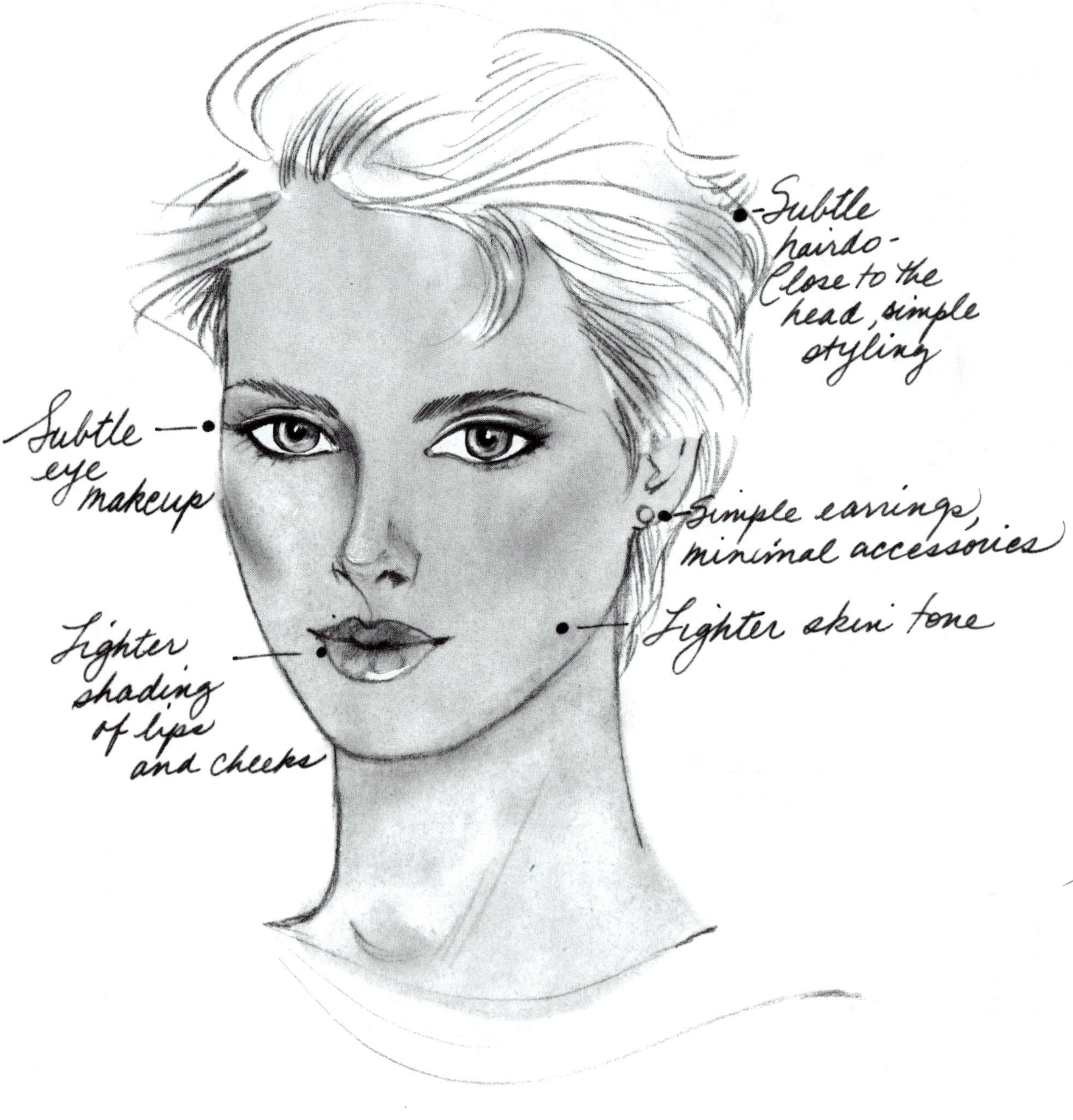

Subtle hairdo - Close to the head, simple styling

Subtle eye makeup

Simple earrings, minimal accessories

Lighter skin tone

Lighter shading of lips and cheeks

Heavier eye and brow makeup

Heavier shading on lips and cheeks

More stylized or flamboyant hairstyle

Flashy accessories

Darker skin tone

THE SOPHISTICATED EVENING FACE
The drama of evening clothes is enhanced by more stylized and defined makeup. Elaborate jewelry is appropriate. The hairstyle can be more flamboyant or stylized, depending on the type of evening dress illustrated.

CHAPTER 4

Moving the Figure

The suggestion that a fashion figure is moving adds drama, excitement, and personality to a sketch. All body movement is governed by the structure of the body. The base of the neck is the center of gravity that determines the vertical (or axial) balance line. When the figure is standing with the weight evenly distributed on both feet, the axial line falls midway between the feet. All the horizontal body lines—the shoulder, rib cage, pelvis, and knees—are parallel to the floor and form 90-degree angles with the axial line.

TYPICAL POSES

The one-leg stand is a typical fashion pose because flowing body lines are created. For this pose, the figure relaxes one leg and supports most of the body's weight on the other leg, which realigns the axial line and horizontal body lines. It is important not to let the figure in this asymmetrical pose lean. To avoid this situation, draw a vertical axial line from the base of the neck perpendicular to the bottom of the page. This line must intersect the heel of the support leg or the figure will tilt. When a figure is leaning against a prop, the axial line falls between the support leg and the prop.

The slant of the shoulder and pelvis blocks are altered when the body's weight is supported mostly by one leg. The shoulder can align with the pelvic block. In this pose, the high shoulder is over the high hip.

In the classic one-leg stand, the rib cage is tilted in opposition to the pelvic block, and the high shoulder is over the low hip. A smooth S curve is created by placing the body's two major masses in opposing directions. This pose is very flattering and shows clothes fluidly, with very little distortion of detail or silhouette. Yet the figure suggests a great deal of movement and action. Notice that the axial line in both of the one-leg stands starts at the base of the neck and always falls at the heel of the leg supporting the majority of the body's weight.

Practice drawing these three figures several times. Concentrate on lining up the base of the neck with the supporting leg, drawing this axial line in a contrasting color felt-tip pen.

THE AXIAL LINE
The axial line governs the balance of any
figure. In a balanced stand, when the weight
is on both feet, the axial line falls between the
legs. In a one-leg stand, the axial line starts at
the base of the neck and lines up with the heel
of the support leg.

DRAWING FROM LIVE MODELS

Courtesy of Charles Bush.

Beginners are often confused when they first try to draw from a live model. The subject looks complicated and difficult to draw after working from photographs. Here are some suggestions to help you begin.

Study the pose before you begin to draw. Analyze the slant of the shoulders and the hip bone. Notice how the head tilts and curves into the base of the neck. Determine which leg is supporting the major weight load. Draw an imaginary axial line from the base of the neck to the heel of the supporting leg, or hold up your pencil and squint to visualize the flow of the pose. Notice how the arms are posed, and relate the elbows to an arc that passes smoothly through the waist.

Now you are ready to sketch the live model. Follow the steps on the next page as you draw a sketch from a live model. For additional practice, stand in front of a full-length mirror with your sketch pad on a tall stool and pose. Sketch yourself, idealizing and lengthening your proportions to the eight-and-one-half-head figure. Check your hand and leg positions in the mirror and draw these. Remember, nothing substitutes for an analysis of the structural elements of the pose before you pick up your pencil.

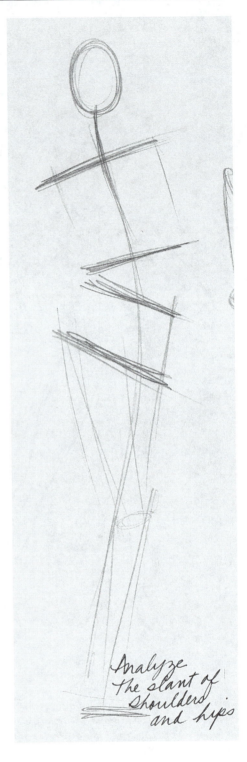

Analyze the slant of shoulders and hips

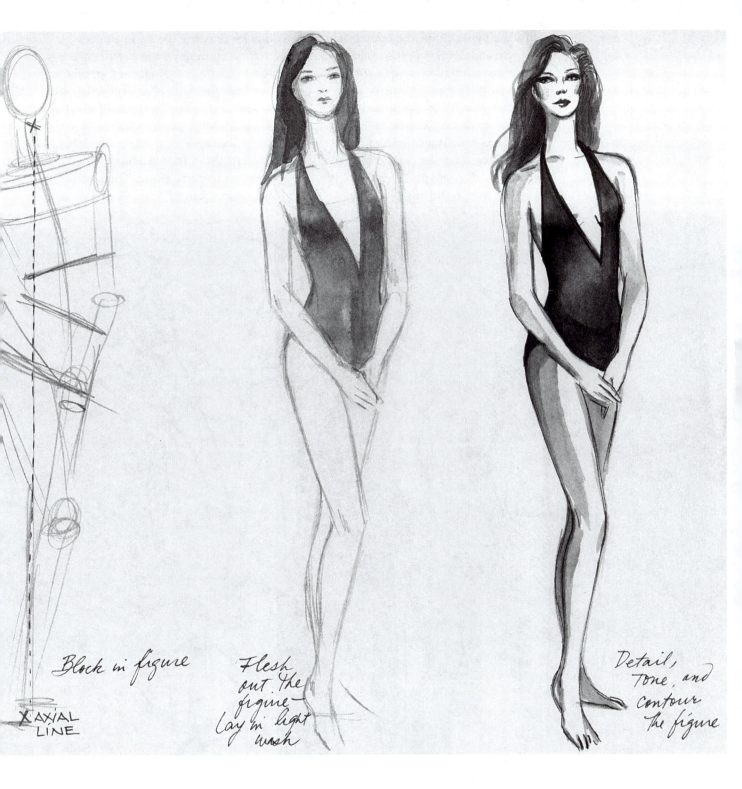

Block in figure

X AXIAL
LINE

Flesh
out the
figure
Lay in light
wash

Detail,
Tone, and
contour
the figure

THE THREE-DIMENSIONAL BODY

As the figure turns, the body planes rotate and develop depth. Arms and legs are often partially or entirely hidden by the torso. Whether you are drawing from a live pose or a photograph, evaluate the pose before beginning to draw. Trace the part of the body that is closest to you (the leading edge) with your eyes. Then begin to lightly sketch the head and torso blocks, drawing the leading edges first. Keep in mind the perspective lesson in Chapter 1. Notice if the torso is blocking the view of an arm or leg. If it is, draw the arm nearest to you first. Then draw the partially hidden arm. Draw the main support leg first. Make sure it falls on the axial line so that your figure does not tip. Then draw the more relaxed balance leg.

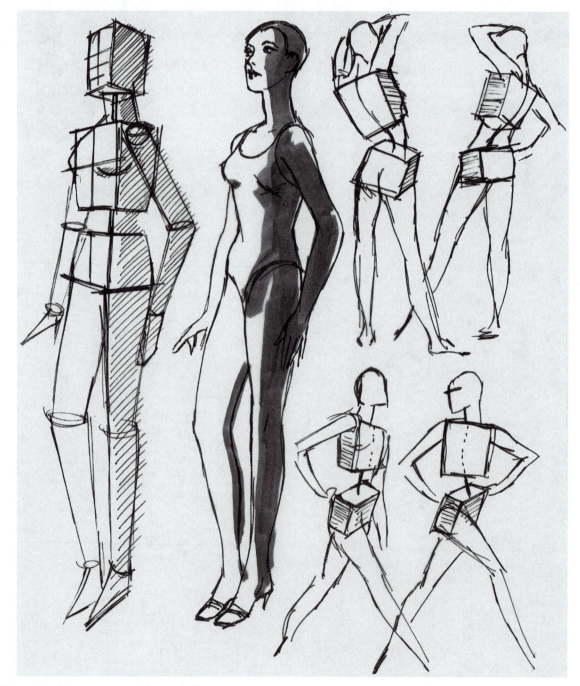

Perspective is important to understand when drawing a moving figure.

Draw the median line (center) on the face and torso blocks. It will shift farther and farther to the side as the figure rotates. On a back view, the median line is the spine, which becomes the silhouette of the profile figure.

Study these sketches and draw a series of three-dimensional figure studies from models in similar poses. Lightly draw the simple box figure blocks before fleshing out your sketch. Remember the one-point perspective lesson in Chapter 1. Visualize the body in three dimensions. Use shading to increase the feeling of added dimension.

THE S CURVE

Fashion sketching, especially when done by designers, is used primarily to show garment detail and silhouette. For this reason, a frontal pose is usually the most suitable. A rigid, straight forward pose can be repetitious and stiff, but the figure becomes exciting when it follows a flowing S curve. The one-leg stand, with well-posed arms that give the shoulders direction and thrust, will show a gar-ment to its best advantage. In addition, the rib cage and pelvis can twist in opposite directions because the waist is very flexible. This twist adds even greater movement to the one-leg-stand pose.

A profile pose can also have a graceful S curve line when the shoulders are thrust back and the pelvis forward.

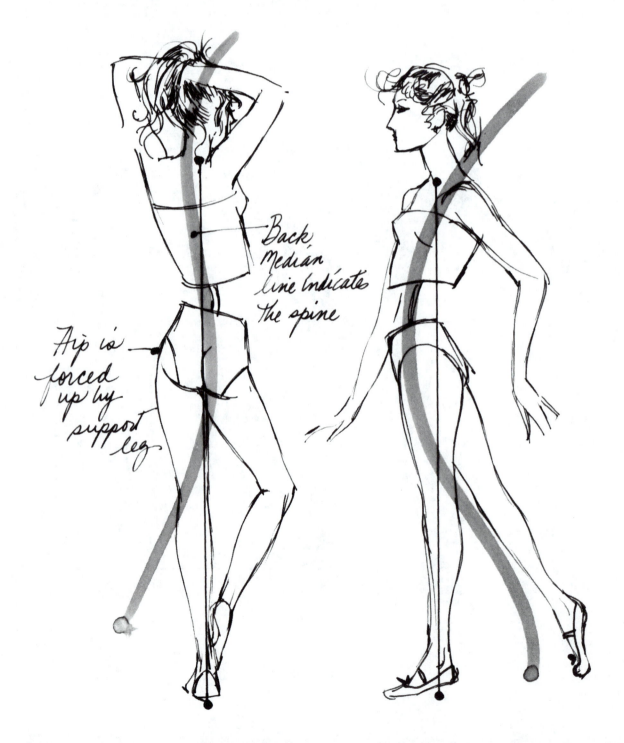

Back median line indicates the spine

Hip is forced up by support leg

The direction and placement of the head and neck are important for creating a flowing, graceful body line. Draw the head at a pleasing angle to the rest of the body.

Practice drawing these figures many times. Start with a broad-nib, light-gray felt pen and draw the S curve first. Then construct a body along this flowing line. Check the axial line frequently and do not forget that the axial line is a guide for realistic support of the flowing pose.

High hip indicates the supporting leg

Courtesy of Charles Bush.

DRAWING FROM PHOTOGRAPHS

Fashion magazines, especially those from Europe, are an excellent source of figures for sketching because they feature trendy styling and innovative photography. A pose is easily adapted from a *swipe* (magazine photograph) when it is used as a suggestion, not a tracing, for a drawing. Analyze the photograph as you would a live pose, determining the axial line of the figure before drawing a line. Notice the slant of the shoulders. Are the hips angled in opposition to the shoulders? Put a piece of overlay or tracing paper over the photograph and quickly rough in the body blocks. Do not trace directly from the photograph because your figure will look stocky and awkward. Put another piece of tracing paper over the rough blocks you traced from the figure and use them as a guide to sketching a finished figure. Refer back to the photograph to make sure the details are accurate.

Block out ten or more figures from magazine photographs. Select several of your favorite block figures to work into finished sketches. Experiment with drawing clothes by observing how the fabric drapes and flows over the body. Use the block figures as guides and try to sketch the figures and garments without using further guidelines. Leave your work for several hours, then compare your sketches with the photograph. Turn the tracing or overlay paper over so you can see the reverse image of your sketches or hold your drawings up to a mirror. Obvious mistakes will pop out at you because your eye adjusts to a sketch that it sees develop over a period of time and tends to compensate for unbalanced symmetrical elements. By reversing the image, you will have a new perspective on the sketch and can analyze its weaknesses.

FORESHORTENING THE FIGURE

Visualizing complicated poses as a series of geometric forms will help beginners analyze and draw the sitting or reclining figure. The axial line for a seated pose relates the base of the neck to the seat. When the weight of the figure is partially supported by an arm, the axial line will fall at a point between the support arm and the seat.

Think of an arm or leg as a cylindrical shape when you want to foreshorten it. Draw the part closest to your eye first. Notice how the part of the body closest to you is larger than the part that is turned away. Draw cylindrical, spiraling lines for the arm or leg as it curves back toward the body. Observation and practice are the

surest teachers for mastering perspective. Quick sketches from life and photography will sharpen your analytical eye and drawing ability.

Perspective plays an important part in drawing a three-dimensional pose. Establish the eye level of the figure you want to draw. At this line, your eye views a flat dimension. Above the eye-level line you will look up at the bottom of the geometric cubes representing the rib cage or pelvic block. Horizontal lines of the figure or garments will have a subtle upward arc. Below eye level the body blocks will be viewed from the top, and horizontal lines will have a downward curve at the center.

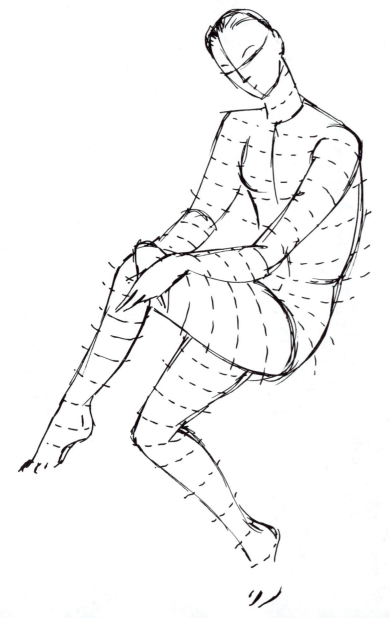

ADDING MOVEMENT TO THE FIGURE

The advanced illustrator is able to give figures realistic action that creates a dramatic drawing. *Loose* drawing has an immediate, spontaneous look that is not overly self-conscious about rendering details. To loosen up your drawing and give it a confident, loose look, use the following techniques and sketch from life or from photographs of a figure in action.

Quickly sketch the body blocks and limbs with a broad-nib, light-colored, felt-tip pen. Use as few strokes as possible to capture the action of the figure. Do not worry about details. Work quickly on live poses—no longer than two minutes. If you are working from photographs, clip out ten or more and use a timer to tell you when to move on to the next sketch. Later, select the best action drawings and use them under a fresh sheet of overlay paper the way you used the tracings of the skeleton in Chapter 2. Draw detailed figures with Prismacolor pencils or fine-line markers, incorporating the movement of the block figure underneath.

Spiral drawing is another effective technique for loosening up your drawings. Start with the head and work through the body with quick spirals, never letting your pencil leave the paper. Practice several times and rework the best examples as you did with the felt-pen action drawings.

You may also loosen up your figures by drawing with a soft piece of charcoal. Wedge the end of the stick, then block in the masses with the broad part of the charcoal and sketch the limbs with a single stroke. Check the proportion of the figure to the crotch line to make sure the legs are at least as long as the torso and head of your figure.

Still another technique is to start with an S curve drawn with a broad-nib, light-color felt pen. Sketch the body around this curve with a soft pencil or fine-line marker. Emphasize the angles of the shoulders and pelvic block.

Whenever you feel stale or tight, review these techniques for refreshing your approach and putting action into your drawings.

Courtesy of Charles Bush

Courtesy of Charles Bush

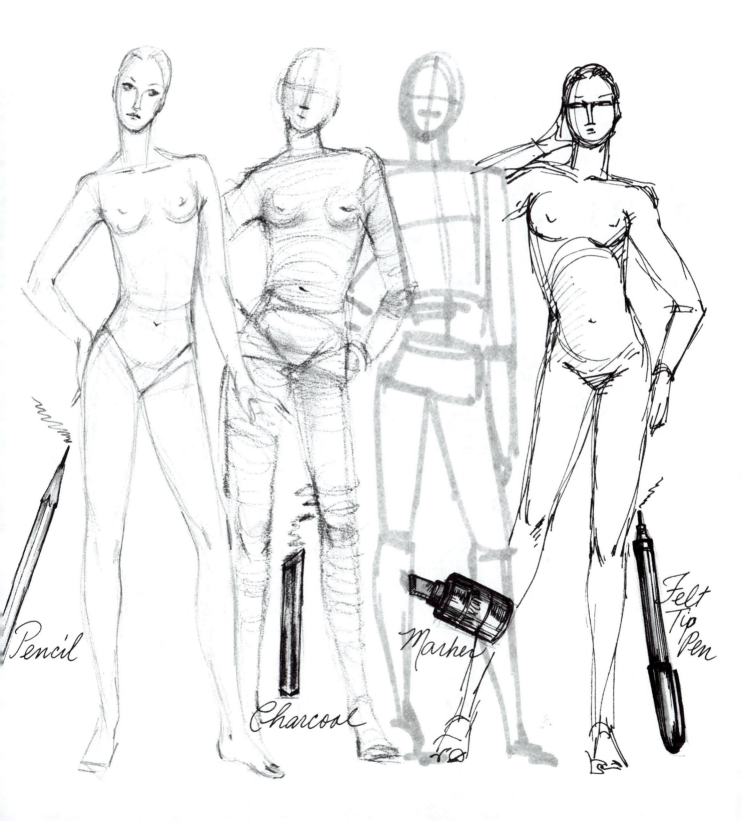

Pencil

Charcoal

Marker

Felt Tip Pen

SCRAP

Start a clipping file of photographs and illustrations that you can use for inspiration. Search out many different ages, images, and kinds of models that inspire you.

THE SKETCHBOOK

Use your sketchbook every day. Carry it with you and doodle. Make quick sketches of everything that interests you. Make drawing an enjoyable habit.

1. Original Photograph

2. Vellum overlay - Block in figure - give swing and movement to sketch

3. Overlay - Block in garment - detail and style

4. Finished sketch on Third Overlay

ACTION DRAWING BECOMES FINISHED ART.
ck in a simple figure on a pice of vellum you
e placed over an action drawing. Draw the
hes on the figure. Detail with pencil or felt
. Try to capture the movement in your
ginal sketch in the second drawing.

THE ARTIST'S MEASURE

As you work with more complicated figure problems, remember the basic proportion lessons from Chapter 2. Use a pencil to quickly measure the figure as you sketch. Measure the figure from the head to the crotch by lining up your pencil point with the top of the head and marking the crotch with your finger on the pencil. Drop the pencil down and indicate the length at the bottom of the figure as a guide to where the feet must fall. This measuring technique can be used for arms and legs in complicated poses where the limbs do not automatically line up with the body. Use the body proportions to guide your pencil measure.

A pencil can also be used to measure and line up a live model's pose. Squint your eye and hold out your pencil to determine the axial line of a pose. Double-check the model's proportions and limb length, then bring the pencil down to your sketch and compare the visual image to your drawing.

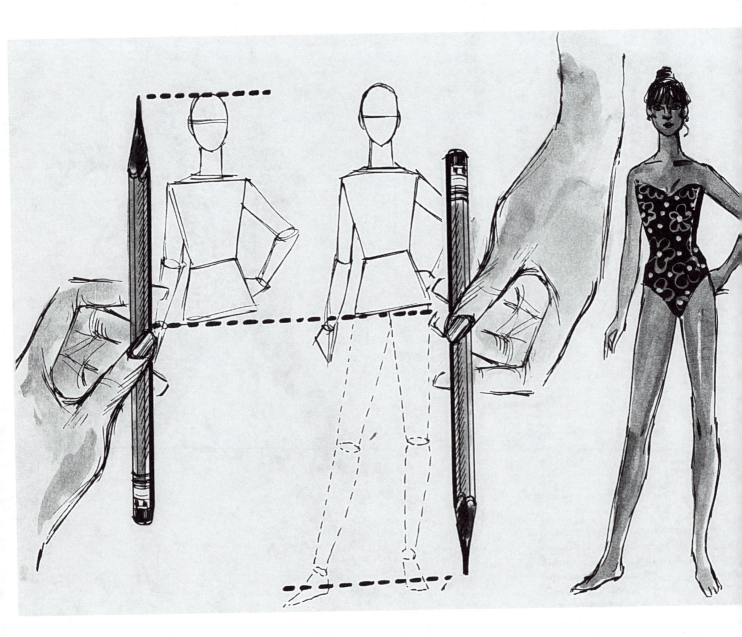

C H A P T E R   5

Drawing Clothes

WHAT IS FASHION?

Fashion is the prevailing style of a specific group of people at a particular time. The style of garments is determined by such elements as the silhouette (the outline of a garment), the fabric, and the details. For example, the silhouette can be loose and boxy, or clingy and fitted to the body. Fabrics can be heavy or light, crisp or soft. And details can be large and dramatic or small and delicate, flamboyant or subtle.

Styles of clothes are continuously changing and evolving, generally shifting in cycles that emphasize different parts of the anatomy. For instance, in the 1960s the focus was on the legs. Garments were short and youthful, with the silhouette shrunk to a small wedge shape that looked like a young girl's dress. Fabrics were crisp and structured and tailored into A-line dresses and jackets.

To keep up with current styles, fashion illustrators and designers must continually update their knowledge of apparel and lifestyle trends. They must be aware of the creations of high-fashion designers and of trends in lower-priced *RTW* (ready to wear). They must understand the influence of foreign designers and the effects of changes in lifestyle on clothing.

As you study these sources, keep in mind that styles usually do not change dramatically. Watch for subtle shifts in emphasis and proportion. For example, jackets rarely jump from short and fitted to long and boxy. Rather, the process will take several years. The silhouette will gradually move away from the body, losing waist definition: The sleeves will become looser, the jacket longer. Shoulder pads may become more pronounced, emphasizing the square shape. Soft, finely woven fabrics will give way to stiffer, more firmly woven ones. The details of pockets and lapels will change. Buttons will decrease in number and perhaps disappear altogether. The relationship of the jacket to skirts and pants will be altered.

All of these large and small elements work together to create the style of a garment. The more accurately you are able to see changes in these elements, the more precisely you will be able to capture the elusive shifts in fashion trends. Exposure and careful observation are the keys to acquiring this knowledge and developing your taste and fashion sense.

An infinite variety of clothes identifies and adorns the people who surround us. Train yourself to see what clothes people are wearing and how they are wearing those clothes. Observe the total effect and the specific details that make an outfit unique. Develop the habit of sketching a detail or garment that you admire. Make drawing a method of recording your impressions.

Stores are stages where appealing apparel is displayed. Shop apparel stores and carefully study the clothes. Try to remember what you see on the rack and sketch it when you leave the store. Draw directly from window displays. The attractive mannequins are good stationary models to show how the latest apparel should fit and be accessorized.

Go to fashion shows. Sketch the models as they parade in the latest styles. Sketch the poses and apparel with quick gesture drawings in your sketchbook.

Sit in a restaurant in a chic part of town and observe and sketch customers. Try to capture the current trends and how real people wear the fashion presented to them by the apparel media and industry.

Exposure to all types of fashion media is essential to every person who creates or illustrates apparel. Look at and collect fashion drawings or photographs that appeal to you. Read trade publications that preview future fashion developments and consumer publications that feature apparel to stimulate consumer's purchases. The following trade publications are important for their visual fashion coverage.

- *Women's Wear Daily (WWD),* Fairchild Publications, 7 East 12th Street, New York, NY 10003. *WWD* is known as the bible of the fashion industry because it is the most important trade publication for women's clothing. Many artists are represented in the daily coverage of the domestic and foreign scene. This newspaper is an excellent source of sketches and fashion news.

- *California Apparel News,* California Fashion Publications, 110 East Ninth Street, Suite A 777, Los Angeles, CA 90079. This west coast newspaper has extensive coverage of the Los Angeles market and features sketches by a variety of artists. The paper also publishes editions to cover midwestern and southern regional markets.

SHAPE—LETS

Drawing by Robert Passantino for Women's Wear Daily.

CONSUMER NEWSPAPERS

- *Local newspapers.* Daily newspapers feature advertisements for current merchandise and fashion editorial sections that are invaluable for the illustrator and designer. Develop an awareness of each major retailer's advertising format and style of illustration. Consider how each format and style relates to customers.

- *The New York Times.* The great collections of major retailers that advertise daily in this newspaper make it an excellent source of sketches for the designer and illustrator. The Sunday edition occasionally includes a fashion supplement.

- *W.* This publication features the fashion coverage of *Women's Wear Daily* reprinted, often in color, for the consumer. Published twice monthly by Fairchild Publications, *W* is now printed in a magazine format. The many sketches and photographs make W an excellent source of inspiration.

SWEATER DRESSING
Eighties 'n Easy

Knits are news!

The witty shapes.
Fresh textures.
Bold patterns.
Attitudinal colors.

There's a ground swell
of new sweaterdressing—
right here, right now—
contemporary and beyond.

Expressing a Junior view:
the sweater that slinks below
the waist and stops short of
the knee—it's back on top.
A powerful statement in
favor of one-piece, sure-shot
dressing. Hooray!

Three city kickers,
from left to right:
The Thermal, knit to match
the texture of your favorite
ski undies, in navy, berry, steel
or lilac acrylic, 38.00.
Juniors on 2.

The Argyle, a whimsical
plaiding of black, blueberry
and cerise acrylic, 24.00.
Metro Juniors, Metro Level

The Stripe, a lean V-neck
in lavender/aqua/pink/maize
or green/navy/ruby/
chocolate acrylic, 38.00.
Juniors on 2.

New York. And a selection in
all our fashion stores.

Sweater Dressings Live at
bloomingdale's

1000 THIRD AVENUE. NEW YORK (355-5900). OPEN LATE MONDAY AND THURSDAY EVENINGS.

These superb illustrations by Antonio for Bloomingdale's are typical of the high-quality artwork run in The New York Times. *Fashion professionals throughout the nation subscribe to this newspaper. (Courtesy of Bloomingdale's, illustrated by Antonio, art direction by John C. Jay.)*

DESIGN REPORTS

Private subscription fashion reports are expensive but excellent sources of future fashion trends. Designers, retailers, and some fashion schools subscribe to fashion reporting services that predict what Europeans are designing, and they show sketches and photographs of what people are wearing on the streets. Many of the reports also cover the American designer and retail scenes. Some of the better fashion reports are *Pat Tunskey's Forecast and Color Box, Nigel French, Here and There, Report West,* and *The Fashion Service.*

DOMESTIC CONSUMER MAGAZINES (GLOSSIES) AND CATALOGS

- *Children's and young girls' apparel Ladies' Home Journal* has occasional articles on children's apparel. *Seventeen* and other magazines geared to the junior customer influence children's styles greatly. "Bubble gum" junior refers to the young teen.

- *Young women. Glamour, Elle,* and *Mademoiselle* appeal to college-age and young career women. These magazines feature articles that promote high audience involvement through store shows and guest editorships.

- *General and high-fashion magazines. Vogue* and *Harper's Bazaar* are the traditional high-fashion glossies. Publications such as *Mirabella, Threads,* and *Victoria* are challenging the traditional fashion journals by appealing to specialty readers. Each carries fashion articles that appeal to special interests or ages.

- *Catalogs.* Consumer magazines have abdicated the role of informing the reader how and what to wear in business and social settings by featuring exclusive and expensive fashions. Photography and selection of models and settings promote high fashion at the expense of educating the reader about new trends. This education process has been replaced by the retail sales catalog, distributed through the mail to generate sales. The phenomenal success of publications such as *Victoria's Secret, J. Crew, L. L. Bean,* and many other retail catalogs has provided the customer with fashion information suited to casual and business life styles. Collect catalogs for their wealth of poses, style details, hair styles, and fashion information.

- Many specialized and general magazines include some apparel articles. Glance through current publications for articles on apparel. Look at pattern-making and home-sewing books and magazines for different ideas.

FOREIGN FASHION PUBLICATIONS

Foreign publications offer many new perspectives on fashion through innovative design and photographs and excellent references for fashion illustrators and designers. The following list covers the most influential and readily available magazines. Subscriptions may be purchased, and

Fashion reporting for the trade is often exaggerated, but careful attention is given to construction details. (Courtesy of FOCUS, published by Pat Tunsky Inc.)

Courtesy of FOCUS, *published by Pat Tunsky Inc.*

individual copies are often sold in major city bookstores and newsstands.

- *Elle.* 90, Rue de Flandre, 75943, Paris Cedx 19, France. This trendy European fashion magazine features youthful apparel and accessories. The European edition differs from *American Elle. Elle Home* covers trends in interior decorating that often relate to apparel.

- *Lei.* Condé Nast, S.P.A., Piazza Castello, 27-20121 Milano, Italy. This magazine, the Italian counterpart of *Glamour* and *Mademoiselle,* features youth-oriented clothing and accessories.

- *Harper's Bazaar.* This magazine is published in several countries. England has *Harper* and *Queen.* In Italy it is called *Bazaar Italia.* This is a leading graphic fashion publication and can be ordered from Bazaar Italia, Corso di Porta Nuova, Linia Italia, 46 Milano, Italy.

- *L'Officiel de la Couture et du Monde de Paris.* Officiel de la Couture SZ, 226 Rue du Faubourg St. Honoré, Paris, 8e, France. This magazine is published by a group of couture and *prêt-à-porter* (French RTW) houses.

- *Vogue.* This magazine is published by Condé Nast in French, English, Italian, and Australian editions. The French and Italian publications are the most forward. Condé Nast also publishes special magazines covering home furnishings (*Casa Vogue*), menswear (*L'Uomo and Homme*), children's clothing (*Vogue Bambini*), and boating apparel (*Uomo Mare*), which represent current interesting lifestyle trends abroad. Condé Nast, S.P.A., Piazza Castello, 27-20121 Milano, Italy.

- *Japanese fashion magazines.* Several excellent Japanese fashion magazines report on the European scene with a unique point of view. *So An* and *An An* cover the youth market. *High Fashion* reports on more sophisticated, trendier styles.

HOW GARMENTS FIT

Now let's look more closely at the interaction between clothes and the fashion figure. Fit is the manner in which a garment conforms to the structure of the body. The way a garment fits depends on the weight and the texture of the fabric, the current fashion silhouette, and the construction of the garment.

Beginners should master the drawing of the fashion figure first. After the proportions of this figure become second nature, you can start to integrate clothing into your sketches. As you begin, you will want to watch how the model's stance and movement change the way a garment hangs. Notice that certain elements of a style are emphasized and others become less important when the garment is worn. Note, too, that the fashion model's slender figure does not look voluptuous even in a tight-fitting swimsuit or evening gown.

To help you integrate the clothes and figures accurately and naturally, be sure to carefully match the proportions of the garment to that of the fashion figure. Analyze the garment's elements and their relationship to understand the look the designer wanted to achieve. What part of the body is being revealed? Where should the garment touch the body and where should it hang loosely? How does the fabric fall? How do the details work?

An understanding of basic garment construction will help as you attempt to answer these questions.

GARMENT CONSTRUCTION

A commercial dress form is divided into symmetrical and balanced divisions. Style lines often follow these guidelines.

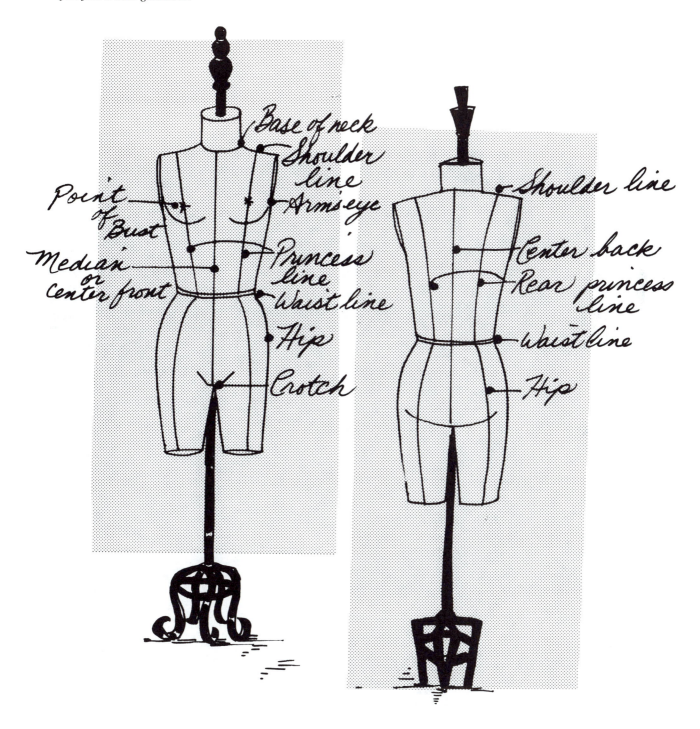

Base of neck
Shoulder line
Armseye
Point of Bust
Princess line
Median or center front
Waist line
Hip
Crotch

Shoulder line
Center back
Rear princess line
Waist line
Hip

DARTS

The dart is one method of fitting a flat piece of fabric to the contours of a body. It is a wedge-shaped piece of fabric that is stitched out of the garment. Darts are used in woven or rigid fabric when the garment is meant to fit the body closely.

Bodice darts extend from the side seam or the waist seam, stopping about 1 inch away from the point of the bust (the highest part of the bust on a dress form) to avoid an exagger-

ated, pointed shape. Darts are used in pants and skirts to take care of the *drop* (the difference between the smaller waist and wider hip). Many variations and combinations of darts are possible.

Search out photographs of garments that use darts and sketch the garments as if they were on a body. See how many variations you can find. Also look at your own clothes to see how darts are used.

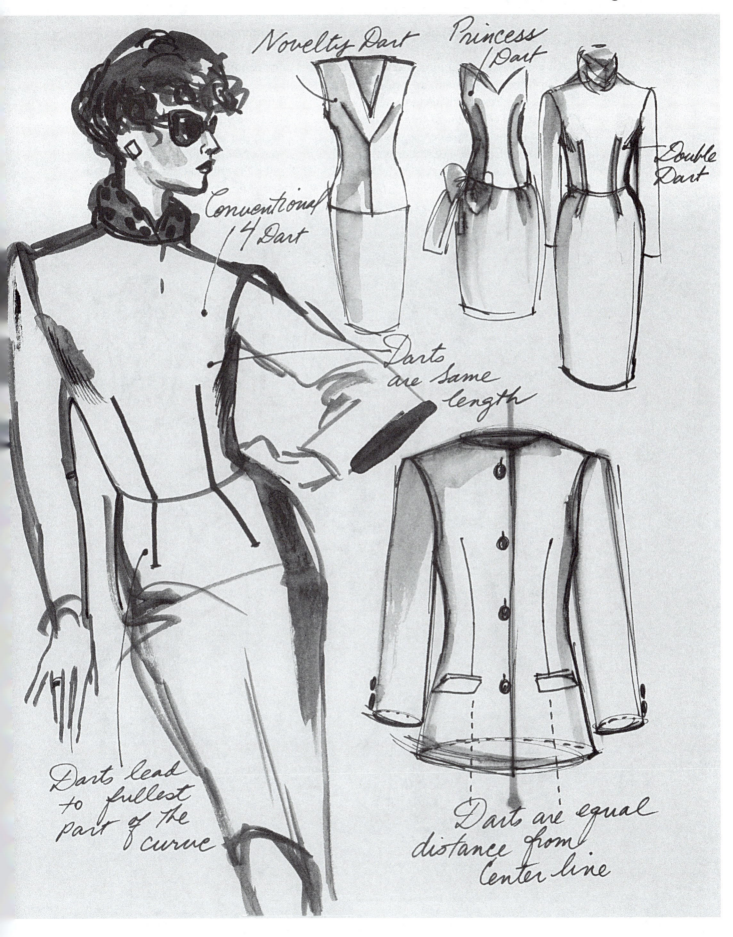

Novelty Dart

Princess Dart

Double Dart

Conventional Dart

Darts are same length

Darts lead to fullest part of the curve

Darts are equal distance from center line

GORES

Gores are vertical pieces of fabric that, when sewn together, shape the garment to the figure. They are often placed on the standard princess lines of the dress form and may also be used to add fullness to a garment. Gores may be placed as novelty style lines wherever a designer wants to call attention to a part of the body. Gores can be accented by stitching or piping for added emphasis. They can be combined with darts or ease (see below) for various effects. Pleats and slits can be added to the gores.

When you are drawing a garment with gores, make sure that the seam line is not broken and that it runs from one edge of the garment to the other. Practice sketching these examples of gores, and collect scrap of other gore treatments.

YOKES

Yokes are horizontal divisions in a garment used for styling and fitting. Yokes are often found at the shoulder line. They are particularly effective when they are used to control ease (gathered or pleated fullness). Yokes can be shaped into curves or wedges. Western (cowboy) shirts feature elaborately shaped front and back yokes. The yoke line is often accented by topstitching, contrast piping, or color blocking.

Hip yokes are used on pants, skirts, and dresses. Skirts styled as a series of tiers are based on yokes that are gathered, then stitched together on horizontal lines. Yoke details are important aspects of garment design and should be observed and sketched carefully.

EASE

Ease has two meanings in apparel construction. Simple, or fit, ease is the extra fabric that must be added to a garment constructed of a rigid fabric (one that does not stretch) so the body can move. Fabrics that stretch naturally do not need as much ease and can fit the body tightly with no darts or gores. For example, most knits have a natural stretch because the fabric construction allows the fabric to expand and recover. When a stretch fiber such as Lycra™ is added to any fabric, knit or woven, the garment will stretch to fit the body like a second skin because the fit ease is built into the structure of the fabric. Leotards, bathing suits, and other active sportswear are often made from stretch fabric because greater flexibility is necessary for vigorous activities.

Ease also means gathers, pleats, or extra fabric added to a garment for style. The ease must be controlled by a smooth area of fabric, a belt, a tie, or elastic insets. Yokes are often used in conjunction with ease to place the fullness were it is most effective. Fashion dictates the placement and quantity of ease. Fabrics tend to become lighter in weight during periods when a full, easy silhouette is popular, and ease is an especially popular design feature for sheer and lightweight fabrics.

Shoulder
Ease

Soft
Pants

Eased
Skirt

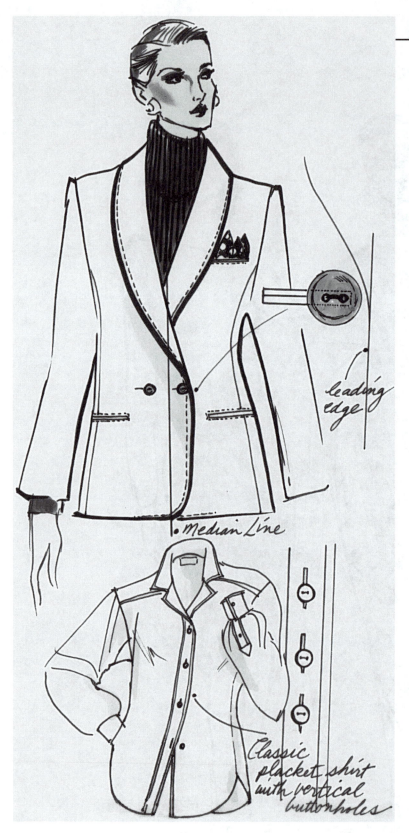

leading edge

Median Line

Classic placket shirt with vertical buttonholes

GARMENT DETAILS

OPENINGS

Buttons and zippers are the most frequently used fasteners for women's apparel. Usually the opening is at the center front or center back of a garment. To position the buttons on the median line of a garment, the buttonhole must extend slightly beyond the center front line. The button is pulled to the edge of the horizontal buttonhole, lining it up with the median line. The button placket extends beyond the median line. When bulky fabrics require large buttons, this extension is wider to visually balance the size of the button. The front edge of the button placket is called the leading edge.

Functioning buttons on a jacket are placed at the top of the front placket where the collar begins to roll and at the bust and waistline. Additional buttons are added between these stress points so the buttons are equally spaced.

Loop buttonholes are placed at the center front line, with the side of the garment that carries the button having an extension. Loop buttonholes are placed at closer intervals because they serve decorative purposes and because they tend to gap.

Zippers are most often hidden, but may be used as decorative fastenings. They can be accented with top-stitching, as in the slot zipper or classic trouser placket. Contrasting colored zippers are sometimes used in active sportswear.

Practice drawing the fastenings shown here. Search out more variations of buttonhole treatments. Sketch the details quickly for practice.

loop

leading
edge

Zipper

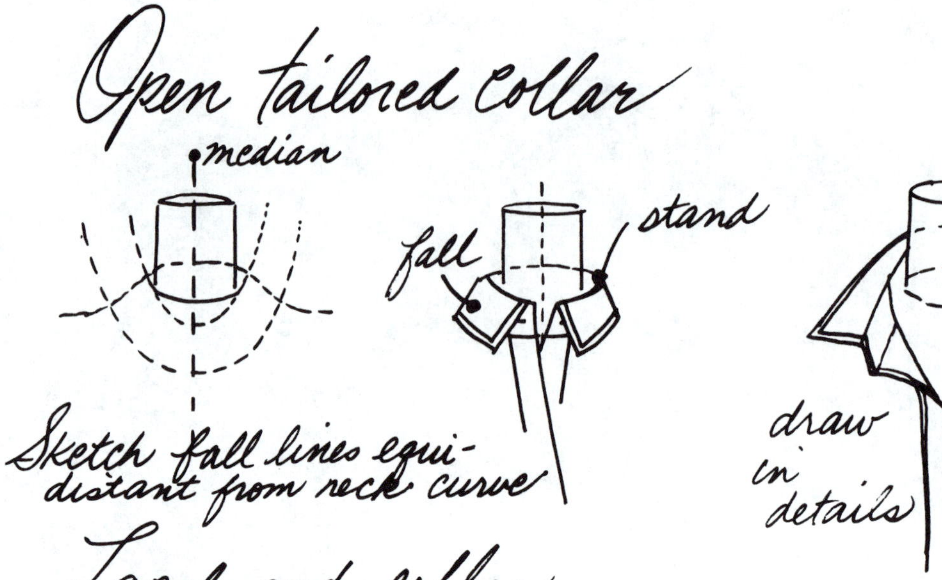

Open tailored collar

• median

fall   stand

Sketch fall lines equi-
distant from neck curve

draw
in
details

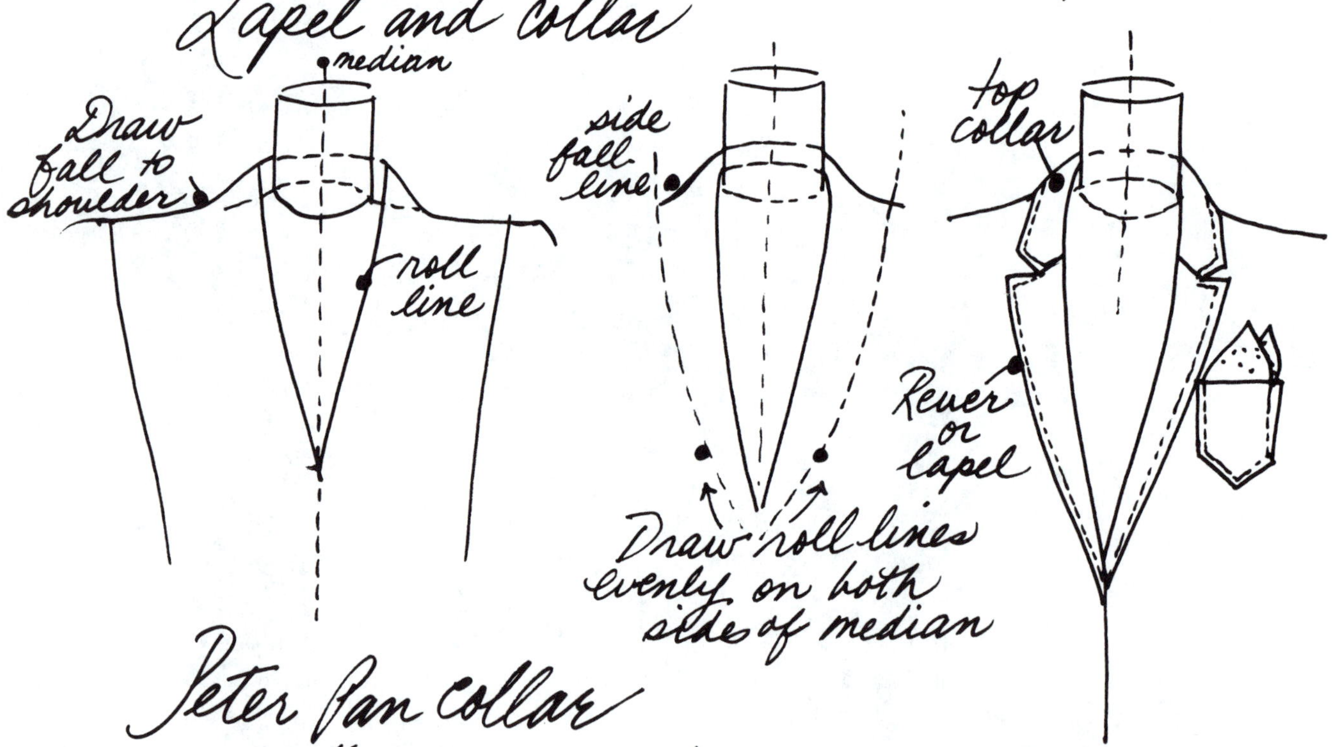

Lapel and collar

• median

Draw
fall to
shoulder

roll
line

side
fall
line

Draw roll lines
evenly on both
sides of median

top
collar

Rever
or
lapel

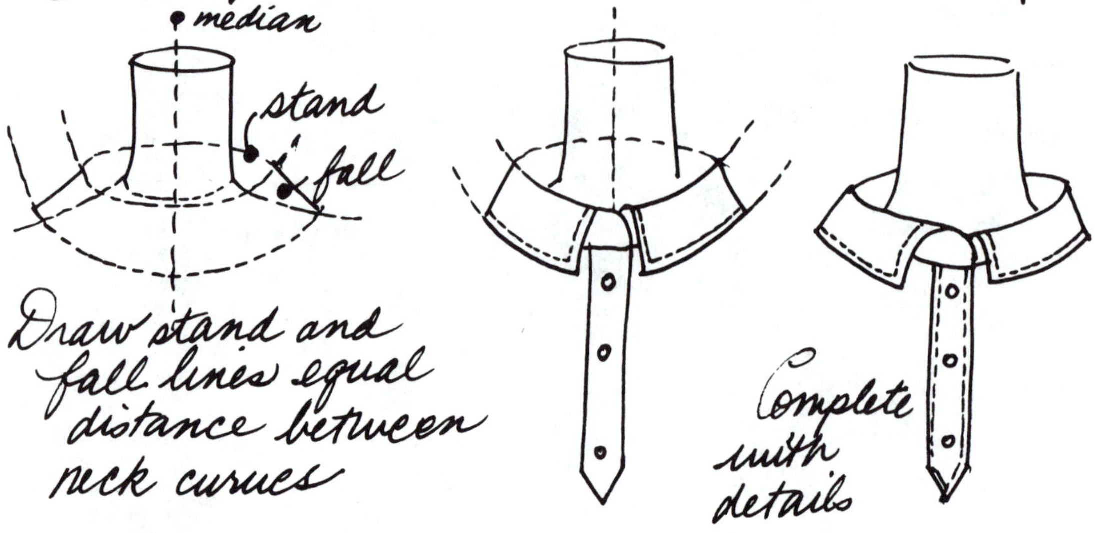

Peter Pan collar

• median

stand

fall

Draw stand and
fall lines equal
distance between
neck curves

Complete
with
details

COLLARS

A collar is an added piece of fabric that encircles the neck and frames the face. Fashion cycles determine the size and kinds of collars that are popular. The illustrator and designer should know the styling possibilities for collar shapes and sizes and interpret them as the fashion period dictates. The collar is an important detail that must be carefully drawn to capture the garment exactly.

Most collars are equally balanced on either side of the median line. Start drawing the back of the collar following the neckline curve in an even arc. Next draw the roll or opening shape. Detail the collar evenly on both sides of the neck. Practice sketching these collars step by step. Sketch collars from magazines and then try some from your imagination.

COLLARS AND NECKLINES
Study these collars and necklines. Collars that have equal sides are called symmetrical. Asymmetrical collars and necklines are different on each side of the garment.

Melton coat with rever

Ascot

Victorian

Hacking Jacket

Poet

Bias ruffle

Collar
and
Drape

Rib-knit
shawl

One
shoulder

Double
lace

Shawl
and
hood

Puff

Roll sleeve + Tab

Raglan

Leg o' mutton

Petal

Set-in Novelty

Drop shoulder novelty

One shoulder drape

Tailored Dolman

Cape

A drop shoulder line has a mature, casual look because the shoulders seem broader.

A sleeve with a shorter shoulder seam looks more youthful than a regular set-in sleeve. The sleeve can be puffed without over-exaggerating the shoulders.

Sleeves are tubes of fabric that surround the arms. The most common type of sleeve is set in at the shoulder line with a seam. Altering the position of the seam from the standard at the top of the shoulder can alter the silhouette of the garment. An artist should notice where and how the sleeve is set in and draw the silhouette and details carefully because they affect the entire shape of the garment. The sleeve itself is styled by changing its size (by adding ease at the shoulder and wrist), its shape, and its length.

A second type of sleeve—which includes raglan, dolman, and kimono sleeves—incorporates part of the bodice into the sleeve pattern. To allow for freedom of movement, these sleeves are usually much looser than set-in sleeves.

Sleeves are affected by shoulder treatments. Fashion often requires a padded shoulder. A slight pad squares the shoulder line and visually deemphasizes the waist and hips. Tailored jackets usually have some padding, even when a strong shoulder is not in fashion. A larger shoulder pad is used to exaggerate the shoulder. To accommodate the pad and allow the arm to move, the sleeve opening must be enlarged and the armseye dropped.

The sleeve shape also affects and is affected by a shoulder pad. A set-in sleeve usually is made with a blunt-end shoulder pad. A raglan or dolman sleeve or a dropped-shoulder sleeve is best made with a rounded pad. Exotic sleeve shapes can be created with different padding methods.

Draw the sleeve length and shape relating to the arm. Carefully observe the sleeves shown here, and draw sleeves from photographs and life. Go through a good fashion magazine and draw each variety of sleeves you see.

SLEEVE VARIATIONS

SET-IN SLEEVES

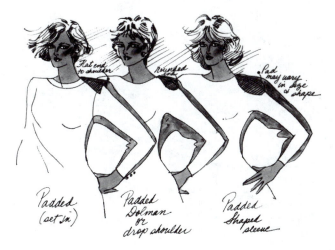

SLEEVES WITH SHOULDER PADS

SLEEVES INCORPORATING THE BODICE

control line
↳ — a seam or elastic that holds
       ruffle ease down

1. Draw Control Line and parallel line where ruffle is to fall.

2. Draw lines of varying distances between the two parallels (erase lower guideline)

Straight Ruffle

3. Lay in ruffles and under-lying curves in fabric

4. Shade and detail contours.

Circular Ruffle

CONTROL LINE

Cascade Ruffle

1.

2.

3.

1. Draw Control line (vertical)

2. Draw an "S" curve going through the control line - indicate ruffle.

3. Fabric folds in triangular shapes, shade and highlight (erase control line)

RUFFLES

Ruffles are shaped in two ways: straight and circular. Straight ruffles tend to be crisper and fuller than circular ruffles. Cascading ruffles are continuous circles set into a vertical seam. All ruffles must be set into a controlling seam or elastic inset to regulate the amount of ease.

To draw ruffles, always establish the control line first. Then lightly sketch a guideline for the bottom of the ruffle. Next, draw uneven ease lines connected to the control line. Then contour the bottom of the ruffle and shade to add dimension.

Observe how ruffles of different fabrics look. Limp, soft fabrics will have smooth, flowing silhouettes when gathered. A crisp fabric such as taffeta will have a bouffant, full ruffle. The smaller the ruffle, the more crisply it will tend to drape. A gathered skirt is actually a long ruffle controlled by a waistband. Sketch many ruffles from photographs and observe how the fabric drapes.

LIGHTWEIGHT FABRIC
Use a light, delicate line to draw ruffles in light-weight fabric.

MEDIUM-WEIGHT FABRIC
A bold, loose line is effective for drawing a cotton sundress with a ruffle neckline. Capture the drape of the fabric

Center the knot and
outer guide lines
equal distance from
the center

Connect knot
to guide lines and
block in

Draw gather
lines and
block in
ties

Detail,
style, and
render

BOWS

Ties and bows are feminine trims typically used as tie belts or softly bowed necklines. Bows can be made from the same fabric as the garment or from contrasting ribbon or lace. Whenever they are used, bows and ties should be drawn as if they were perfectly tied. They should have body, and the streamers should flow gently, as if a soft breeze were blowing them. A limp, bedraggled bow will make a garment look old and used.

Cut a crisp length of grosgrain or satin ribbon that is at least 2 inches wide and tie it into a bow. Sketch it several ways, rearranging the ties each time. Try to capture the twists and turns of the ribbon. Then apply this lesson to bows you see on garments.

Ellipses form the waistband and skirt flare— equal distance from center dividing line

Pleated front trouser

Classic Scottish Kiltie

Engineered Box Pleat

Inverted Pleat and Ease

Asymmetric Engineered Knife Pleat

PLEATS

Pleats are a way of adding fullness to a garment. They can be worked into tops and pants as well as skirts. Most pleats have a linear look that is emphasized when the pleats have been pressed into the fabric so they are permanent. Pleats can be made in many sizes and styles. When they are left unpressed, pleats look like soft folds in the fabric. Pleats can be emphasized with top-stitching. A pleat that is stitched down or worked into a seam is called an engineered pleat.

Study the mechanics of these pleats. Observe a classic pleated skirt and render the precise execution of the crisp pleats. Notice how pleating in a soft, delicate fabric such as chiffon is different from pleating in a heavy-weight, day-wear fabric such as wool gabardine. Pleats in soft fabrics are usually very small and have a gathered or ruffled effect.

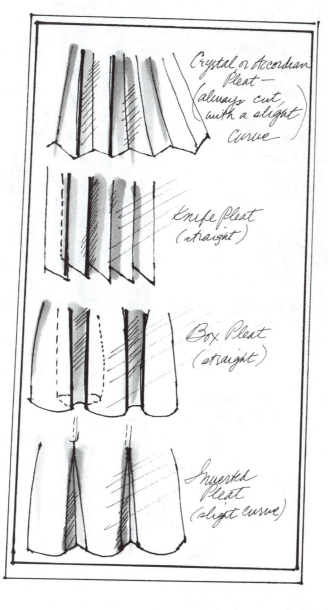

Crystal or Accordian Pleat — (always cut with a slight) curve

Knife Pleat (straight)

Box Pleat (straight)

Inverted Pleat (slight curve)

Exaggerated shirt pockets

Patch pocket

Chanel style

Kangaroo pocket

Safari jacket

POCKETS

Pockets are generally used in pairs positioned symmetrically on either side of the median line of a garment. Pockets are also used singly, as in the traditional blazer breast pocket, or they may be used in mismatched pairs for dramatic design impact. Pockets look best when they are appropriately sized for the garment and the function they are to perform.

Patch pockets are extra pieces of shaped fabric sewn on the outside of the garment. Other pocket styles include up-right flap, welt or buttonhole pockets, hidden pockets, and flap pockets. Many variations of these basic kinds are also used.

Observe pockets and their placement on photographs of garments. As with any small garment detail, sketch pockets precisely and place them carefully on the garment.

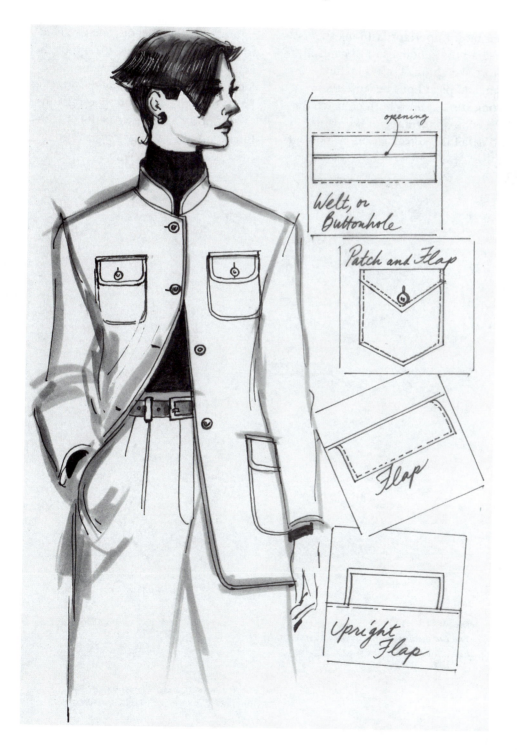

PANTS

Long pants make a person seem taller because one expanse of fabric covers the body from the waist to the floor. High-heeled shoes, hidden by long pants, extend the illusion of height even more. The illustrator enhances the illustration further by drawing pants or a long skirt on a taller than usual figure to emphasize the sweep of the long garment.

The silhouette and fit of pants are their most important fashion aspects. Observe the subtleties of fit carefully before sketching. Always include seam and pleat lines because these strong vertical lines both enhance the long, slim appearance of the pants and detail the construction. Almost all pants have a center front seam line. Most pants have a zipper opening in the side seam, center front seam, or center back seam. Indicate this with a stitching line.

It is very important to sketch the entire figure when drawing pants because the leg detailing and position must be accurate. There is no skirt to camouflage mistakes in balance or proportion. When drawing the longer figure, the length is, of course, added to the leg. However, the torso must be kept in proportion or the figure will look awkward. Sketch models wearing pants from life and from photographs. Draw sporty and dressy pants in combination with a variety of tops.

DRAMATIC PANTS
The full evening pants will drape gracefully,
like a long skirt.

High-heeled or thick-soled shoes increase the
illusion of height, especially when hidden by
the pant leg.

THREE MAJOR PANT SILHOUETTES
The flap on a pant fly may go right over left like a conventional woman's garment or left over right like men's jeans.

JACKETS

Classic spectator sportswear and suit jackets are precision-tailored garments that depend on subtle differences of detail and fit to be successful. The size of a lapel, for instance, can easily date a jacket. Subtleties of fit, the size of the shoulder pad, length, sleeve styling, lapel and pocket details are the components of tailored jackets. Sportswear designers must pay particular attention to these details to style a commercially successful tailored jacket.

Blazers and suit jackets are only one end of the jacket spectrum. A jacket is any outer-weight garment that covers the torso. Study the casual and dressy jackets below. Relate the image of the face and figure of the model to the activity and age of the person who would wear the outfit you are sketching. Hang several jackets on hangers and study their details. Meticulously sketch them as if they were on a body. Try the jackets on and compare your images in a mirror to your sketches. Make corrections and try to sketch other examples more accurately. Concentrate on making the details as clear and realistic as possible in your first drawing. As your sketching ability improves, you may wish to emphasize certain details and eliminate others to create various effects.

SKIRTS

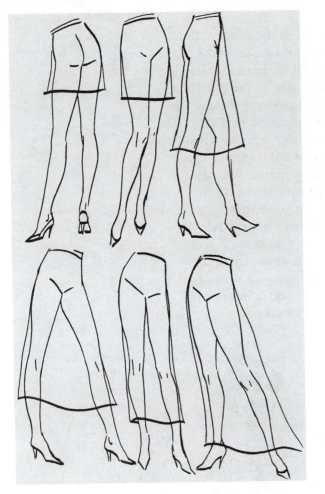

Skirt styles are characterized by four factors: shape, length, kind of fabric, and detailing. A skirt hangs from the waist, and the hemline mirrors the direction of the slant of the hipbones.

The length is determined by the relationship of the hemline to the knee. It is very important not only to place the hemline correctly but also to draw the leg shape accurately so the leg "reads" as the correct length for the skirt.

Skirt shapes fall into four general categories: slim, straight skirts; dirndls (gathered, full, straight skirts); flared skirts; and pegged skirts. The shape combined with the *hand* (crispness or softness of the fabric) establishes the major silhouette characteristics of the skirt. Hang several skirts tightly on clip skirt hangers. Observe how the fabric falls. Draw a skirt and carefully draw the undulating shape of the hemline. The fuller the skirt, the more character the drape of the skirt will have.

Details such as the shape and width of the waistband, pockets, trims, and pleats are the finishing touches.

Observe skirts carefully and draw many. Try putting a powerful electric fan behind a model with a skirt on and drawing the fabric as it blows in the breeze. Refer to the section on drawing pleats (page 115) and apply these techniques to drawing pleated skirts.

Don't forget that the shoes must relate to the length and style of the skirt being illustrated. Study appropriate shoes during each fashion period so that your sketches capture the current look.

Hint: Skirt always goes around body!

SLIM SKIRTS

The slim skirt has little excess fabric so the body shape and motion are clearly visible. Slits or pleats are usually necessary for movement.

FLARED OR CIRCULAR SKIRTS

This silhouette is the most flattering and has the widest possible styling variations. The hip is slim, and ease is added with gores, flounces, pleats, or additional circles for a very full effect.

GATHERED OR DIRNDL SKIRTS

These skirts have straight sides and are gathered into a waistband. In a crisp fabric, they make the hips look wide.

PEGGED SKIRTS

This skirt shape has a full hip and is tapered at the hemline. Pegged skirts exaggerate the hips so they are used less often in fashion cycles.

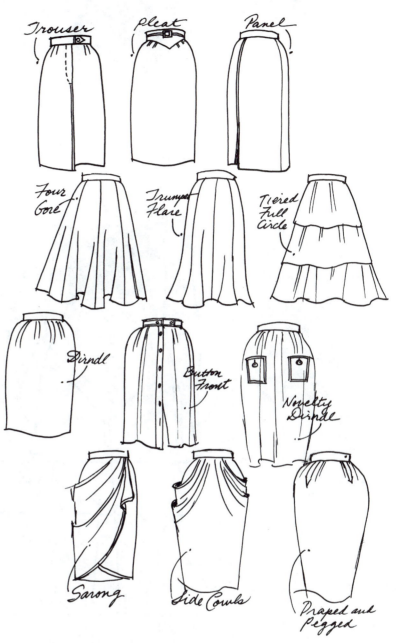

Trouser Pleat Panel

Four Gore Trumpet Flare Tiered Full Circle

Dirndl Button Front Novelty Dirndl

Sarong Side Cowls Draped and Pegged

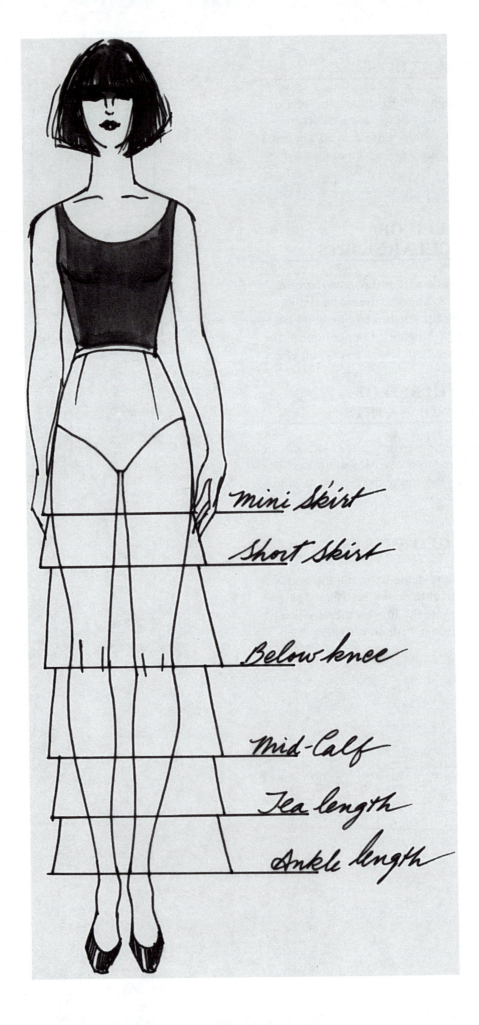

mini Skirt

Short Skirt

Below knee

Mid-Calf

Tea length

Ankle length

DRESSES

Dresses combine the drawing techniques of blouses and skirts. When the dress has a waistline or is belted, the drape of the fabric and the slant of the hemline are controlled by the angle of the hip, just as skirts are. A dress that has no belt and hangs from the shoulders (called a chemise, shift, or float) is controlled by the angle and size of the shoulders. The hemline of the shift will be parallel to the shoulders.

Dresses are usually made in lighter fabrics than sportswear jackets and skirts, and they have fewer traditional styling formulas than a classic blazer or shirt jacket. Variety and versatility characterize dress styling.

Dresses are often designed for a specific age of wearer. Therefore it is important to match the visual age of the model to the probable customer the dress was styled for. Hairstyle is a key factor in establishing visual age. Youthful, romantic dresses look appropriate on models with soft flowing hairstyles. A more expensive dress looks best when drawn on a model with a sleek, well-controlled hairstyle and well-defined makeup.

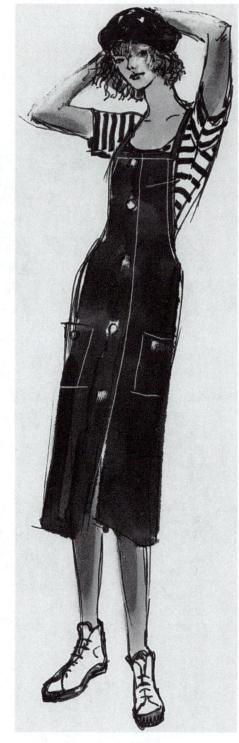

A fine, delicate pen-line sketch gives the dress a young look. The fabric looks light and lacy when handled in a fresh, direct way.

JUNIOR DRESSES

The perfect model for junior dresses is a young, fresh high-school girl. Junior clothes are usually exaggerated, often styled with a sense of humor. Pose your models informally, and consider using light-hearted accessories, trendy makeup, and youthful accessories.

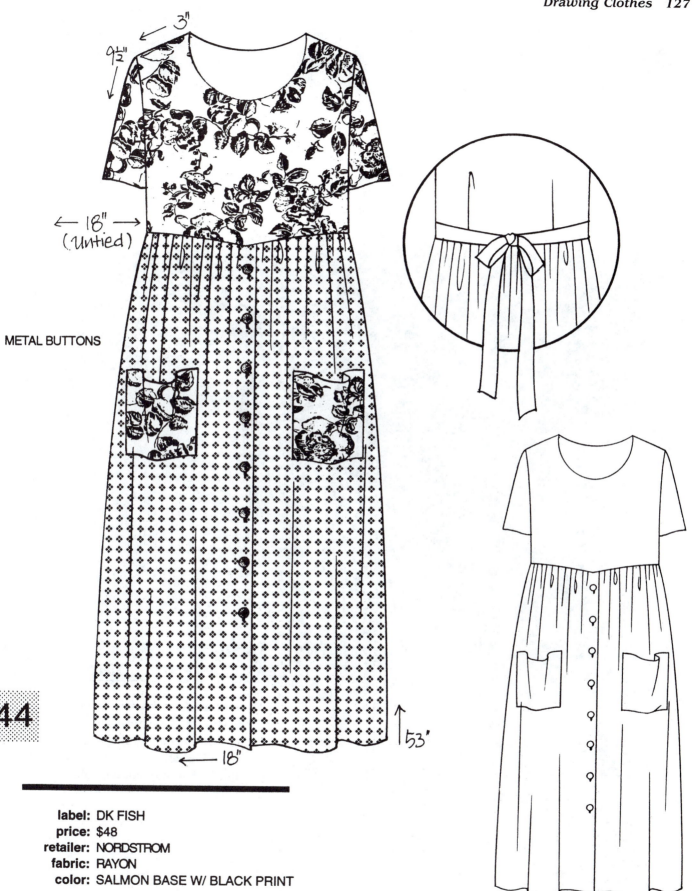

3"

9½"

← 18" →
(Untied)

METAL BUTTONS

44

← 18"

↑ 53"

label: DK FISH
price: $48
retailer: NORDSTROM
fabric: RAYON
color: SALMON BASE W/ BLACK PRINT

This simple sketch effectively communicates exactly how the dress should be constructed. (Courtesy of Report West, a fashion reporting service.)

DESIGNER
AND EVENING DRESSES

The customer for this type of dress is
a sophisticated individualist.
Consequently, the evening dress
model will usually reflect the most
elegant, high-fashion makeup and
hairstyles.

MISSY DRESSES

This broad category refers to women's dresses that come in even-numbered sizes (6, 8, 10, 12, and so forth). The models should have a youthful but sophisticated look and casual hairstyles. The shirt dress is a classic missy dress silhouette.

SWEATERS

Aran-Style Pullover

Scandinavian Jacquard

Sweaters are very versatile garments that can be worn for almost any occasion except the most formal. The yarn and stitch give the sweater its character. Bulky yarns can be knitted into intricately textured Irish fishermen's patterns for a casual garment. Fine shetland yarn is knit into jacquard patterns called Fair Isles. Knits can be sophisticated city suits or fluffy mohair novelty sweaters.

Sweaters usually have very few seams or style lines. The sleeves can be set-in or raglan. Side seams are used, but the clinging nature of the interlocking knit stitch makes a sweater naturally hug the body's curves. *Ribbing* (a tight, elastic knit banding) is used to finish the sleeves and bottom hem of many sweaters. This distinctive touch is typical of pattern changes used in sweater styling.

Before sketching a sweater, study the textures and patterns. Estimate the volume of the sweater by imagining the body underneath. Block out the silhouette and then add the pattern work.

Novelty Yarn Cardigan

Intarsia

Bulky Knit Cable

Cable Cardigan

Fair Isle Jacquard

COATS

Coats are essentially tailored garments constructed in heavier fabrics than sportswear jackets. Seam and style details, such as lapels, topstitching, pockets, and flaps, are similar to the jacket details but drawn in a larger scale.

Coats are most often made in bulky fabrics for warmth. Camel's hair, melton, blanket-weight plaids, and fleeces are typical materials. Thicker fabric is best drawn with heavier lines. Round the corners of the silhouette and style details like pockets and collars to add to the illusion of bulk. Choose warm-looking accessories, such as gloves, boots, scarves, and hats, as appropriate accents for coats. Balance the scale of buttons and belts to the large volume and heavy fabrics used to style a coat. Fur collars and cuffs are popular accessories.

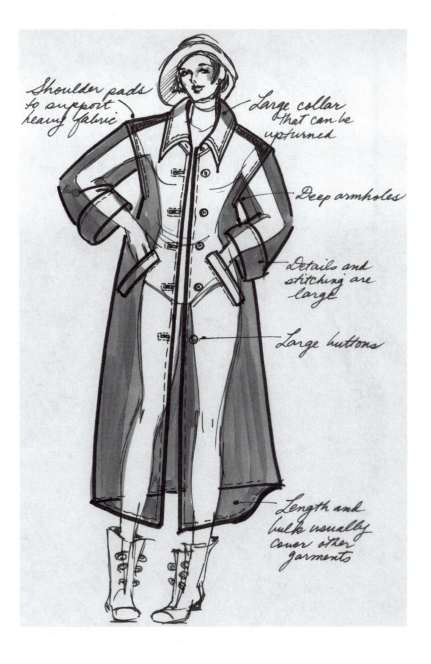

Shoulder pads to support heavy fabric

Large collar that can be upturned

Deep armholes

Details and stitching are large

Large buttons

Length and bulk usually cover other garments

C H A P T E R 6

Rendering Fabrics

Clothing is soft "sculpture" supported and animated by the human body. The fabrics from which clothing is made may be woven, knitted, or felted and come in a tremendous variety of textures, colors, patterns, and weights. *Hand* refers to the way fabric feels.

Designers select fabrics to help create the style that is the fashion look of the period. When fashion decrees tailored, shaped clothing, crisp-hand fabrics in medium weights are used to create geometric shapes. When bulky silhouettes are popular, large amounts of lightweight, soft, or crisp fabrics can be styled with gathers and full-ness to create a rectangular silhouette. Thick, soft-hand fabrics, often interfaced and cut in boxy or tent shapes, also give the effect of volume.

Drawing clothes requires keen observation of how different fabrics drape and fit the body and how these fabrics look when they are styled in garments. Study the way fabric drapes on the body before beginning to draw a garment. A soft fabric flows and clings to the body. Draw it with smooth, downward flowing lines. Crisp fabric has its own form and stands away from the body when gathered or flared.

Get into the habit of feeling fabrics. As you touch a crisp, lightweight fabric, imagine how it will lightly puff when gathered into a full skirt. Feel the soft, fluid drape of a wool jersey, and visualize it clinging to a torso, slipping sensuously over the hips, and falling into a soft, fluid skirt. Collect your tactile and visual impressions to understand how to draw fabrics.

Crisp Hand

Soft Hand

FABRIC HAND
A soft fabric will drape from the shoulders and cling to the body's contour. A crisp fabric has inherent stiffness that makes it stand away from the body and that creates a full silhouette.

WOVEN FABRICS

HEAVY, CRISP FABRICS

A crisp silhouette emphasizing geometric precision is achieved by styling in a medium to heavyweight fabric. Architectural shaping refers to the geometric shapes achieved through padding the shoulders and using interfacing to produce crisp lapel and pocket details. Tucks and welt seams are typical tailored details that accent the structured silhouette. When you sketch tailored garments, simplify the hairstyle, makeup, and accessories. Concentrate on drawing the bold silhouette and structural details with a strong, well-defined line.

Sharp corners

Straight hems

Bold, well defined silhouette

Crisp press line on slacks

HEAVY, SOFT FABRICS

The heavy, soft fabric in this suit has a sensuous yet casual drape. The model's hair and slouchy pose emphasize the heavy texture of the wool melton. Use a bold line when drawing the silhouette and a finer detailing line for the lapel and topstitching. Wrinkles and folds should be well shadowed, suggesting the weight of the fabric. Round the edges of the hem boldly to emphasize the drape of the skirt.

Slightly rounded details

Soft gathers

Deep shadows in folds

Carefree, relaxed pose

Rounded folds

Curved hem

LIGHTWEIGHT, CRISP FABRICS

Lightweight, crisp woven fabrics can be styled in garments with a great deal of volume. Gathered, bouffant skirts and full sleeves are best in this type of material. Taffeta, organza, and moiré are typical lightweight, crisp fabrics. Use a light, smooth, precise line for rendering this silhouette.

Gathers should be drawn with uneven lines and should flow outward into puffy shapes. Bows curve upward with crisp precision. Avoid deep shadows that make the fabrics look heavy. Emphasize the highlights that are inherent in these fabrics.

Crisp bow

Silhouette is full and has a crisp line

Breezy, flowing linework

Emphasize light, transparent fabric

LIGHTWEIGHT, SOFT FABRICS

Lightweight, clinging fabrics such as chiffon, voile, georgette, and crepe follow the body's curves. These fabrics should be drawn with a smooth line for both the silhouette and details. Prints on lightweight fabrics seem softer and more feminine than when printed on crisp, midweight base goods. A delicate pattern is most effective when it is loosely rendered with white space from the paper used as highlights. Avoid heavy shadows and very realistic rendering of the print or the fabric will seem heavy.

Woven fabrics can be cut on the bias (the exact diagonal between the warp or lengthwise grain, and the filling or horizontal grain line). This diagonal is the most flexible part of most woven fabrics, so when a garment is cut on the bias, it will fit the body with a soft, clinging flare. Fewer seams or dart lines have to be used to style a bias-cut garment. Bias skirts have fluid hemline curves.

Bias garments are usually more expensive and sophisticated than garments cut on the straight grain because more fabric is used. When a pattern is cut on the bias, it should be carefully matched to compliment the garment. When a plaid or check is cut on the bias, the pattern becomes a diamond.

The master designer of the bias-cut dress is the Paris couturier Vionnet, who made the bias dress her signature styling technique early in the twentieth century. The bias cut is still popular because it flatters the figure and gives woven fabric the drapability of soft knits.

Crisp silhouette

Undulating hemline

Slim fit at hip

Clings to body contours

Movement from flare

STRETCH KNITS

Knit sweaters are distinctive garments because banding, novelty yarns, and intricate stitches can create a great variety of styles. Knit fabric is different from sweater knits because it is made to be cut and sewn into garments. The advantage of styling with knits is that they stretch (because of their interlocking-loop construction), which makes them comfortable and easy to care for.

Knit fabrics are made in a great variety of weights and patterns and often look like wovens. Heavyweight knit goods have the same styling requirements as woven fabric. Other knit fabrics are not made to simulate wovens but have a unique knit appearance and hand. Cotton, silk, or synthetic interlock has a smooth jersey *face* (the surface of the fabric) and clings to the body's curves. Knit jersey stretches over 20

CUT-AND-SEW SWEATERS
Bands of ribbing are used to control the fit of sweaters cut from knit yardage to simulate a hand-knit look.

Cut-and-sew knit striped fabric should be matched when seamed like a woven garment.

percent of the original size, so seams, darts, and fit ease can be eliminated. Knit garments often fit snugly and Lycra™ is added to knits when great stretch and *recovery* (return to the original size) are required. These garments stretch to fit all the body's curves with no construction details other than side seams required.

BATHING SUITS
Lycra™, a very stretchy yarn with good recovery, is used for swimsuit fabrics. Few fit lines are required.

STYLED KNITS

Cut-and-sew knits are also styled as soft dresses, tops, skirts, and pants. They tend to have a lean, clinging line when gathered or pleated. The body shape is accented in even the fullest garments. Even though a soft knit is cut on the straight grain line, it will drape like a bias-cut woven garment. These soft garments often have more style details than stretch knits. Gathers, pleats, belts, tucks, and elastic shirring are typical ways to control cut-and-sew knits. Banding can be knit separately and sewn on cut-and-sew knits to imitate a sweater look.

Study the pictures of the knit garments shown below. Notice how the soft, sensuous flow of the fabric is captured in the bold, fluid line of the illustration. Sketch several cut-and-sew knit garments from photographs. Try to draw the fluid drape of the fabric.

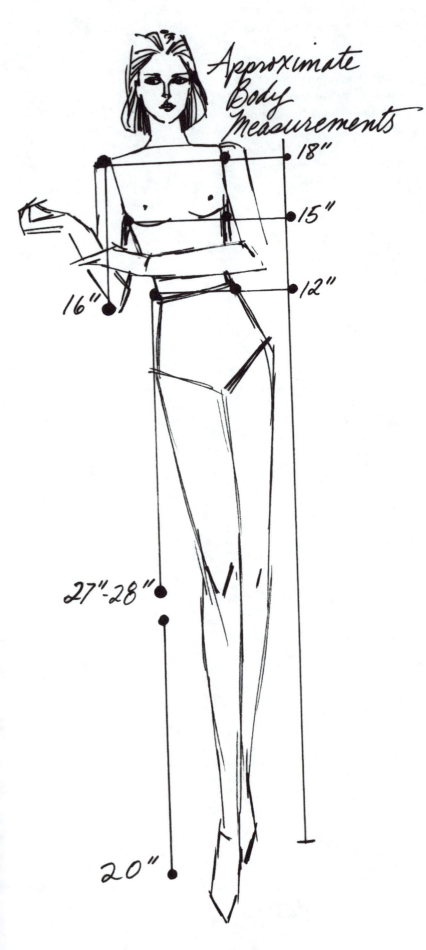

Approximate
Body
Measurements

18"

15"

12"

16"

27"-28"

20"

PATTERNED FABRICS

Patterned fabric presents an additional challenge to the illustrator, who now must sketch the figure and the garment and render the pattern. The first consideration is *scale* (the size of the pattern as it relates to the size of the model's body).

SCALE

It is important to accurately translate the scale of the fabric's pattern to the size of the figure you are drawing. If you are working with actual fabric, you can measure the vertical and horizontal repeat of the pattern (where a single motif unit is repeated to form the overall pattern). Then fit the repeat size to body measurements. For example, a motif with a vertical repeat of 6 inches would be repeated about four and one-half times in a knee-length skirt. Use a tape measure to determine approximate length and width of a garment by measuring your own body or a similar garment. You can use that number to determine the size of the pattern on your drawing.

To draw the pattern, first block in the boldest parts of the pattern with a light sketch line on the garment's silhouette. Sketch parts of the pattern that might be visible and lose the part that would be cut off at the edge of the garment. A combination of media is often used to render fabric. Small details are easily drawn with pencil and fine-tip felt pen, while paint and broad-based markers easily fill in the background. When sketching patterned fabrics, most artists draw a rather large figure so they can render the print in a convenient size.

• *Measure scale and repeat of fabric*

• *Block in motif— 6" repeat*

• *Fill in background*

• *Detail with paint to indicate smaller motif*

A tight pattern indication shows a tighter, crisper and more commercial illustration

LOOSE RENDERING VERSUS TIGHT RENDERING

Realistic rendering of a motif is not necessarily the most effective way to illustrate a patterned garment. Often the pattern can be rendered partially to accent the silhouette of the garment. Compare the two illustrations of the dresses on this and the next page. The realistic illustration is called a *tight rendering.* Every part of the print is carefully, almost photographically, rendered.

The second illustration is *loosely rendered.* The print is suggested, but large areas of the garment are left unrendered. Shadowed accent areas highlight the pattern rendering.

The kind of rendering an illustrator should use depends on several factors:

A loose pattern indication shows a looser, more editorial feeling — with fabric rendering less detailed

1. *The personality of the garment.* Some prints look best carefully rendered. Experimentation and observation will help you approach a finished rendering with a vision of how it should look when completed.

2. *The skill of the artist.* Many illustrators gravitate toward a style—either precise or loose—that is compatible with their drawing skills. However, good artists develop their drawing skills to the level at which they can easily use any style of illustration.

3. *The time element.* When an artist is rushed, a loose rendering is an effective way to quickly illustrate a print garment.

Tighter rendering of
fabric pattern creates
less editorial, more
sale-oriented feeling.

Looser rendering of fabric pattern creates lively, editorial feeling

BUILDING THE
FINISHED RENDERING

1. Lightly sketch the figure and block in the pattern in the correct scale.

2. Build up layers of colors (or tone if you are rendering black and white). Let each application of

felt pen or paint dry thoroughly before working over it.

3. Add the silhouette and detail lines with black pen or Prismacolor pencil.

Sketch the figure in pencil—

Get movement in the figure by starting with the body underneath the garment

Block in the garments

Create a flowing feeling & indicate folds

Add
a wash
light
e-
ase
ncil
nderneath)

Bring in
darker
wash,
add
detail
with fine
line marker,
pencil, or
brush.

Add white
paint to
"punch up"
detailed
areas

Darts distort stripes

Bias stripe used as a design device

Mitered bias four gore

Bias three gore

Straight flare

Stripes seem wider at the hem because they are gathered together at the top.

Stripes are parallel to the hemline, broken by gathers in the fabric.

STRIPES

Stripes are popular fabric designs. In woven fabrics, stripes are most often printed or woven in even parallel lines following the *warp* (also called *selvages*) of the fabric. Knit stripes, especially T-shirt and sweater knits, are almost always knitted horizontally.

Before beginning your illustration, notice the direction the stripes are cut on each part of the garment. Stripes are often cut on a contrasting or bias grain line for effect. Note also the size of the stripe in relationship to the garment. As you block the pattern in, keep the stripes evenly spaced unless the garment is gathered. Gathering will pull the stripes together at the gathering line. Darts also distort the stripe layout.

Scale the stripes appropriately for the garment. Do not attempt to draw stripes in exactly the correct amount, but render the lines to approximate the scale.

Any fabric with a linear design should be treated as a stripe. Seersucker is a good example of a stripe pattern that is created by texture and contrasting color.

CHECKS

Gingham and Shepherd's Checks
Checks conform to rules of geometric placement not unlike those applied to stripes. Unfitted garments are most effective in checks because darts and seams alter the smooth grid of the fabric.

Build a check by placing the vertical grid as you would a stripe on your rough sketch. Then fill in the grid with the horizontal stripe. Keep the checks even in both directions. Accent the boldest part of the pattern as a final touch. Study how subtle design elements are accented by changing the direction of the check to the bias grain line. Remember to relate the size of the check to the size of the garment.

Houndstooth Checks Houndstooth checks are a variation on gingham or shepherd's check. They are achieved by weaving a cross grid into a twill weave. From a distance, this pattern looks like a simple gingham unless it is enlarged for dramatic impact.

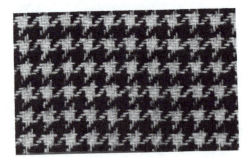

Pencil in the primary check on a grid

Lay in Primary Check with Marker

Lay in secondary check

PLAIDS

Plaids are more complicated geometric patterns than checks are. The most important things to analyze before beginning to draw a plaid garment are the special breakdown of the pattern and its scale.

A plaid is built by the intersections of horizontal and vertical stripes. The blending of yarns creates a wide variety of color and pattern possibilities, from bold tartans to subtle glen plaids. To analyze these complicated patterns, separate the two stripe directions and render the vertical repeat after you have drawn the horizontal stripe.

Measure the repeat of the plaid and block in the pattern on a light sketch of the garment. Notice how a bias grain line alters the direction of the plaid on various parts of the garment. Felt pens in different colors or tones of gray are good for rendering plaids because they are easy to control, and the intersecting lines build tone intensity when they cross, just as the stripes in the actual fabric pattern do.

Because plaids can be complicated to work out, you might want to begin by drawing a rough sketch and working out the scale and placement of the plaid. Then trace over the rough sketch on vellum. The finished drawing will be cleaner and more accurate.

Establish the size of repeat of the plaid and relate it to the garment. Lay in major directions of the plaid — then tone and render.

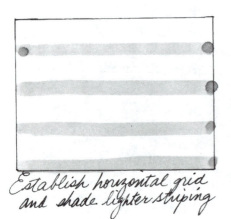

Establish horizontal grid and shade lighter striping

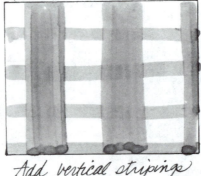

Add vertical stripings of the plaid

Detail the light and dark areas of the pattern

BIAS PLAIDS

Cutting the entire garment on the bias is an interesting design device. Measure the block of the plaid on the diagonal and scale it to the garment as you did the straight plaid.

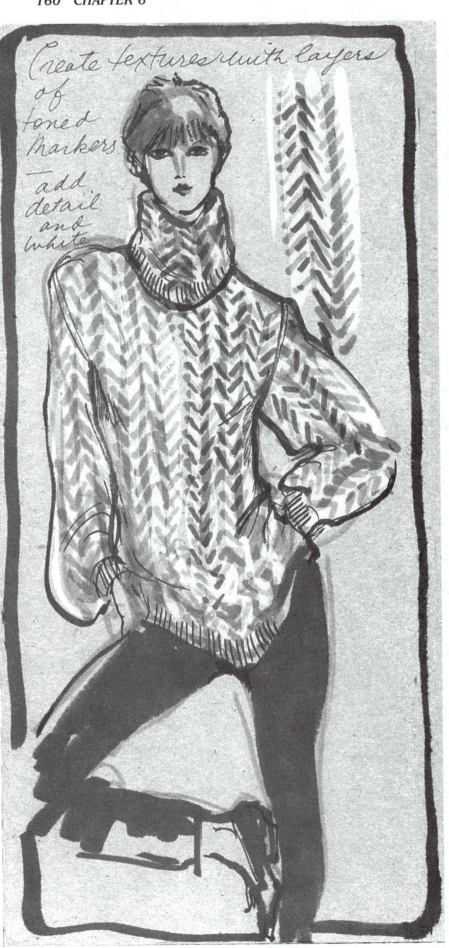

Create textures with layers of toned markers — add detail and white

TEXTURED FABRICS

MENSWEAR SUITING

Herringbone   Twill is a fabric woven to give the appearance of diagonal lines. The herringbone pattern is created when a twill is reversed in narrow stripes. This fabric is thus essentially a stripe, but the stripes are defined by the direction of the diagonal lines rather than by color. Two or more colored yarns generally further define the weave. Herringbones are often cut on the bias and alternate grain. A plaid is often superimposed on a herringbone ground.

To draw a herringbone pattern, lay out the direction of the stripe with a light-tone felt pen on all parts of the garment. Detail the reverse twill pattern with a fine-line marker or sharp pencil.

Tweed Contrasting yarns define the basket weave of a typical tweed. Accent-colored nubs are usually used to spark the basic color of the tweed.

To begin your rendering, use an undertone of broad-nib felt pen or a light wash. Work over the base tone with Prismacolor pencils or felt pens in a cross-weave texture. Leave open space in your pencil work so the toned ground looks like a subtle highlight. Paper with a rough surface helps to create highs and lows of color that are typical of a tweed. Draw the pockets, lapels, and other style details with a black fine-line marker.

Build up tones with markers — add details with fine-point pen

—

Punch up texture with white opaque pen or paint

ADDITIONAL TECHNIQUES FOR TWEEDY FABRICS

Spatter Paint Technique   Spatter painting with a toothbrush is an effective way to render a tweed or other textured fabric. First paint the garment with the basic tone of the fabric. This is the color most visible from a distance. Then trace over the silhouette of the area to be rendered and cut this shape out of a second piece of paper. Tape the outline exactly over the area to be rendered with masking tape (this will not damage the surface of your paper). You are now ready to mix the accent tones of the tweed.

Using a good quality of designer gouache or watercolor, mix your second color with water until it is the consistency of heavy cream. Dip the bristles of an old toothbrush in the paint. Test the spatter on a scrap of paper. Scrape a pallet knife lightly against the bristles, flicking the paint so it spatters lightly on the paper. When you are satisfied with the effect, spatter paint on the finished art. You may use two or more colors if you allow the area to dry between applications. Wash the toothbrush between applications.

This technique approximates airbrush rendering and can be used to create many interesting effects.

Salt Paint Technique Paint an area on your sketch with transparent watercolor or dye. Keep the area quite wet. Sprinkle table salt delicately over the painted surface. The salt causes the paint to collect around each grain and creates an interesting surface effect.

Allow the area to dry thoroughly before brushing off the salt. Now you may work back into the drawing with pencils and felt pens or paints to heighten the effect the salt has created.

Both the spatter paint and salt techniques require some experimentation to master the methods. Remember that you should always test the reaction of the original colors and the consistency of new paint before applying it to your work. If the paint is applied over a dry wash, it will not run.

TAILORED SUITING

Corduroy Corduroy is a linear plush fabric that conforms to the layout rules of striped fabrics. Corduroy's pile (called *wales*) gives the fabric a soft luster. Begin your rendering by laying out a linear pattern in a light-tone felt pen. Leave highlights on parts of the garment. Study real corduroy fabric or a garment to see how it reflects the light. Shadow the lapels and folds in the fabric with a soft pencil. Use deep shadows. Reinforce the linear quality of the fabric with a pencil or fine-line marker. Detail the style elements of the garment with a dark fine-line marking pen.

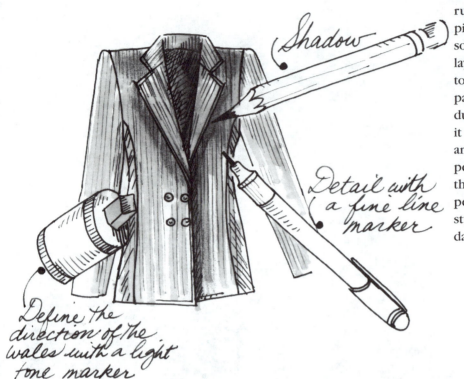

Shadow

Detail with a fine line marker

Define the direction of the wales with a light tone marker

Linen   Linen has a slightly glazed surface that reflects light. Leave highlights of untoned paper to capture the glaze. A slub yarn is characteristic of linen and best rendered over a light wash and highlights with a fine-line pencil or pen in a slightly darker tone than the ground. Keep the style details and silhouette crisp and precise. Topstitching is very visible on linen's smooth surface.

Hopsacking, Raw Silk   Tone the garment with a light color wash or felt pen. Study the fabric and leave appropriate untoned areas as highlights. Detail the texture with a pencil on rough paper to accent the heavy, nubby yarns used to construct these fabrics.

LUSTER FABRICS

Luster fabrics reflect a great deal of light because they are woven with smooth, shiny yarns.

Lamé   Metallic yarn called Lurex™ is the most lustrous yarn available and is woven with other yarns to create lamé. Notice the highly reflective areas that occur in the top folds of the garment. Random glints highlight the mid-tones and deep shadow areas in the folds of the garment. In addition to the usual highlights, accent the most brilliant areas of the garment with a highly concentrated mixture of opaque white paint. Use metallic paints or pencils when working in color.

Satin and Crepe de Chine. Crepe de chine, satin, taffeta, and other smooth reflective surface fabrics create highlights in broad areas of the garment although there is no metallic "super" highlight as in lamé. Jacquard patterns are sometimes woven into the fabric, and satins and crepe de chine can be printed.

Before starting your drawing, study the illustration on this page for a typical shadow and highlight pattern for lustrous fabric. Begin with a wash or tone with a light-colored felt pen. Build up the tone with several overlays of color. Leave original paper highlights on a loose rendering. Shadow with smooth, flowing, darker tones of the same cast as the base color. When you render the silhouette and details, keep the line smooth, light, and crisp.

Tones are darker at the edges of the figure

Watercolor wash

Pen Crosshatch work also Creates Volume

Leave white spaces on paper to act as highlights

Lightest paint closest to viewer

Sequins
Tone the ground
with marker
or wash

Highlight
sequins with
opaque
white
paint — Punch
up individual
sequins with
fine line
marker

Sequins and Rhinestones *Sequins* (also called *paillettes*) are small disks of reflective metal or plastic sewn onto a carrier fabric. They form a dot pattern of highlights on a medium tone when reflecting light. Study the pattern sequins make when highlighted from a photograph or a real garment.

Begin rendering a toned ground with wash or a broad-nib felt pen. Highlight the most reflective areas of the pattern with dots in a dense white paint. If your illustration is in color, tint the white slightly to tone to the ground color.

Rhinestones react like sequins in reflecting light and can be rendered with the same technique.

Beading   Beading may be applied to fabric to cover the entire surface or to create a great variety of patterns. Fine beaded garments are very expensive because each of the small beads must be handsewn to the fabric. Beaded garments are usually very heavy, even if the fabric they are sewn onto is as light as chiffon. If a garment is only partially beaded, the weight of the beads will make that portion hang very straight.

Beads reflect the light individually. A solid beaded garment should be rendered with spots of highlights. Beads are too small to render individually unless you are executing a close-up drawing of the pattern.

Sequins and Bugle beads defining and adding shoulder and cuff interest

Moiré Moiré is taffeta with a characteristic pattern that looks like a watermark. This motif is best rendered over a light tone with a fine-line pen in a darker tone. The salt technique is an excellent way to render the basic color of the fabric. This fabric reflects light like satin, so many areas of the illustration should be highlighted. Notice how a medium-tone area can have accented light highlights that form the moiré pattern.

Moiré

Tone the ground with wash or marker sprinkle with salt over wet paper and paint. Detail with fine line marker, brush, or pencil.

Velvet, Velveteen, Velour Velvet and velvet-like fabrics absorb light because of their deep, rich pile. Highlights occur only around the edges of the garment. A wet watercolor wash applied several times is an effective way to render pile fabrics. Build the densest color at the center of the garment and allow highlights where the fabric is gathered and at the edges of the garment. Velvet is effective when rendered in dark, rich colors. Light tones are difficult to render convincingly because deep contrasts cannot be built up. Render style lines and details in dark velvets with opaque white paint and a fine brush line or darker detail lines. Be sure to wait until the wash has completely dried before detailing the garment. Round the corners of collars, pockets, trims, and the general silhouette to capture the bulky nature of these fabrics.

LEATHERS

Suede   Suede surfaces have an uneven pile that catches and reflects light. This "mottled" surface is characteristic of sporty leather garments. Render suedes by interpreting the texture with different tones of the base color, building in varying grades of color. To duplicate the irregular tex- ture, use a rough-textured paper and a charcoal or soft pencil to pick up the texture of the paper. Another method is to use a transparent broad-nib felt pen on textured paper. Work back into each layer of tone with a marker or Prismacolor pencil to emphasize the shadows and detail the seam and stitching lines.

Use a textured or grainy paper

Lay in a light tone with a wash

Build up soft shading with a pencil

Add crisp detail

Smooth Leather, Kid Smooth leathers are finished with a reflective surface that is rendered like satin or crepe de chine. Medium or heavy-weight kid leather usually has stylized highlights. Many fine leathers are as thin and pliable as lightweight fabrics. Less expensive smooth leathers may be quite stiff and bulky. Leather sur-faces may be embossed, overprinted, or handpainted with a pattern.

Before beginning your illustration, study the hide and analyze the weight and surface. Try to feel the leather. As you work, reinforce the natural paper highlights with opaque white accents.

Use wash or marker

Create high contrast (for shiny leather) by "punching" up details with white paint

QUILTING

Two pieces of fabric are jointed with a stitched pattern to form quilted fabric. A filling of fiber or down is usually added as insulation. Quilting is an age-old method of creating a warm, heavyweight fabric from two lightweight fabrics.

Geometric quilting patterns are popular for robes. These are done on large machines that make a variety of patterns. Outerwear jackets and coats, especially active ski wear, also feature quilt details. Handsewn quilting motifs are creative and flexible means of detailing all kinds of apparel. Contrast-color stitching, patterned fabrics, colorful backings, and puffy fillings are variations that make quilting a unique design device.

Trapunto is a trim similar to quilting, but it is done in only one area of a garment. A spot motif is typically stitched into the fabric and stuffing is added to accent parts of the design.

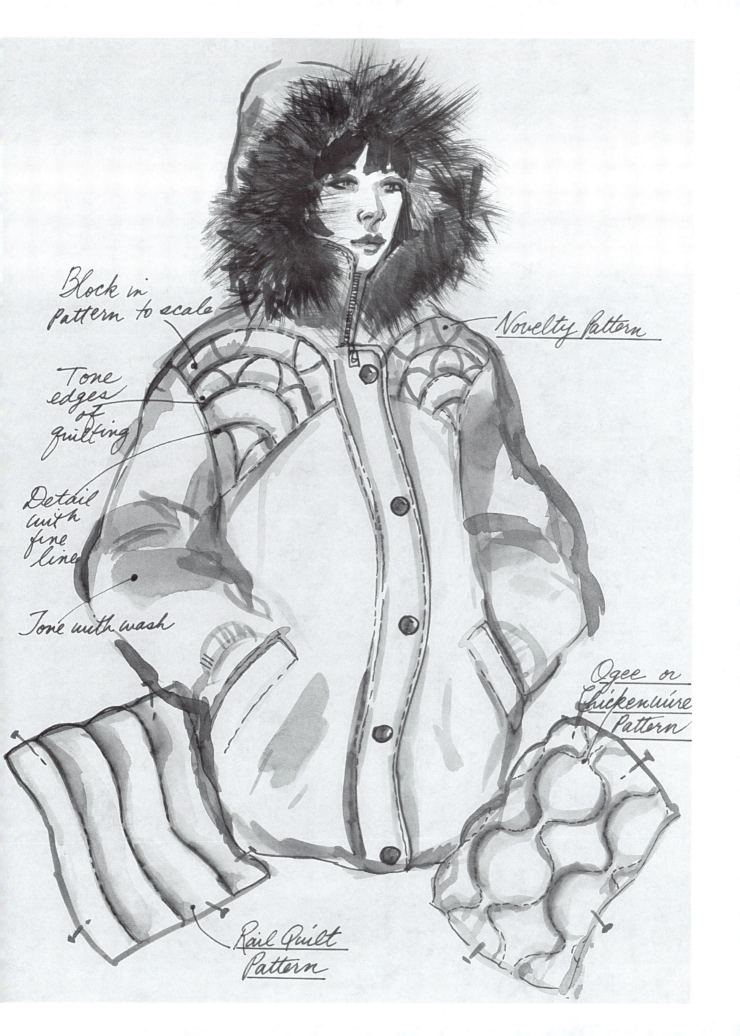

Block in
pattern to scale

Tone
edges
of
quilting

Detail
with
fine
line

Tone with wash

Novelty Pattern

Ogee or
Chickenwire
Pattern

Rail Quilt
Pattern

SHEERS

Sheer fabrics are transparent, revealing the body's contours. Sheers are natural fabrics for evening wear, and sheer cover-ups may be worn over swimwear. Undergarments and linings are designed to be seen.

Both knits and wovens can be sheer and can have a crisp or soft hand. Chiffon and georgette are two typical soft-hand sheers. They are often used in draped garments because they cling to the body. Organdy, dotted swiss, and eyelet are crisp, bouncy sheers.

The body shape should be lightly drawn first, with the silhouette of the sheer garment sketched over it. As you render the fabric, subtly reinforce the body contours with a flesh tone or darker shade of the fabric color. The details and silhouette should be rendered with a fine, light line.

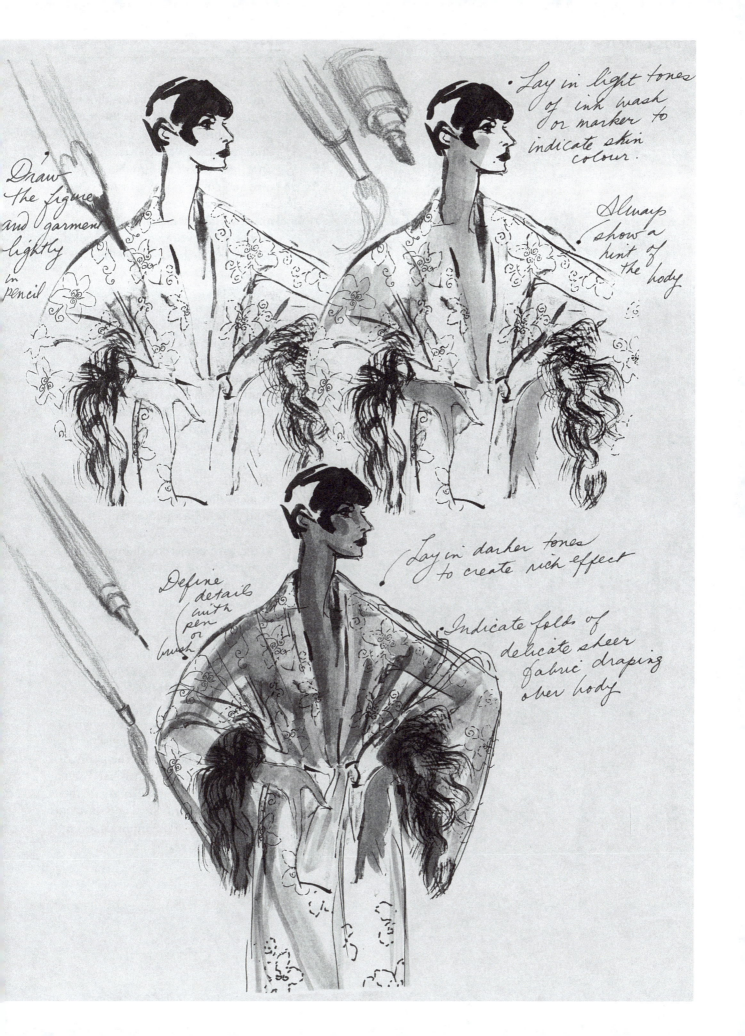

Draw the figure and garment lightly in pencil

Lay in light tones of ink wash or marker to indicate skin colour.

Always show a hint of the body

Define details with pen or brush

Lay in darker tones to create rich effect

Indicate folds of delicate sheer fabric draping over body

LACE

Lace has a transparent quality that is similar to a sheer with an additional motif to be rendered over the transparent fabric tone. There are many kinds of laces: widely spaced motifs on a lightweight net ground, lace edgings and ruffles, dense, heavy cotton laces, and white embroidery on a cotton lawn fabric that is called *eyelet*. Lace can be dyed in a range of colors, but the classic colors are white, black, and flesh-tone.

Dark colors are best rendered with a fine-line marker over a flesh-toned body. White lace is most effective when rendered on a colored board. Tan and shades of taupe or gray are neutral colors that will not detract from the finished illustration. Use a fine brush and a dense opaque white paint to detail white lace.

Begin the illustration of a specific lace by analyzing the predominant pattern from a swatch or photograph. Lightly sketch it on the basic figure, scaling it to the garment as you did with fabric patterns. Work on a fairly large figure so the motif is large enough to render easily. Tone the body and under garments or lining with felt pen or wash. Let this base color dry completely before working over the sketch with the fine-line marker or white paint for the actual lace pattern.

Expensive lace garments are sewn so darts and seam lines are invisible. The pattern is cut out where the garment has to be shaped and then hand sewn back together with a seam that conforms to the motif. Style and fit details in the lace should be minimal, even in less expensive garments.

Use combinations of white wash and opaque paint

"Punch up" lace pattern with a fine outline

Use thick white paint to create feeling of stiff fabric

RENDERING WHITE LACE

A contrasting illustration board sets off the pattern of white lace. A neutral-color board is most effective.

FURS

In the past, traditional furs were limited to natural colors and a small selection of "fun furs," which were dyed in fashion colors or stenciled to resemble other animals. Mink was the most common fashion fur, and beaver, rabbit, seal, sable, chinchilla, and broadtail were novelties. Today many fashion designers have entered the fur market and have introduced new methods of styling furs. Fashion dictates the way furs look, and the conservative "little fur piece" is out of fashion. Concern with environmental and animal rights issues have also affected the fur market. Fake furs have gained in popularity and importance as the public's resistance to real fur grows. New kinds of furs have become popular. When endangered species limited a specific kind of fur, designers used novel methods of stenciling or clipping available pelts to imitate the real thing. Render fake fur with the same techniques used for real fur.

Each fur garment is styled around pelts with unique markings. Illustrators should work from actual garments or good photographs. Instead of attempting to render every hair, a bold loose style is the most effective approach to capturing the rich and varied texture of furs.

Charcoal or a soft conté crayon worked over a paper with a toothy (textured) surface is an effective way of rendering the plush depths and highlights of furs.

Draw the edges and collar details of bulky furs with thick, rounded corners. The long-haired furs will have greater volume. Lynx and spotted long hairs should be rendered with a great deal of white paper left open. Detail the fine hair lines with charcoal, a dry brush, or a fine-line marker. Keep the illustration loose and open. Soften the spots in long-hair fur and give them an imprecise quality.

Block out fur
pattern, lay in
light tone with
marker

Add tone with pencil and
medium-tone markers, highlight with white dry-brush
technique, and
"punch up" with pen

Mink pelts have a characteristic dark stripe down the center of each strip, or pelt. A fine line indicates the direction the pelts have been worked. Smudge some areas of the charcoal and deeply shadow others to capture the rich depth of the fur. White highlights painted over dark areas with opaque watercolor are effective. Be guided by an actual garment or photograph when you render the shadows and highlights.

SEAL, BEAVER

Seal and beaver are such deep, rich pelts that—much like velvet—they absorb rather than reflect light. Highlights tend to occur around the outer edges of these plush furs. Render these furs with deep, dark tones near the center of the garment, and highlight and feather the soft silhouettes of the fur with a fine marker.

Beaver

Lay in wash
or light
marker tone

Establish the
direction of
fur pattern

Add black and
dark marker or
paint to
finish
fur pattern.

Spotted patterns are most effective on a light ground. Keep the spots irregularly rendered. The spots are well defined on a flat fur. Light shadows are typical of the edges of the large smooth pelts. Render animal-print fabrics the same way as fur.

1. Establish the direction of the fur pattern — lay in wash or light marker tone

Add black and dark marker to finish pattern

Chinchilla and Fox

Horizontal pelt - with darkest areas between each pelt

CHINCHILLA

Chinchilla is one of the most regal furs. It is characterized by deep tones of dark gray at the lower side of each pelt. Coats are most often designed in deep ribs to emphasize the rich toning of chinchilla fur. The silhouette of a chinchilla garment is a series of curves to capture the look of the rows of pelts.

CHAPTER 7

Rendering Techniques and Materials

Learning to draw in a clear, easy manner, without gimmicks, should be the primary goal of a fashion illustrator or designer. A knowledge of what the figure is and how the body moves is the first key to fashion illustration. The second key is a visual concept of the way garments are constructed and how fabrics drape as they surround the body. When you have assimilated this knowledge and developed a high level of skill with easily controlled media such as pencils, felt pens, and Prismacolor pencils, then explore and master more complicated media.

A good art supply store offers a wide range of papers and materials, and trained sales personnel can explain and demonstrate media. This is where you will find new products, so shop art supply stores frequently. Note that many have catalogs so phone and mail order is available.

Most kinds of art products are manufactured in various qualities, and prices will depend on the quality. Serious students should buy the best materials they can afford. *Artist-quality* brushes, paint, and paper will be easier to handle and will produce professional results more easily than inexpensive products. *Student-quality* art supplies are less expensive but often produce inferior results. Inexpensive paper may not accept paint as well as an artist-quality paper. Brushes that shed their hair spoil a painted surface. Weigh the cost of art supplies against the quality of the product you wish to produce.

This skilled artist uses a bold, dry brush line to give his illustrations a painterly quality that is dramatic for high-fashion apparel. (Courtesy of Steven Stipelman.)

DRAWING PAPERS

Papers vary widely in weight, quality, size, finish, color, surface characteristics, use, and price. The list of paper terms that follows suggests basic varieties and their uses, but nothing substitutes for experimentation and experience in selecting a specific paper for a special effect. Begin to purchase a variety of papers and experiment with colors and quality. It is always best to buy extra sheets to cover possible mistakes. You can always keep odd paper scraps for working out experimental ideas.

Illustration board is the "workhorse" paper for drawn and painted illustrations. It is a good-quality watercolor paper mounted on cardboard for greater stability. A *cold-pressed* or slightly "toothy" surface is the best for drawing and painting because it withstands repeated erasures and reworking.

Illustration board is available in several weights and surface patterns and a wide range of colors. It is fairly expensive, however, so as a beginner, you will want to work out a rough soft-pencil sketch on a less expensive bond paper. To transfer this image to the illustration board, use a soft lead pencil to cover the back of your rough sketch. Use two small pieces of masking tape to secure the drawing to the illustration board. Then use a sharp, hard (#3) pencil to draw over your sketch. Remove the rough drawing and clean off any carbon smudges with an eraser before working further into the illustration.

Inexpensive illustration board may have sizing on the surface. This surface will resist a watercolor wash, and you cannot paint a smooth color area on it. To remove the sizing, delicately wash the surface with a clean rag or paper towel and warm water. Apply the wash to a slightly damp board for the smoothest results.

Professional illustrators often draw directly on the illustration board. Sure

drawing skills produce a looser, more interesting sketch than the transfer technique. Strive to build your drawing skills so that you feel comfortable lightly sketching your rough drawing directly onto illustration board.

Collect several subtly colored illustration boards and novelty papers. Buff, ecru, gray, and taupe are good neutral tones that will enhance your illustrations. Colored paper is especially effective for rendering white garments. Use a toothy, or rough-surfaced paper when sketching with charcoal or pastels. The rough surface enhances the soft, sensuous charcoal line. Smooth-surface papers take fine pen lines and delicate line drawings best.

Vellum is a semitransparent paper often used by illustrators for *camera-ready work* (precisely rendered drawings ready to be printed). It is a sturdy paper that does not tear as easily as tracing paper. You can place vellum over a rough drawing and trace the sketch in finished form. Vellum will accept washes, ink, markers, and a variety of pencils as well as tonal screens. Coloring the back side of vellum will produce a smooth surface, even if you use a broad-nib marker. The surface is durable enough so that mistakes made in water-soluble markers can be wiped off the surface with a damp rag or paper towel. Vellum can be mounted on a more durable board for presentation.

Build a supply of different papers so you can select the appropriate vehicle for any drawing or medium you wish to attempt. Add several *hot-press illustration boards* (they have a smooth, slick surface) so you can mount or mat your best work for a truly professional presentation. Hot-pressed illustration board will not accept most paint, pencil, and markers because it has a slick surface, but it is less expensive than cold-pressed illustration board.

BASIC DRAWING PAPER TERMS

- *Tooth (also called bite).* The texture of a paper. In a good paper, a textured surface is created by the arrangement of fibers. These little peaks and valleys are visible as a textured line when the paper is drawn on with a lead pencil, crayon, or charcoal. More tooth makes the surface bulkier, more absorbent, and the lines drawn upon it rougher.

- *Feel.* This refers to the comparative bulk, finish, snap, and feel of the paper. The term is similar to the hand of a fabric.

- *Grain.* The direction the paper fibers run as the paper is made. The grain line affects the folding capability of the paper and the way it tears.

- *Hand, high-surface, hot-press, smooth, slick, or plate finish.* These terms all describe a smooth, hard-surface paper that is appropriate for a delicate line drawing. This finish is difficult to erase and paint on because the fibers absorb less of the medium and feather easily when erased or dampened.

- *Medium-surface, vellum, kid, or cold-press finish.* These terms describe a toothy surface with a slight texture that accepts almost any technique, from airbrush and paints to marking pens and pencils.

- *Rag paper.* A paper that contains 25 to 100 percent rag, or cotton pulp. The greater the rag content, the more erasing and wetting the paper can take.

- *"Pound" substance.* The weight of a paper in pounds, determined by the weight of a ream (500 sheets) in the paper's basic size. For example, one ream of bond paper 17 by 22 inches weighs 16 pounds and is called a 16-pound bond paper. Ledger bond weighs 32 pounds in the basic bond paper size of 17 by 22 inches, so it is designated as 32-pound ledger bond.

- *Point.* The thickness of illustration board, matt or mount boards, and papers are measured by the point. A point is .001 inch (a thousandth of an inch).

- *ST.* Single-thickness illustration board is approximately 1/16 inch or 60 points thick.

- *DT.* Double-thickness board is approximately 1/8 inch or 110 points thick.

- *TT.* Triple-thickness board is approximately 3/16 inch or 165 points thick.

- Bond paper (16 pound) is about 3 points thick.

- Ledger bond (32 pound) is about 6 points thick.

APPLIED PAPERS

Color screens. These are pressure-applied, transparent acetate sheets in a wide range of colors that are often used in professional illustrations. Because these overlays are transparent, they may be used over a drawing and then reworked with paints, pencils, or marking pens. The colors are available in many graduated tints.

Printed color sheets. Opaque printed color paper that may be used in a collage and must be applied with glue.

Shaded screens. Many kinds of patterns are available in black printed on transparent acetate screens. The patterns are then applied to paper by pressure. The basic range is a dotted surface that ranges from a light gray to a dense gray surface. These patterns are helpful devices for doing black-and-white camera-ready artwork.

Typefaces. Pressure-applied screens containing alphabets and numerals are available in a great variety of styles and sizes. These typographic elements are applied like the color and tonal screens.

Tissue paper, book endpaper, novelty papers. A great variety of novelty papers is available for collage illustrations. Usually such papers may be purchased by the sheet.

The geometric screen focuses the eye on the face and enhances the strong graphic quality and bold line of Passantino's work. (Courtesy of Robert Passantino.)

APPLIED-PAPER TECHNIQUES

Acetate Screens   Machine-made screens of transparent acetate, over-printed with color or pattern, can be purchased at most art stores. They are easily applied to tone an area on a sketch, creating a smooth, professional look.

Sketch the basic illustration on a smooth piece of paper or illustration board. You may shadow the illustration before applying the screen. Carefully place the full sheet over the illustration and cut a piece slightly larger than the area you wish to cover. Be careful not to apply any pressure to the screen. When the shape is cut, place it on the illustration and cut out the exact contour with a mat knife. Be careful to cut only the film and not the paper the illustration is on. Lightly press the sheet to "tack" it in place, then burnish it firmly with a smoothing tool (a teaspoon works well). Be sure to press down the edges of the screen securely. Detail shadows, highlights, and style lines with paint, pen, or pencils after applying the screen.

Because of their transparency, several color screens can be applied over the same area, creating blended colors. Experiment with scraps of colored screens to see how colors mix and other media work with the blends you create.

Screens give a clean even tone on Fashion Figures

Cut with sharp blade.

Cut section of screen of approximate size you will need

Press down
Cut around area to be shaded — lift off...gently!

Tissue Paper and Novelty Collage Materials Colored tissue can be used as a collage (pictures created by assemblies of paper and objects). Brilliant colors are available in single sheets or as packages at most art stores. To apply with liquid laundry starch, carefully paint the area to be covered with starch. Press down the precut piece of tissue paper and repaint the area with another coat of starch. The tissue color will bleed, so wash the brush after each application and let the piece dry before applying paint or additional tissue layers. The tissue will often wrinkle, forming an interesting texture. The double application of starch makes the tissue look glazed.

The glory of Summer. Brassy light
dry wind and sparkling waters.
Sea breezes; mists dissolving
into the heat. Childrens'
laughter, kites and
balloons float to the sun.

A different effect is achieved when the tissue is mounted with rubber cement. Precut the shape you want. Apply a thin, even coat of rubber cement to the back of the tissue and to the top surface of the paper it will be applied to. Let both sides dry completely. Carefully place the precut shape and smooth the tissue into place. This application gives the tissue a matt surface.

Any kind of paper can be used as collage material. Paper can make a distinctive color or texture area, and your illustration can be finished with paint, felt pens, and pencils. Collage is a versatile and quick method of illustrating. Collect scraps of interesting paper and experiment with several collage approaches to illustration.

PASTELS AND CHARCOALS

Pastels are dry color. When applied to paper, the colors may be blended with the fingers or with a paper-blending stump. To fix the colors to the paper permanently, a spray fixative, available at a well-stocked art supply store, must be applied over the finished illustration. Hair spray may be used if no fixative is available.

This technique is difficult to use for fashion illustrations for several reasons: (1) It is most effective when it is applied directly to the page with no under drawing, which requires advanced drawing skills; (2) it tends to be messy and imprecise; (3) special papers with a very toothy surface are most effective.

Care is needed to master this medium, but an accomplished artist can achieve fresh, spontaneous drawings in charcoal. Pastels and charcoals lend themselves especially well to the rendering of furs. *Conté crayons,* stick drawing pastels from France that are available in black, white, and sepia tones, are fine traditional drawing pastels.

To create a pastel or charcoal sketch, draw quickly and boldly directly on a toothy drawing paper. Concentrate on drawing the silhouette and shadows instead of the tiny details of the garment. Create smooth areas of tone by blending the charcoal with a *tortillon stump.* This looks like a pencil but is made of paper. The point can be made quite sharp to tone small areas. Use the point on the side to tone larger areas. Do not overwork the sketch because it will become dirty and muddy. Enhance the spontaneous drawing style by using color boldly and directly. Preserve the drawing with a coat of spray fixative.

This technique
gives a very
spontaneous
and unplanned
look—

There should be very
little under-sketch
work

Charcoal and Pastels
are best used on
a grainy paper

PAINTS AND PAINTING EQUIPMENT

PAINTS

Paint is pigment mixed with a *binder,* a glue that makes the color adhere to a receptive surface. Binders are dissolved and extended by water or *mineral spirits* (turpentine). The vast majority of color fashion illustration is done with water-base paints because they dry rapidly, are relatively inexpensive, are easy to work with, and dry with a matt surface suitable for camera-ready art.

Water-base paints are available in two main kinds: transparent and opaque (also called *gouache*). These two types of paint may also be mixed. Both are compatible with dyes and acrylic (polymer emulsion) paints—in fact, with all paints that use water as an extender. Water-base paints are not compatible with oil-base paints.

Transparent watercolors are available in individual tubes, in bottles as liquid watercolor, and in solid cakes contained in palette sets. Palettes usually have twelve or more colored cakes and are very economical and portable. These solid colors should have a drop or two of water added to each cake several minutes before using. The water will break down the binder, and intense color will be readily available. When either cake or tube watercolor is mixed with enough white paint, an opaque surface results. This is *gouache,* or *opaque watercolor.* To paint a light, transparent color, thin the pure color with water, not white paint.

Dyes are extremely concentrated liquid pigments. When painted full strength on a white surface, dyes produce a brilliant, transparent tone. Dyes come in bottles with eye-dropper tops, so a small amount can be dropped onto a palette or into white paint and then brushed on paper. A

great variety of colors is available. However, dyes fade quickly in sunlight, so do not leave an illustration colored with dyes in direct sunlight.

Liquid watercolor is available in eye-dropper-top bottles that are similar to those that contain dyes. Liquid watercolors are usually more costly than liquid dyes or cake watercolors, however.

Transparent watercolor paint tends to produce a looser, more painterly illustration than the opaque techniques. Opaque surfaces are most effective when they are applied as tightly rendered color areas within an illustration and reworked with a well-defined outline and precise detailing.

Gouaches, also called *designer colors,* are more frequently used in fashion and commercial illustration. These are good quality paints that can be easily mixed to produce a smooth, even surface. A high degree of control over color and paint density is possible. Designer colors are available in tubes. The medium-sized tubes are most practical because they will not dry out before they are used up. A wide variety of colors plus black and white are available as well as many tones of premixed gray to facilitate the rendering of black-and-white camera-ready art for commercial illustration purposes. Beginners should have a good selection of these paints.

Acrylic paints produce a dense opaque surface with a slight gloss. They can be extended with water and used to tint white designer color paint with the same methods used for dyes and watercolors. Experiment with this paint medium to determine if you wish to add it to your technical repertoire.

BRUSHES

Brushes are available in many qualities, the finest of which are red sable watercolor brushes. Brushes are numbered to define the size—the smaller the number, the finer the brush size. The beginner should buy a range of brush sizes in the best quality brush the budget will allow. Several small brushes for detail work are important (select an 000, 0, and a #1). Medium sizes are #2 through #5; select a #3 and a #5 to begin. Buy a #7 or #8 for larger washes and one medium-sized blunt *sky brush* (fine artists typically use this brush to paint washes depicting sky and clouds) for painting larger areas.

Nylon brushes are preferred for painting with acrylics because the paint's polymer binder produces a texture that is quite thick, and thus stiffer brushes are required. Oil paint effects can be achieved with these slightly firmer brushes, which have a natural "snap."

White sable brushes are also acceptable for painting with acrylic paints and are also excellent for ink applications. Both these media are very hard on brushes, and white sable brushes are very durable.

Clean and store your brushes carefully. Never leave brushes in water for extended periods of time because the glue that holds the hairs in the *ferrule* (the metal band holding the hairs to the handle) will loosen, and the hairs will bend permanently. Wash your brushes with a mild hand soap, rinse with clear, warm water, and let them dry naturally. With care, good brushes will last many years.

The following list may help you in your selection and use of brushes:

- *Japanese (sumié) brush.* A long pointed brush often made with a bamboo handle that is used for painting Japanese characters and for brush painting.

- *Nylon bristle brushes.* Used for acrylic paints because of the large amount of paint they can hold and because of their "snap" or resiliency. Available in flat, round, and chisel shapes, and in a range of sizes.

- *One-stroke, lettering brushes.* Flat, broad-tipped sable (or mixed-hair) brushes designed for lettering.

- *Oval, "sky" brushes.* Blunt-end brushes used for broad washes, especially sky tones in fine art painting.

- *Pointed brush.* Needle-sharp pointed hairs with which you can paint fine line. To paint washes with this brush, load with paint and use the brush on its side.

- *Red sable.* The best-quality hair for a watercolor brush. The hair is obtained from kolinsky (red Tarter martin) weasel tails. These brushes are soft, resilient, and durable.

- *Student-quality brushes.* Less costly hair made from black sables, squirrels, ponies, and oxen are used to make these less-expensive brushes. Although they often resemble the red sable quality, these brushes rarely perform or last as well.

MISCELLANEOUS EQUIPMENT

Buy a plastic palette for mixing colors or save clean white Styrofoam egg cartons. Blotters or absorbent paper towels are an important painting aid: Use them for cleaning brushes or lifting excess paint from an illustration. Use a large glass or jar for fresh water to rinse an unwanted color from your brush.

A smooth drawing board made from soft wood or masonite board is important. To make painting easier, raise the board in the back and draw on a slanted surface. Buy a clip or push pins to secure your paper or illustration board to the drawing board.

A light box is a handy tool for transferring drawings to translucent papers. You can purchase a professional box that is made to sit on a table or is free-standing, or you can make your own. All light boxes have solid bottoms and

sides and a cool light source, such as a fluorescent tube, inside. The top of the box is frosted glass. Work is placed on the glass, and the light below makes the work easy to trace.

BASIC COLOR TERMS

- *Primary colors.* Red, blue, and yellow: the foundation colors that can be combined to form all the other colors.

- *Secondary colors.* Combinations of two of the primary colors: orange = red + yellow; purple = blue + red; green = blue + yellow.

- *Tertiary colors.* Colors created by combining three colors, for example, brown = red + yellow + blue.

- *Black and white.* Colors at the opposite ends of the gray scale that combine with pure colors to create shades (black + color) and tints (white + color).

- *Chroma.* The intensity of a particular hue.

- *Color wheel.* An arrangement of colors radiating out from the primary and secondary colors.'

- *Complementary colors.* Colors directly across from one another on the color wheel.

- *Hue.* Pure color.

- *Saturated colors.* Pure, full-strength, intense color with no black or white to alter the tint.

- *Shade.* Color + black, which gives a darker tone to the hue.

- *Tint.* Color + white or transparent color diluted with water.

- *Value.* The amount of light or dark in a color (luminosity scale).

PAINTING TECHNIQUES

Experimentation and practice are the key ingredients to mastering the techniques of mixing colors and handling brushes and watercolors. Nothing substitutes for the trial-and-error process of mixing a color or developing a technique by trying to duplicate an illustration you admire or envision.

Begin painting by doing the following exercises to master transparent and opaque washes. Repeat the exercises several times, first using black and white, then substituting a color. Then begin to experiment with color mixes. Duplicate illustration and painting techniques from this book and your scrap collection. Experiment with paint without expecting to produce a finished illustration. Such experiments and "doodling" will help you develop the skill of mixing color accurately.

Learn from your mistakes as well as from the successful illustrations you produce. Hold a finished illustration up to a mirror for a new perspective. Put a finished piece of art away for a day or so, then reevaluate your achievements and analyze how your work could be improved.

Watch professional illustrators whenever possible and imitate their work methods. Attend fine arts classes for tips that may improve your technique. Ask an illustrator or instructor to critique your work. Rework past pieces, using the directions you received from the illustrator or instructor.

Remember, you can learn how to match and mix colors only by doing it.

This superb gouache rendering is accented and highlighted with pencil and pen. (Courtesy of Catherine Clayton Purnell.)

FALL NEWCOMERS

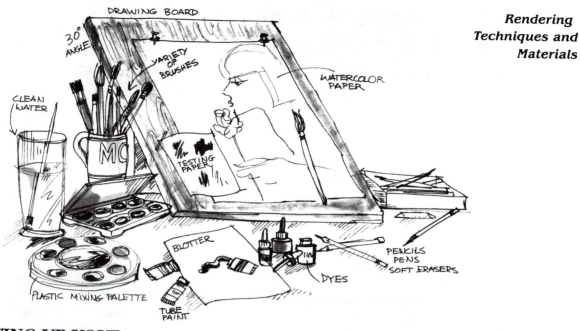

SETTING UP YOUR WORKING SPACE

1. Store brushes in a container with the points up in the air. The size and kind of point will then be easily visible, and the hairs will not bend. After using, always clean brushes with mild soap and flush with warm water.

2. A palette of twelve or more color cakes is a good basic investment. Before using the colors, add a drop of water to each cake to break down the binder so the color is in solution and ready to use. After a number of uses, the palette may be cleaned by rinsing with a gentle flow of warm water.

3. Use a plastic palette for mixing paint for washes. For the smoothest coverage, premix the colors thoroughly in one of the wells on the palette before painting.

4. Clear water is necessary for mixing paints and rinsing brushes between colors. Change the water frequently to keep colors brilliant.

5. Dyes and tubes of paint are additional aids that should be added to your supplies as your budget allows. A tube of white designer color is a must for a beginner.

6. A paper towel or blotter is used to mop up water and excess color and to dry brushes.

7. Drawing pencils and felt pens should be handy. Use them to work into the illustrations when the washes are completely dry.

8. Before you apply paint to an illustration, test a dab for color and consistency on a spare piece of paper.

9. Elevate your drawing board to a 20- or 30-degree angle so that the paint can flow down into the area you want to cover.

TRANSPARENT WASH TECHNIQUES

Gray-scale Washes

1. Draw a series of 2-inch squares on illustration board or good-quality watercolor paper.

2. Paint two or three squares with a small amount of clear water and wait until the paper absorbs most of the water. This priming makes the paper accept the paint smoothly.

3. Put a small amount of water in a well of your palette. Tint it with a dab of black paint from your black watercolor tube or cake. Mix the pigment and water well. Paint the first square with a medium-sized (#7 or #8) brush.

4. Paint from the top of the square downward. Work one stripe after another, overlapping them slightly and blending the overlap area with your brush so you have a smooth, even wash.

5. Add more black paint to your palette and paint successively darker squares. Paint at least twenty squares. Cut the squares out and select ten gray tones that are evenly graduated from a pale gray tint to a deep shade of charcoal.

6. Paste the squares in the corner of a 7-by-14 inch white board, using rubber cement. Apply the cement to the back side of the paint swatch and the board. Let it dry until it is tacky. Carefully place the swatches over the corresponding cement and press in place. Make sure the ten squares are arranged in two rows, with an even distribution of space around the grouping.

Rendering with a Transparent Wash

1. Lightly sketch a figure on good watercolor paper or illustration board. Mix a light gray tint and paint it as the flesh tone of the figure. (Did you remember to prime the area with water before painting?) Let this wash dry completely before continuing.

2. Mix a medium gray tint and paint the garment in your sketch. Let some of the paper remain white where the highlights of the garment would fall. Work the shadows and folds of the fabric with a deeper shade of gray. Let this wash dry.

3. Build shadows into the folds and edges of the garment. Tone the hair, again leaving highlights of white paper. Shadow the cheekbones and eyelids with one of the gray tones in your palette. Allow the washes to dry completely.

4. Detail your finished sketch with silhouette and style lines done with a very fine brush and black paint or a fine-line marking pen.

Practice several figures. Notice that the transparent wash technique can create a dramatic, loosely rendered illustration. Render some garments from photographs. Instead of gray tones, use tints of pure color from your palette. Dilute brown paint and tint with a touch of red and yellow to paint a skin tone.

1. Block in - lay in lightest skin tones

2. Block in middle tones lay in shadows

3. Block in darkest tones - leave highlights, apply final shadows

4. Add final details, "punch up" with black

OPAQUE WASH TECHNIQUES

Gray-scale Opaque Washes

1. Draw 2-inch squares on a piece of good watercolor paper and prime with water as you did in the last gray-scale exercise.

2. Squeeze an aspirin-sized dab of white designer color into a bowl in your palette.

3. Dilute the white paint with several brushfuls of water (use a #7 brush). Mix the water and paint thoroughly until it is of brushing consistency.

4. Add a drop of black paint to the white mixture and mix it again (use the brush for mixing). Completely blend the black paint and the white paint until no streaks are visible.

5. Paint the first square from top to bottom with slightly overlapping strokes. Smooth out any streaks with your brush.

6. Continue mixing deeper tones of gray from white and black paint extended with water. The secret to streakless washes is to thoroughly premix the paint in the palette before painting it on the paper. Paint twenty squares in graduated gray tones. Cut them out and select ten squares that are evenly graduated from a gray tint to a deep charcoal shade. Mount as you did the transparent wash examples.

Compare the two kinds of paint. Notice how the dense opaque washes cover pencil lines and kill most of the quality of the paper. Opaque paint lends itself to tightly rendered illustrations; transparent washes have a looser, more painterly feeling.

Lay in sketch in pencil— Block in where pattern of fabric is and sketch to scale

Erase guidelines. Float light wash for fabric and other large areas.

Detail fabric pattern with fine line or brush. Leave some areas less detailed to create "breathing space"

Rendering with an Opaque Wash

1. Lightly sketch a simple figure on watercolor paper or illustration board. Mix an opaque light gray wash with black and white and paint the skin tones.

2. Mix a gray wash the color of the lightest portion of the garment. Allow each painted area to completely dry before beginning the next. Remember to prime your paper with water before painting each area.

3. Work back into the basic wash with deeper tints of gray to accent the folds and shadows of the garment. Use an opaque white paint for highlighting the basic colors.

4. Detail the silhouette and style lines and the features with a fine brush and black paint or a fine-line marker.

Work out several more illustrations using the opaque-wash technique. Use a fashion photograph to guide you in the way the fabric falls and reflects light. Observe the shadows and highlights in garments and hair. Duplicate them with your gray-tone paints.

Experiment with a combination of transparent and opaque washes in the same illustration. For example, render the skin tones with an opaque wash and paint the garment with a loose, transparent wash, emphasizing paper highlights and brush strokes.

COLOR RENDERING

The majority of professional fashion illustration is done as black-and-white art for newspaper advertising. Colored fashion illustrations are used for camera-ready art for color-print-media design plates (especially for theater costume design) and commercial design presentations. Color work is also extensively used in print fabric designing.

A basic knowledge of painting and mixing a wide range of colors from the three primary colors is helpful to any artist. In practice, most professional artists use a great variety of pre-mixed paints, dyes, and marking pens to cut down the elaborate mixing necessary to create colors from scratch.

Refer to a color wheel. Notice how the basic, or primary, colors—red, blue, and yellow—are combined to form the secondary and tertiary colors. Note also how a tone can be subdued by adding the color opposite it on the color wheel (its complementary color).

Experimenting with this range of artists' aids is essential to developing an eye for color matching. Begin to learn how to mix colors by substituting a primary color for black. Develop a range of tints from the pure hue to a pale pastel shade of the color. Deepen the pure color in steps to achieve near black. Select ten equal steps of these tints and shades plus the saturated

Wash
Charcoal Stick
Charcoal Pencil

color and mount them as you did the gray scales.

To improve your color-matching ability, mix paint to match several fabric swatches. Remember, watercolor dries slightly lighter than it is when wet. Refer back to the discussion of rendering fabrics (Chapter 6) and repeat several exercises for each fashion problem presented.

Color Rendering of the Head

1. Mix an opaque skin tone by extending a drop of white paint with water in a well of your mixing palette. Tint this to a skin tone by adding dabs of red, brown, and yellow. Mix thoroughly and test on your trial paper. Correct with additional dabs of color until you are satisfied with the shade.

2. Paint the basic skin tone on the face, leaving the eyes white. Tint the remaining skin tone in your palette several shades darker with brown paint. Shadow the cheek bones, nose, and top edges of the forehead with this tone. Allow to dry.

3. Paint the iris with an appropriate color. Use the eye color to tint a small amount of flesh tone and paint the eyelid with a complementary shadow. Use a red, coral, or pink to color the lips. Do not overemphasize these colors; keep them natural.

4. Mix a hair color. Paint the hair with a transparent wash with loose brush strokes. Leave white paper highlights. Let the basic hair tone dry thoroughly. Mix a darker color of the hair shade and detail the flow of the hairstyle with a fine brush.

5. Detail the whole drawing by outlining the features, blackening
   the pupil, finishing the eyebrows and eyelids, and so on.
   Reinforce the hairstyle lines
   with black paint unless it contrasts too strongly with a light
   hair shade.

6. Mix a pure, dense white and
   apply to the whites of the eyes
   and the teeth if they are visible.
   Highlight the tip of the nose, the
   black pupil, and perhaps a touch
   at the bottom lip.

C H A P T E R   8

Designing the Ilustration

Skillfully drawing a fashion figure is only one phase of fashion illustration and presentation of designs. The figure should also be well positioned in the space of the total composition. A well-drawn figure—the positive image—is enhanced by the design of the setting (the negative space that surrounds the image). In addition, an illustrator or designer usually has to arrange several elements on one page. For example, the fashion layout artist who plans print media has to integrate the following elements for a typical newspaper ad: several fashion figures, a headline, the body of copy, the store logo, and miscellaneous print information. A designer usually illustrates several figures or a group of garments and adds swatches of fabric and colors and handwritten instructions on a typical fashion plate.

The total space must be planned so the eye focuses on the main point of interest and flows logically through the subordinate elements. Well-designed illustrations have a pleasing appearance that will attract the viewer and enhance the figure. In addition, a limited drawing ability can be camouflaged by a well-designed presentation that stresses the skills of the artist.

The successfully designed layout should do the following:

1. Capture the interest of the viewer.

2. Direct the eye toward the most important element on the page.

3. Support the center of interest with explanatory print areas or descriptive materials.

4. Reinforce the subject matter with an appropriate format.

5. Avoid the extremes of monotony and confusion through careful planning of the positive images and the negative space that surrounds them.

The creative application of the principles (guidelines) to the elements (components) of design results in a successful layout. Think of baking a cake. The recipe tells a cook how to combine the ingredients and at what temperature to bake them to produce a delicious cake. To an artist, the principles of design govern the way the elements or ingredients should be combined to create a successful illustration.

This delicate airbrush rendering of a face for a cosmetic product is effective because of the range of light and dark tones that contour with no hard edges. (Courtesy of David Horii.)

Contrasting areas of line and mechanical screened tones move the eye through this complicated layout. Notice how the car frames the figures and directs attention to them. (Courtesy of Mia Carpenter.)

CONTRAST

The focal point and the subordinate elements are distinguished by varia-tions, or contrasts, in value, line and form.

VALUE

The eye is drawn to the high-contrast areas of an illustration. A bold, dark area is most effectively seen against a lighter value or a white background. A white circle on a black ground rivets the eye because of the high contrast in values. However, equal areas of light and dark are monotonous. To maintain interest, vary the size of the value areas in a composition.

The contrast of light, generalized line and detailed tonal rendering focuses the eye on the product. The gesture, and attention of the models directs the viewer to the copy area. (Courtesy of Gregory Weir-Quiton.)

LINE

Interest can be created by the direction, weight, and character of lines. A bold, crisply drawn line has an interesting character even before it describes a specific object. A light, smooth line suggests light fabric, delicate details, or sleek limbs. A bold, heavy line best describes a bulky fabric, the silhouette of a garment, or a bold, masculine face.

Compositions that have strong linear direction assume a definite personality based on traditional perceptions of directional lines. Using several weights of line in a single drawing lends interest and emphasis to the composition.

- *Horizontal lines* are restful and tranquil.

- *Diagonal lines* are exciting and express action, but they should be avoided by beginners because undisciplined use of angles can be confusing.

- *Vertical lines* seem to reach or climb. They represent power and growth.

- *Curved lines* remind the eye of natural forms. The eye takes longer to perceive a curve than a straight line. Curved lines seem lyrical and tranquil.

FORM

Contrast is created with form when large, bold areas are accented with small details or crisp, smaller shapes. This is contrast of scale—large compared to small. When you plan contrasts of form, remember that a small dark space can "read" (seem to the eye) as more important than a lightly outlined larger shape.

for your body. running bras.

32-38 B, C, S100, 38 D $10.50 Body Fashions, 19. S100.55

The Broadway

The bold central focal point of this layout dramatizes the silhouette of the garment. A wide range of gray tones moves the eye quickly from the top to the bottom of this illustration. (Courtesy of Paul Lowe.)

RHYTHM

Rhythm is the repeated use of a similar value area, shape, or line technique to create a unified whole. Repeating the same form creates a repeated rhythm that can be successfully accented by changing the shape, line quality, color, or value of the accent unit. The one black sheep is immediately seen in a herd of white sheep.

UNITY

Unity, or harmony, is the logical emphasis of the focal point and the subordination of less important elements of the composition. Harmony unifies the elements of design to fulfill the visual goals of an illustration. Unplanned use of color, line, value, or form will detract from the impact of the focal point. For example, picture an advertisement for a discount drugstore or market. These ads are composed to cover every part of the newspaper page with a jumble of copy and unrelated illustrations. Almost no neg-

ative space is left. As a result, the eye has no place to pause, and the viewer is confused. The purpose of the ad is to sell inexpensive merchandise, and the image of the store is that of a bargain retailer.

More sophisticated merchandise is sold by developing an exclusive image to appeal to the selective customer. A successful fashion ad uses well-designed images to enhance the consumer's perception of the styles illustrated. The personality of a fashion store should be integrated with the visual message of the merchandise so the store image gains prestige from the advertisements.

BALANCE

Balance is an aesthetically pleasing arrangement of elements on a page.

Formal, or symmetrical, balance is created by an equal distribution of similar shapes on either side of a median line. In other words, the two sides are mirror images of the other. For example, the human body is symmetrical. Formal balance seems strong, dignified, restful, and static.

In informal balance, dissimilar shapes are positioned in the layout so that they are balanced by "weight" (their density or darkness) and by their relationship to each other. Asymmetry creates a more dynamic illustration than a symmetrical arrangement. Unless they are carefully designed, however, asymmetrical formats can easily seem unbalanced or random.

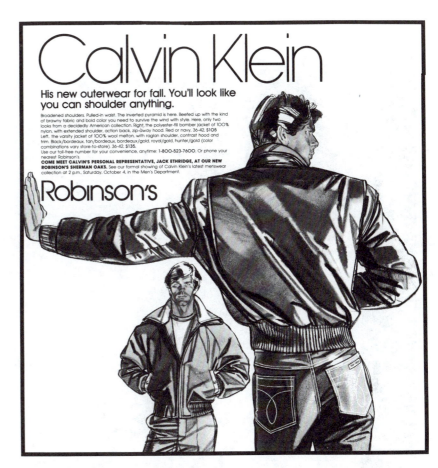

This bold symmetrical layout balances the headline with the central figure. The subordinate figure is well integrated into the positive space. Consequently, the negative space highlights the elements of the illustration. (Courtesy of Steve Bieck.)

These figures arranged rhythmically on a slightly asymmetrical axis break up the space beautifully and direct the eye through the illustration. The wide variety of lights contrasting with black and medium tones adds more excitement to the layout. (Courtesy of Mia Carpenter.)

Sleek FOLKLORIC

T.F.S.
THE
FASHION
SERVICE™
FORECAST

1987 · SPRING · 1987

assy PARADOX

*Complicated subject matter requires
careful planning to avoid confusion
and allow the eye to logically follow the
figures through the illustration. The
consistent style and line accented by
dark areas unifies this complicated
illustration. (Courtesy of The Fashion
Service, David Wolfe.)*

LAYOUT SKILLS

Axial

Band

Formal

The layout sketch is a plan for the organization, or *make,* of the page. The way the page should look is governed by these factors:

1.   The personality of the subject matter.

2.   The size of the page.

3.   The size and number of elements (figures, swatches, body copy, headline, logo, etc.) that must be incorporated into the layout.

4.   The image of the store or advertiser.

These conditions establish the *problem,* or the limitations of the page's make. The limitations of a problem do not hinder the artist's creativity. Rather, they focus attention on the specific requirements of the project and eliminate many possible solutions to designing the piece.

Advertisements are usually planned by several specialists. The layout artist designs the page, designates where the logo, copy, and illustration should be placed. The illustrator or photographer must carefully follow the layout plan for the specific page make. If a specification is missed or ignored, the artwork may be unusable, resulting in the loss of valuable time and money.

A design presentation should be planned like a good retail store advertisement. The designer must consider the subject matter and the audience who will see the presentation. If a designer is sketching for a boss or pattern maker, a simple pencil sketch of the front and back of the garment with sewing instructions and a fabric swatch will be enough. If the presentation is for a store buyer, the illustration will need figures that are well rendered in color and a complete set of swatches, trims, and price nota-

tions. The designer plate is a selling tool just like a store ad. The designer should set up specific requirements that will govern the graphics presentation of the garments. Besides the basic layout criteria, some additional considerations for a design presentation are the drawing skills of the designer and the time allotted for the project.

The beginning designer or illustrator should list the requirements of a particular project first so they are clearly in focus and not forgotten during the execution of the project. Establish a realistic deadline and time yourself so you know how long each phase of the project takes.

The second step to executing a project is the *thumbnail,* or layout, sketch. A thumbnail sketch is a rough drawing that shows the position of all the elements on the page. The size and position of the figures and other elements are roughly indicated on bond paper or vellum in pencil or felt marker.

The western eye reads a page from left to right and top to bottom out of habit. (Japanese perception is opposite to the Western tradition, and their print media reverse these rules.) A figure on the left-hand side of the page that is looking to the right seems to be entering the illustration. A figure on the right seems to be leaving the field of interest. For this reason, the dominant focal point usually is on the left-hand axis of a composition.

The principles and elements of design discussed in the first part of this chapter strongly influence good layout design. For instance, negative space is as important as positive space. The white area guides the eye to the focal point of the page and should be as carefully planned as the positive images. Lavish use of negative space implies that the advertiser does not have to cover every inch of space with copy or an image of the product. The prestigious object can be surrounded with space that enhances it. Other rules discussed previously include the following: Avoid using equal amounts of light and dark; vary the line and values on the page to guide the eye's attention to the focal point of the illustration; and avoid using strong diagonal elements until you are more experienced because they can be confusing.

Beginners should work the layout sketch the same size as the finished illustration. The figures may be sketched freehand, redrawn from photographs or scrap, or traced from earlier sketches. Make several layout sketches and select the best one for the finished artwork.

Grid

BASIC LAYOUT FORMATS

Above all, remember that there are no set rules governing page layout or determining which format is most acceptable for a particular subject matter. However, there are some typical layout formats that can be adapted to a great variety of subject matter and requirements. They are: axial, band, formal, grid, group, and path.

Study these layout formats, their descriptions and the fashion examples of each. Use these examples for future reference when you tackle complicated layout projects. Remember that these are guidelines and not dogmatic formulas. Go through a good glossy fashion magazine and identify as many typical layouts as possible. Experiment with the layout problems that follow in the next section.

Group

Path

Axial

Dadmy
Geneve

AXIAL COMPOSITION

Think of a tree trunk and branches breaking up space in a pleasing way. The subordinate elements should balance off the central axis. Make sure that the positive space results in an even distribution of negative areas so the composition is interesting and dynamic.

BAND COMPOSITION

The elements in this format are tightly placed on a vertical or horizontal band. The figures should touch and overlap in interesting relationships, and you should avoid leaving arbitrary space between the figures. Mix the values and patterns in the band to keep the eye reading through the composition. The negative space at the sides of a band look best if it is asymmetrical.

FORMAL COMPOSITION

Formal composition is the identical
grouping of the same elements on
either side of the axial line. This format gives the illustration a static sim-
plicity. The negative areas on either
side of the blocks should be divided
with uneven spaces to make the elements most interesting.

GRID COMPOSITION

A grid composition fills the whole area of the page with a pleasing mix of elements. To be effective, this composition should have a variety of large and small images rendered in a range of values that emphasize the most important area of the composition. This format gives a feeling of rich abundance to the items illustrated. However, great care must be taken so the grid format does not get too cluttered or confusing. The grid format is effective when illustrating a group of accessory items.

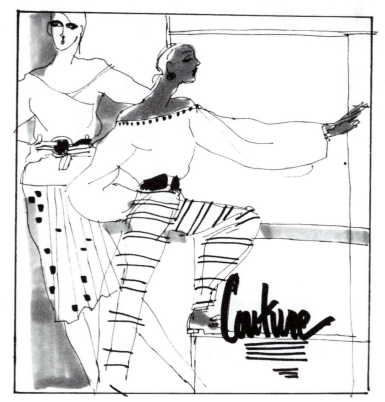

GROUP COMPOSITION

The group format is a cluster of tightly grouped elements that forms an interesting overall contour. The contour must be crisp and well defined, and the elements must interact within the grid so there is no confusion about the central element and the subordinate themes.

PATH COMPOSITION

The path format should lead the eye on a "walk" through the composition, as if on stepping-stones across a stream. There should be a natural flow through the composition. Remember that the eye will tend to read down the page from left to right, so organize the elements accordingly. Vary the negative areas and connect the elements of the page with interesting value, line, and form variations. In this way you will make sure that the eye does not "fall off" the "stepping-stones."

LAYOUT PROBLEMS

GENERAL CRITERIA

1. Use a rectangle, 8-by-11 inches for each exercise. The rectangle may be used vertically or horizontally. Draw a bold, sharp outline on layout bond paper with precisely drawn 90-degree corners.

2. Render in pencil and gray-tone felt pens.

3. Use two of the typical formats for each set of criteria, and do not use a format more than once.

Too stiff - too expected a layout

More animated - more movement - headline is important - copy leads the eye around the ad

Problem 1

1. Three figures

2. Three geometric shapes representing fabric swatches

3. A two-word headline, handwritten or typeset

4. Handwritten copy

Problem 2

1. Five figures with one dominant figure

2. A two- or three-word headline

3. A copy area indicated by gray-tone lines

4. The store logo

Problem 3

1. Two figures within a geometric shape rendered in a half-tone gray

2. The store logo

3. A copy area indicated by gray-tone lines

4. A three-word headline

O.K - but stiff - doesn't get the viewer involved

Leads the eye into and through the ad - creates more of an atmosphere.

METHODS

1. Study each problem and visualize a possible format that will effectively arrange the elements. Refer to fashion illustrations for additional ideas.

2. Collect scrap of store logos of varying sizes, and use a print copy book or instant type book to trace off headline copy.

3. Trace or draw some of the elements on bond or tracing paper, and cut them out so you can move them around the basic 8-by-11 inch rectangle to experiment with positioning.

4. Work out rough layouts and label each format used.

5. Discuss your layouts with an instructor or designer, and select one layout for each problem to render as finished artwork in tones of gray.

Good use of space —

This headline indication is more important as a design element —

(Many times you will like two layouts equally —)
.... The problems of being creative...

STYLIZING YOUR DRAWINGS

CONTOUR DRAWINGS

Contour drawing teaches your hand to draw a bold dramatic line with no *stuttering* (sketchy, interrupted lines). Save your first contour drawing to compare it with the drawing you can produce after several days of practice. Notice how dramatically your ability increases. Use these techniques to loosen up your drawings every so often when you get tight.

Start with a large, clean sheet of bond paper. Draw with a #2 soft lead pencil. Sketch a partner or sketch yourself by facing a large mirror. Do not look at the paper as you draw.

Imagine that your eyes are directly connected to the pencil in your hand. Look at every detail of the subject. Force your eyes to explore every part of the head you are drawing and imagine the vision flowing through your

body and out of your pencil. Travel over each part of the subject slowly and carefully. Move the pencil as fast as your eyes move. Concentrate on really looking at every detail.

Empathize with the subject. Some areas should be drawn with a different line. The smooth planes of the face require a lighter, smoother line than the texture of the hair or clothing. To emphasize the definite contours of the face, vary the pressure you put on the pencil. Make your pencil line match the surface your eyes are seeing.

Initial results are often very disoriented, but if you concentrate on capturing volume and proportion, your powers of observation will develop so you can produce a dynamic image.

ABSTRACT DRAWING

Abstraction requires that the artist observe the subject carefully and analyze the strongest and most important structural elements. These are reduced to their simplest form and carefully stylized to produce the desired effects.

The abstraction is usually influenced greatly by the apparel styles of the period. When fashion features a slim silhouette with strong vertical style lines, the abstract figure will naturally be simplified to simple vertical shapes. During periods when full, rounded silhouettes are fashionable, the curved flowing line and rounded oval shapes will be exaggerated to emphasize the fashionable shape.

Successful abstractions depend on a good initial concept. Begin by sketching a realistic face, and gradually eliminate and simplify the features. Bold use of geometric shapes can replace the hair, mouth, and eyes. Eliminate some of the features and test the effect. Keep the proportion and layout of the features fairly realistic.

A beginning illustrator or designer can develop a simplified figure and face that is effective for presenting quick sketches while working on improving his or her drawing skills.

EXAGGERATING THE FIGURE

High-fashion illustrations can be enhanced by subtly altering the proportions of the figure and simplifying the realistic details. Emphasize the main theme of the fashion silhouette by exaggerating the shape. The proportions of the body between the neck and the hips should remain realistic so the clothes do not look awkward. The head may be drawn smaller and stylized for effect. Length should be added in the neck, thighs, and lower legs.

ELIMINATION DRAWING

Elimination drawing reduces a fashion figure to the most dramatic essentials and is a very effective method for illustrating high-fashion apparel. However, you should consider the audience before abstracting a drawing. When the drawing is supposed to sell the garment, a realistic rendering is the best choice. The customer is interested in the silhouette and a faithful drawing of the details. Abstract drawing is effective for editorial coverage because the newspaper or magazine selects the garment to illustrate a fashion point and a direct sale is not the desired result. The editorial illustration is designed to stimulate a sophisticated audience with a new fashion trend.

BEFORE

• Too much linework

• Excess of detailing... seams, stitching

• Many tones— overworked and seemingly painstakingly drawn.

AFTER

• Minimal linework

• Broken lines ---- leaving the eye to complete lines

• Seems to be a spontaneous, emotional statement.

A professional artist knows intuitively what to emphasize and what to underplay or delete in an illustration. The beginner can gain this knowledge by experimentation. Here is one way to go about it: Work from a tightly rendered sketch of a fashionable outfit or from a preliminary drawing of your own. Place tracing paper over the illustration and trace the most dramatic parts of the silhouette and pertinent details of the garment. Simplify the figure and face. Do several tracings, eliminating more details and emphasizing the important fashion elements of the garment with a heavier line or exaggerated shape. Use various media and experiment with the results. Compare all the sketches with the original. Professional illustrators often use this technique to perfect a drawing.

Study the examples of elimination illustration shown here. Experiment with garments and subjects that lend themselves to editorial illustration.

COMPUTERIZED ILLUSTRATION

Computers are new tools for fashion illustrators and designers. They can be used in a number of ways. An illustrator may sketch a fashion figure on a digital computer tablet with a stylus (a tool similar to a pen), and the tablet then relays the image to a video screen. The sketches often look stiff because the stylus and computer pad lack the flexibility of traditional illustrations.

Illustrations may be entered into the system via a scanner. The illustration may then be altered on the computer.

A video camera can input a photograph or colored illustration into the computer. The image may be manipulated through reduction, flipping, additions, corrections, etc. Printers have improved greatly, and sophisticated images without the "grid" look of early technology may be printed. Sophisticated color systems, capable of many color nuances, are still very expensive. Service bureaus allow the designer to use sophisticated equipment on a per-project basis by using a portable disk and having the service bureau print from a disk.

...e artist draws with a data pen on the tablet ...scans a photograph or sketch and the ...age appears on the screen. The keyboard ...ows the artist to select commands to alter ...e image by recoloring, enlarging, flipping, ...changing the pattern of the garment. The ...age can then be printed on the color printer ...photographed from the screen. (Courtesy of ...rber Garment Technology.)

COMPUTER AIDS
FOR ILLUSTRATORS
AND LAYOUT ARTISTS

Personal computers (PCs) cut down the work of the layout artist by allowing the development of design formats on the video screen. Illustrations, headlines, and blocks of copy can be manipulated until the layout meets the artist's satisfaction. The layout artist can design pages for a catalog, for example. The copy may be typed directly into the computer. A typeface for both headlines and body copy and the format of the page are developed on the computer.

The layout artist who works with a computer can send work to a client via a telephone, a modem, or a receiving computer. Thus the layout artist does not have to visit the client to make changes, saving a great deal of time.

More sophisticated computer systems are being used for illustration by the fashion industry. Computers allow the artist to select from a wide variety of media to "draw" with, including a computer line that duplicates pencil, pen, brush, or marker line. Colors can be easily changed, eliminating tedious rendering time. Technology designed primarily for the commercial art and printing fields is being applied to fashion design and illustration, and applications grow more sophisticated daily.

COMPUTER AIDS FOR FASHION DESIGNERS

Fashion designers can save a great deal of time by working with a software program entitled, *SNAPFASHUN*™. The concept for SNAPFASHUN™ evolved from a trend report, published by Bill Glazer, that documented the hottest fashion details found domestically and in Europe. After a decade of successfully selling REPORT WEST, Glazer published a "pictionary" of the bodies and details collected and realized the huge volume of information he had amassed could be computerized. Software was developed that allowed a person with limited sketching ability to "snap" fashion details together to form new styles. New details are added monthly, and the manufacturers, purchase of SNAPFASHUN™ updates provides their design staff with a constant flow of information on the hottest details and bodies in the market.

Other graphic software manufacturers, such as Gerber/Micro Dynamics, and ModaCad, have integrated design packages into their grading (changing the size of a pattern) and pattern making systems. The designer begins by sketching a figure on the computer tablet or scanning a sketch into the computer, and then modifying it.

Both types of software have the advantage of producing the many sketches needed to develop a sample garment in all stages of production. The drawings can be modified as *versions,* garments that resemble a successful style but have different details. A great many designs can be stored in the computer for future use. Seasonal colors can be entered into the system for use on a variety of styles. The designer can experiment with style and color combinations and minimize the number of trial samples that have to be actually cut and sewn.

Many manufacturers now have computer systems that manage stock, accounts receivable and payable, pattern making, grading, and marking. Fewer have equipped their design rooms with computers, but the trend to computer-assisted apparel production is clearly on the upswing. Innovative programs such as SNAPFASHUN™ that can be updated with the latest details clearly will accelerate the trend to automate the design process.

SNAPFASHUN™ combines a sketching system with a library of thousands of garments and garment details allowing the designer to create variations of proven garments. (Courtesy of Bill Glazer, Associates.)

COMPUTER AIDS FOR THE SHOE INDUSTRY

The shoe industry has the most advanced computerized design and pattern systems. The foot is a three-dimensional form, and the difficulty of designing precise patterns has stimulated a great deal of innovation in this area. The advanced systems integrate shoe pattern making and grading with the manufacturing steps. The designer may draw, erase, and modify the color and texture of a shoe style on the computer prior to molding the lasts.

The shoe industry uses three-dimensional computer graphics because the designer must shape the parts of the shoe to the contour of the foot. (Courtesy of Gerber Garment Technology.)

COMPUTER AIDS IN TEXTILE DESIGNS

The textile designer benefits from the computer's ability to recolor prints instantly. Colors are selected from a large range stored in the computer's memory, and a design can be recolored in many different ways. The designer can review all the color combinations on the screen and print the best. A design can be enlarged, reduced, duplicated many times, rotated, or flipped to give a large variety of different effects. If a textile artist had to paint each of these combinations, it would take a great deal of time.

Computerization of design and illustration is in its infancy, with limitless possibilities for the future. Illustrators and designers will continue to find more uses for computers, and less expensive systems will become available as computerized graphics evolve.

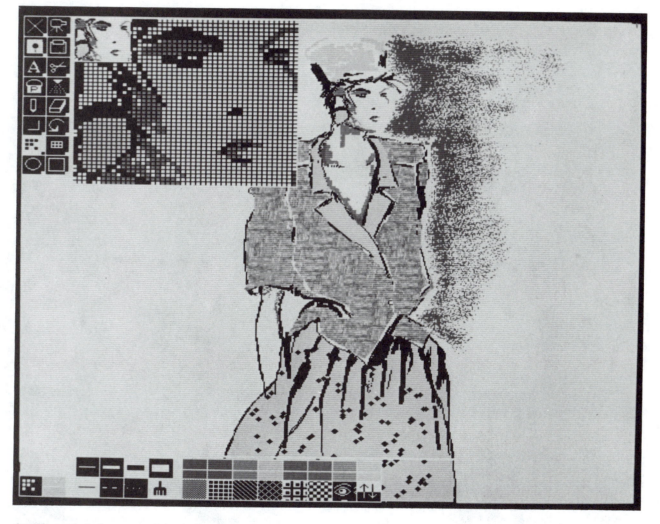

An enlargement of any part of the drawing can be made so the drawing can be changed. Notice the various line qualities that resemble ink, pastel, paint, and felt pen. The small boxes are symbols of the commands the artist can use. (Courtesy of Gerber Garment Technology.)

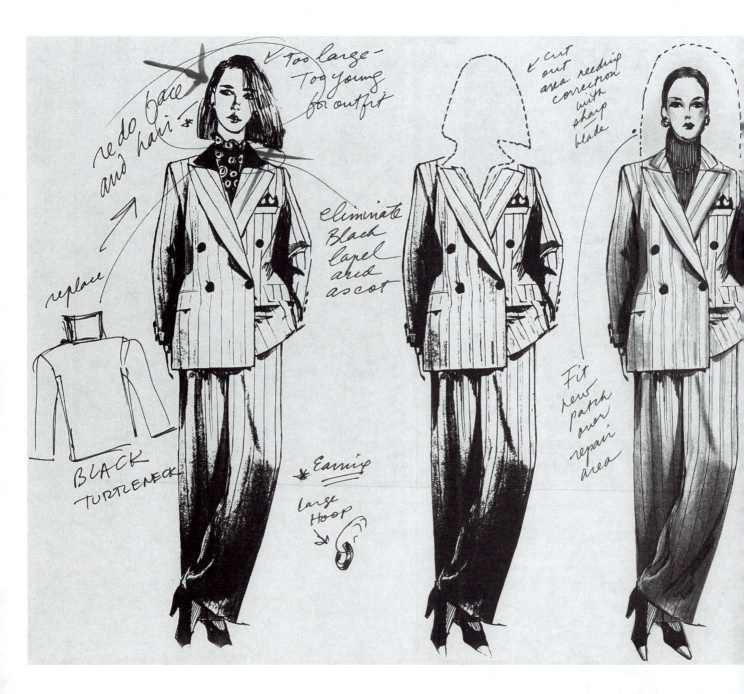

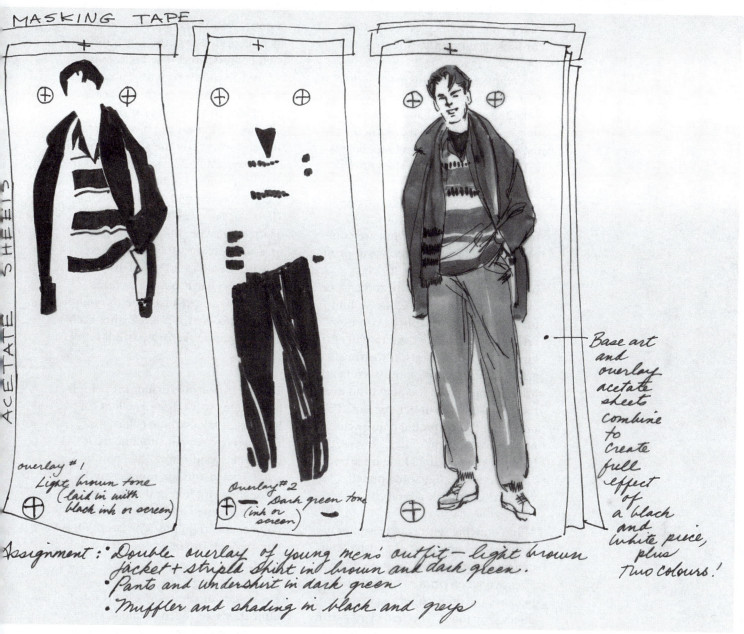

MASKING TAPE

ACETATE SHEETS

overlay #1
Light brown tone
(laid in with
black ink or screen)

Overlay #2
Dark green tone
(ink or
screen)

Base art
and
overlay
acetate
sheets
combine
to
create
full
effect
of
a black
and
white piece,
plus
two colours!

Assignment: • Double overlay of young men's outfit — light brown
jacket + striped shirt in brown and dark green.
• Pants and undershirt in dark green
• Muffler and shading in black and greys

CAMERA-READY ARTWORK

Camera-ready art, photo-ready art, and the *mechanical* are all terms for illustrations that can be photographed for print reproduction. The fashion illustrator works from a layout sketch and the actual garment to produce a crisp line and tone illustration. When the artwork is done to size, a paste-up artist pastes it on the mechanical with the appropriate headline type, copy, and logo. Usually the graphic portion of the advertisement is computer gen-

erated. When the artwork is not done to size, it is sized up or down by the camera and then integrated into the mechanical by the printer.

The most advanced technology allows a sketch or photograph to be scanned into the computer. The image may then be sized and fitted into an advertisement, and all copy is also generated on the computer. The graphics are sent to an image generator that converts the computer information into printing film ready for the press. The computer and image generator can also produce four-color separations for high-quality printed pieces.

As computers enter the production picture, fewer people are needed to create the copy, art, and camera-ready image. Many artists have learned to use software type-setting technology to allow them to create the entire advertisement.

To prepare camera-ready art, the black-line and tone drawing are completed first. The illustration will print clearly if you render it with clear black line, wash, pressure screens, or other matt media on a white vellum that can be photographed with no reflective shine. The camera will "forgive" many corrections. If the finished art needs correction—a redrawn head, for example—paste the new head over the mistake with rubber cement. The outline of the corrected paper will not photograph and will save you hours of rework time. Line up artwork and type with a light-blue pencil, which does not photograph.

A line drawing with no tones of gray is the easiest and least expensive kind of art to reproduce. This type of art is effective when printed on newsprint because the poor paper quality reproduces gray tones with less clarity than does better paper. Gray tones do add dimension and complexity to an illustration, and camera-ready art is usually rendered in black-and- gray tones. When a special color job is desired, the press is inked with a colored ink instead of black ink.

A job of two or more colors requires color overlays that work with the black-line art. After the black-line art is done, a clear acetate or vellum sheet is placed over the illustration for each color desired. The areas to be colored are outlined with a sharp, light pencil line. Registration marks are placed in two areas outside the artwork border on the black illustration and in exactly the same places on all subsequent color overlay sheets to guide the printer in lining up the acetate screens with the black-line art. The color areas are filled in with opaque gouache, ink, or transparent pressure screens. Ruby-red screen may be used instead of a dense black screen because it photographs as black, yet the artist can see through it to cut out a complicated shape. Each color requires a separate overlay sheet.

This method is inefficient for complicated color work, but excellent for low cost, two- or three-color jobs. Each acetate screen should have a color ink swatch from the Pantone color system and the number of the color the printer is to match. The press is cleaned and reinked for each color that is required. The print job is run through the press for each color used.

Evaluate your camera-ready art jobs after they have been printed. Analyze how much darker a gray tone has to be rendered to print well on each kind of print stock. Remember which wash or line technique prints best. Save all your printed artwork for reference, and include the best pieces in your portfolio.

PRESENTING YOUR ILLUSTRATIONS

MATTING

A mat is a frame cut from illustration board. To make a mat:

1. Select a medium-to-dark neutral tone of single-ply illustration board that complements the color of your illustration. Avoid white or cream mats, which get dirty and offer little contrast to most plates. Limit the mat size so it can be carried easily in your portfolio.

2. Measure the board with a T square to ensure 90-degree angles at all corners. To make sure the outer edge of the mat is smooth, use a paper cutter to cut the overall size down from the 30-by-40-inch board size. Draw the size of the window with your T square and a sharp pencil on the front side of the board. Sides should be an inch or wider for strength.

3. Use a very sharp mat knife with a large handle. Hold the knife at an angle facing the window to form a bevel. Use a braced T square as a guide to cutting a straight line. Several passes with the knife may be necessary. A mechanical mat knife may be set at a bevel angle and guided with greater ease. Cut completely through the board until the window falls out. Save the window and recut the edges for a smaller mat.

4. Attach the illustration with masking tape from the back of the board.

Groove for mat knife

A good mat is cut at an angle allowing a bevel of the board's core to show

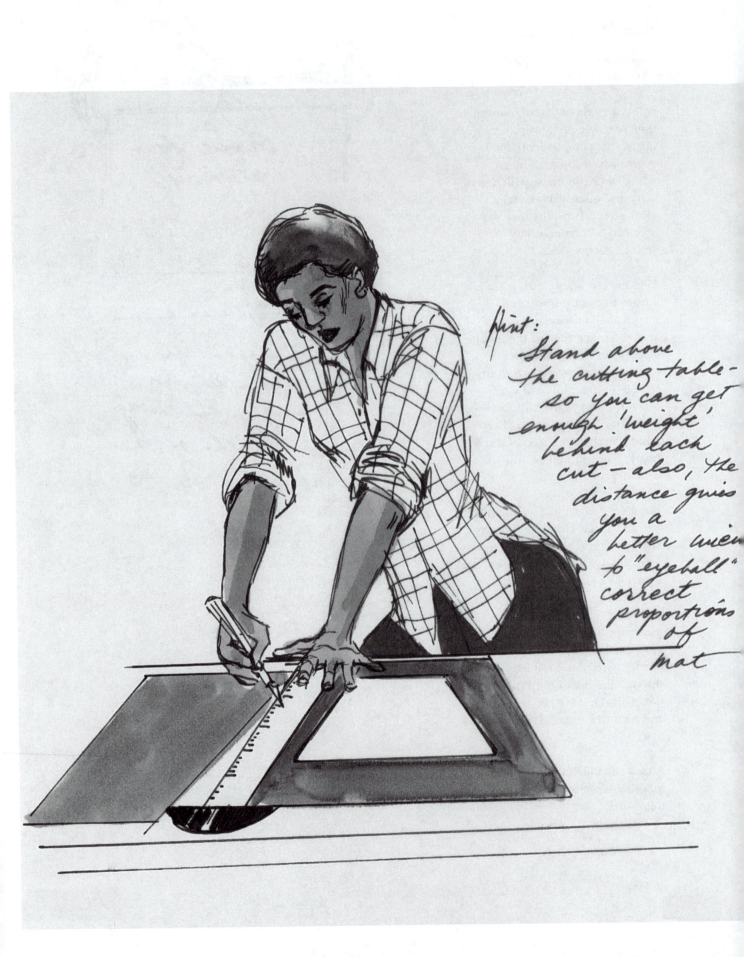

Hint:
Stand above
the cutting table-
so you can get
enough 'weight'
behind each
cut — also, the
distance gives
you a
better view
to "eyeball"
correct
proportions
of
mat

MOUNTED ARTWORK

Matting commercial artwork may make it seem too "precious." Another appropriate way to present commercial illustrations is to front mount them on illustration board or colored paper. A portfolio or series of illustrations can be visually tied together by mounting them on the same color or on a range of complementary colors. This method of displaying artwork is particularly appropriate for slipping into the plastic pages of a commercial portfolio.

A commercial job should be covered with a plain sheet of vellum or tracing paper taped to the back of the illustration. This protects the image and allows the client to add identification or to note changes without damaging the illustration.

MULTISECTION ARTWORK

Designer presentations are often done in several sections and joined with colored art tape. This allows the presentations to be portable for easy display and mailing. To prepare multisection art, first make sure that the boards relate well in size. Tape the hinge with a contrasting color tape that complements the art, and finish outlining the edges of both boards with the same color tape.

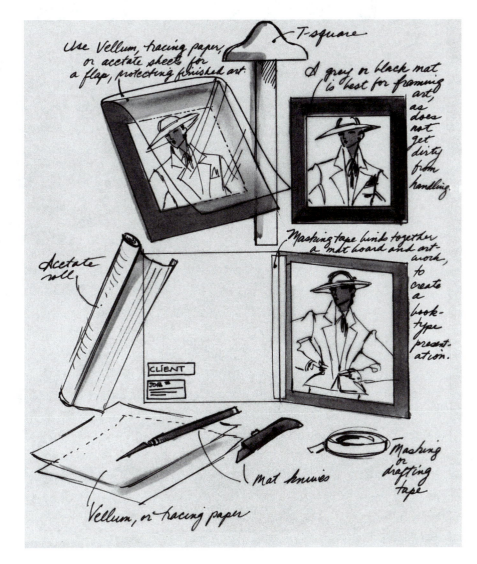

Portfolio
Review *

* Hint: Try to relax!

PORTFOLIO
AND RESUMÉ

A *portfolio* (also called a book) is a representative collection of an artist's best work. The material should demonstrate the kind of work the artist wants to be hired for but not be so narrowly focused that related jobs are eliminated in the eyes of the interviewer.

A *resumé* is a brief summary of work experience and education. The resumé is headed with name, address, and telephone number. Work experience should be listed by date and employer, with the most recent job first. A brief description of the job and specific duties should also be included. The schools attended and degrees received should follow the work experience. A resumé should be neatly typed and fit on one page. Professional resumé services will write and print a resume for a fee.

To begin your portfolio, collect school projects and artwork that has been printed. Before graduation, review this work with an instructor to evaluate your strengths and weaknesses. Ask for suggestions for filling gaps in your work. Try not to be too specific about the type of design you want to do after leaving school. A period of apprenticeship will help you gain a concrete idea of the requirements of specific jobs and enable you to develop more realistic career goals.

Research a company before an employment interview. Shop a manufacturer's line, then select designs or illustrations from your pool of work that are suitable or slightly more fashionable than the apparel produced by the interviewing company. Study the advertisements and catalogs of a retail store before interviewing for the job. Shop the store and have a firm grasp of the kind of customer and merchandise the store deals with so you can relate your experience to the image of the retailer or employment agency.

When you prepare your portfolio, select consistent material so your artwork appears to have been done by one person. Make sure to show enough variety to emphasize your strengths. A portfolio is often judged by its weakest example, not the strongest. Show from twelve to fifteen pieces of work. Make sure the illustrations are clean and neatly mounted or matted. Published material is especially effective because it shows that other people thought enough of your work to purchase it.

As a job seeker, you will be evaluated in many ways. The total package is important. Stress your desire to participate in the team effort needed to make the company a success. Do not carry a huge portfolio, which is awkward to look at and spoils the image of the person carrying it. A portfolio should be a neat, flat case of a reasonable size containing your well-edited material. Three-dimensional or oversize examples of work can be photographed, printed on a 5-by-7-inch or 8-by-10-inch format, and mounted on illustration board.

Occasionally a design applicant will be asked to do sketches appropriate for a specific line or job. It is reasonable for a beginning applicant to do a limited number of these assignments, but never leave any sketches with an interviewer without receiving remuneration or a concrete job offer.

PREPARATION FOR THE INTERVIEW

To avoid excessive nervousness, prepare carefully for the interview. The following tips will help:

1. Carefully plan what to wear on an interview. An artist or designer should reflect current fashion to a greater degree than a person interviewing for a business position, although you should take care not to seem too frivolous. You should also avoid very casual clothes that might make you seem less serious and as if you would not be a motivated employee. Dress in daytime business wear, expressing your creativity by wearing innovative colors and styles. After you have the job, observe your coworkers and carefully analyze their apparel. Creative people who have contact with clients usually wear more formal business clothes, so very casual dress could designate you as a worker who will always be in the back room.

2. Know the exact time and place of the interview. Arrive on time or a few minutes early. Know the interviewer's full name (and how to pronounce it) and title.

3. Investigate the specific facts about the company. A retail store is easy to shop, but also check the public library for annual reports (available if the company sells stock) or other information. Research the clients of an advertising agency. Look for advertisements and evaluate the image a manufacturer is trying to achieve through its ads.

4. Accepting a job is a two-way street, so prepare questions to ask the interviewer. Ask about growth potential, training programs, and advancement possibilities.

5. Fill out an employment application neatly (in pen) and completely. Bring two copies of your resumé and leave one with the application. Give the other to the interviewer.

6. Greet the interviewer by name, and shake hands firmly. Smile and be as relaxed as possible. Listen and respond alertly to questions. Look the interviewer in the eye.

7. Do not chew gum or smoke.

8. Ask about the requirements of the job as early in the interview as possible. Then you will be able to relate your skills and abilities to those requirements. Be prepared to answer questions about your goals and abilities. Show your portfolio as reinforcement of your career goals.

9. Answer questions truthfully and to the point. Do not over-answer questions. Do not make derogatory remarks about your present or former employers.

10. Ask for the job if you are interested in accepting the position. Accept an offer on the spot if you want the job. If necessary, arrange for a specific time to think it over. Call the interviewer with a response even if you have decided not to take the job.

11. Thank the interviewer for his or her time and consideration. In several days, follow up with a note summarizing your interest in the job.

CHAPTER 9

Sources of Inspiration

Fashion illustration is a synthesis of fashion awareness and graphic skills. The fashion illustrator must develop an eye for current style details and cultivate an interest in fashion trends. Awareness of lifestyles and interest and participation in other current trends is another of the pleasurable requirements of a fashion illustrator.

A creative artist has the ability to combine elements in a unique way to produce a new visual image. Artists have a keenly developed awareness of familiar things that they see from their unique perspective. An artist is also curious to experiment and take advantage of accidental events to cre-

ate a new visual order or a new arrangement of design elements. The artist tries to solve problems—with no guarantee of success; the artist is an experimenter.

The fashion illustrator is an artist who focuses these skills and perceptions on the presentation of decorative human form. A fashion artist must also be sensitive to the demands of the commercial world, so the high-fashion message is interpreted for a specific customer without becoming so diluted it grows dull. The commercial image must generate excitement and enthusiasm for a garment without making the garment seem too radical.

Fashion trends traditionally originate in European *prêt-à-porter* (ready to wear) and Paris couture. Several times each year the American fashion press, fabric designers, store buyers, manufacturers, and designers cross the Atlantic to absorb the European fashion predictions for the coming season. They edit, copy, and export the creative European fashions for the American consumer. A fashion illustrator should read as many foreign and domestic fashion magazines and reports as possible. Often slide shows and fashion shows are presented in major American cities. Attend these and make sketches to record the fashion trends. Develop your fashion taste to enhance your graphic skills.

COLLECTING SCRAP

Cut out any picture or photograph that captures your imagination. Keep these clippings (scrap) in folders and refer to them often. Refer back to Chapter 5 for a list of influential foreign and domestic fashion magazines.

SKETCHBOOK

Select a handy-sized book with plain pages and cover it with a decorative fabric or paper so it is inconspicuous. Carry your sketchbook with you when you shop the stores, attend a show, or travel. Develop the habit of recording memorable images to be worked into future illustrations. A scrap collection and a well-used sketchbook unite fashion exposure with drawing skills—the inseparable tools of the fashion illustrator.

The illustrator often works closely with the apparel designers and store buyers to convey their fashion message visually to the consumer. These professionals can provide fashion expertise, but they rely on the illustrator's graphic and layout skills to enhance the original concept of the garment. To develop your graphic taste, constantly refer to the following sources.

MUSEUMS AND FINE ART BOOKS

Museums are invaluable sources of inspiration. Attend special shows devoted to a specific artist, period, or craft. Explore the general collection of period fine art and take courses in art history. Frequent museum book stores and purchase books and postcards of paintings or drawings that you admire. Sketch directly from works that you see in museums and save your sketches for future reference.

CONTEMPORARY FINE ART

Galleries and museums featuring the work of current artists offer many inspirational techniques and themes. Fine artists are often more experimental than commercial graphic artists are and tend to preview trends and techniques that flow into commercial illustration years later.

COMMERCIAL ARTS

Commercial illustrators and photographers produce a continually innovative body of work—often with very advanced rendering skills that are easily incorporated into fashion illustrations. Read *Grafix*, a quarterly magazine devoted to republishing outstanding international examples of innovative commercial illustrations.

Read children's books for specialized illustration techniques in juvenile illustration.

MOVIES, VIDEOS, AND TELEVISION

Original and timely films often influence lifestyle and fashion trends.

Music videos also influence fashion. Many apparel manufacturers and retailers have begun to use music-oriented videos to publicize their fashions. Rock stars understand how to wear avant garde apparel for shock value and are often trend setters. Watch the award shows, such as the Academy Awards and the Grammies, to see innovative costumes, makeup, and hairstyling.

Occasionally a television show will start a fashion trend. Television producers are beginning to appreciate the vast appeal of fashion and invest in innovative costumes instead of buying ready-to-wear clothes for their actors. Designers and illustrators should tune into every phase of modern life that has an impact on apparel fashions.

HOME FURNISHINGS

The way people style their homes often reflects the way they decorate their bodies. Stylish interiors also provide appropriate settings for fashionable garments. Observe the trends published in shelter magazines, *House & Garden, Metropolitan Home, Casa Vogue, Elle Interiors,* and *Architectural Digest.* Collect scrap of accessories and setups that can be used to enhance fashion figures.

Artists are guided by the people and things they see and emulate. They must be sensitive to the visual images that surround them. Constant exposure to a wide variety of visual stimuli will enhance your taste and enlarge your store of possible solutions for specific illustration problems.

USING PERIOD ART AS INSPIRATION

Art from the past is always used by artists as a foundation for their creativity. Students of fine arts often copy paintings and drawings to absorb the techniques of the masters. The true artist is a synthesizer—a person who creates a new visual order out of existing elements. Creative fashion illustrators can also be inspired by period artists and can integrate the work of those artists with appropriate current fashions.

A knowledge of art history can help you focus on artists and periods that are rich with inspiration. Perhaps the serendipitous (accidental) discovery of an artist that appeals to you is more inspirational than a methodical search for historical sources. Exposure to as many visual stimuli as possible is the key to collecting a body of inspirational references.

Decorative art periods are valuable sources of inspiration. The art nouveau and art deco movements offer a rich source of visual inspiration. Japanese woodblock prints (*ukiyo-é*) have unique arrangements and colorations. Poster art from the last half of the nineteenth century is a rich source of decorative human form.

Period art can inspire by suggesting techniques, color schemes, layouts, or perspectives that can enhance modern fashions or fashion illustrations. Combine the elements of the period pieces with modern styles to create a new visual order.

The modern interpretation focuses on the interplay of textures in the hair, robes, and faces.

Two Women *by Utamaro Kitagawa, Japanese, 1750–1860. Japanese woodblock prints depicting scenes of everyday life, called* ukiyo-é, *had a tremendous influence on nineteenth-century European art. The novel treatment of space and perspective was widely imitated. Utamaro was a leading artist who specialized in portraying beautiful women. These two women capture the viewer's attention because of the contrast of the white skin with the dark hair and the intricate pattern of the kimonos. (Courtesy of the Collection of the Grunwald Center for the Graphic Arts, UCLA.)*

*Henri de Toulouse-Lautrec, French,
1864–1901. This familiar artist worked in
Paris during the late nineteenth century. His
realistic posters of dancers and entertainers of
the Montmartre district showed a gripping
insight into the personalities of his subjects.
Lautrec's posters were not decorative collector's
pieces like those of his contemporaries Mucha
and Chèret. The modern viewer appreciates
Lautrec's bold style and fine artist's eye for
reality. (Courtesy of the Collection of the
Grunwald Center for the Graphic Arts, UCLA.)*

*The espressive pose and vigorous line inspired
the modern fashion illustration.*

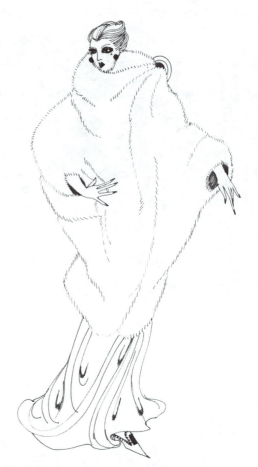

The delicate rendering and flowing line of the Erté drawing was emulated in this illustration.

Erté (Romain de Tirtoff), Russian, 1897–1993, detail of the poster 1979. Romaine de Tirtoff, who adopted the name Erté, emigrated from his native Russia and worked briefly as a designer for the house of Poiret. He became a major contributing artist to Harper's Bazaar, Vogue, *and* La Gazette du Bon Ton. *His drawings and designs are noteworthy because of their precision, imagination, humor, and superb drawing technique. Erté produced a continuous body of fashion illustrations throughout the twentieth century. His fashion and theater design work was most popular during the 1910s and 1920s. (Courtesy of the Collection of the Grunwald Center for the Graphic Arts, UCLA.)*

*Alphonse Mucha, Bohemian,
1860–1939, Monaco–Monte Carlo
poster. Alphonse Mucha designed art
nouveau posters during the last half of
the nineteenth century. Sarah
Bernhardt was so pleased with a poster
Mucha did for the play* Gismonda *that
she contracted with Mucha to create all
her posters. He designed commercial
posters for many products from beer to
bicycles. Mucha's posters were widely
collected by contemporaries and have
remained popular during the twentieth
century. (Courtesy of the Collection of
the Grunwald Center for the Graphic
Arts, UCLA.)*

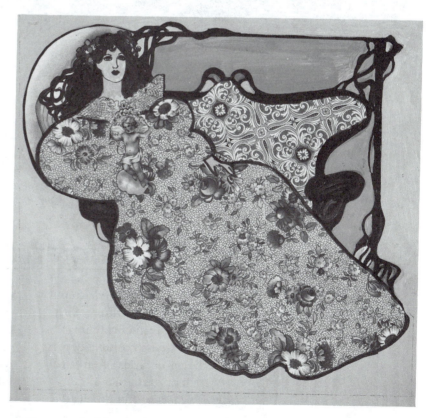

*Collage areas build up intricate pattern layers
on this illustration that has an art nouveau
flavor.*

Howard Chandler Christy illustrated many short stories and fashion "situation illustrations," including this typical romanticized illustration of western life for Harper's Bazar *[sic] (Courtesy of* Harper's Bazaar.*)*

PERIOD FASHION ILLUSTRATION

Fashion art has paralleled style trends through the twentieth century, with echoes of fine art influencing form and content. Museum costume departments and larger libraries often have copies of such magazines as *Vogue* and *Harper's Bazaar* from the early 1900s. *La Gazette du Bon Ton* and *Delineator* are two out-of-print magazines from early in the century that have high-quality illustrations. These valuable periodicals contain a wealth of information for the fashion designer and illustrator.

Charles Dana Gibson illustrated a series of society cartoons for Harper's Bazar *[sic]. His definitive rendering technique makes his sketches of fashionable women of the period the prototype of beauty, called the "Gibson Girl." (Courtesy of* Harper's Bazaar.*)*

1900–1930

Fashion emerged from the cumbersome, overblown costumes of the nineteenth century to a slimmer yet mature silhouette, which finally evolved into the flapper silhouette of the 1920s. Women became more active, and their clothing was gradually streamlined and pared down to accommodate the new lifestyle of the twentieth century, but this evolution took almost twenty-five years.

Paris couture directed fashion. Early couture designers such as the House of Worth, Paquin, Poiret, Vionnet, Chanel, and Lanvin began to design costumes that could be worn by ordinary women as well as clothes for their royal counterparts, clothes for everyday events, not just grand occasions. These, in turn, were copied by seamstresses all over the world from illustrations in the new fashion magazines.

Wealth was taken for granted by many women, who faithfully supported custom dressmakers and the couture. The masses emulated hand-crafted fashions by sewing for themselves or ordering ready-made garments from the newly emerging catalogs such as Sears and Roebuck. Illustration during these early decades ranged from the fantasy creations of Erté, the famous Russian costume designer and illustrator, to the practical catalog illustrations produced to sell garments to the masses. Theatrical posters advertised famous plays and movies of the period and publicized the stars' costumes and individual styles. Other fashion artists of note during this period were Valentine Gross, Barbier, Sem, Vuillard, Pierre Brissard, George Lepape, Helen Dryden, Drian, Ruth Eastman, Marie Laurencin, John Martin, Howard Chandler Christy, and Charles Dana Gibson.

Drian worked exclusively for Harper's Bazar [sic] during 1913 and 1914, illustrating covers and fashion articles in this monthly woman's magazine. (Courtesy of Harper's Bazaar.)

After World War I, the first youth-oriented decade of the twentieth century emerged. The shape of garments was a slim rectangle with no hint of a natural waistline. Hemlines rose to their highest point in 1927. Makeup, especially lipstick—an innovation—was an important accessory. Hair was bobbed and styled like a man's. As an alternative to formal dress, spectator and active sportswear were developed for resort wear. Art greatly influenced the designers and illustrators of the 1920s.

The fashion world was shaken by the crash of the New York stock market in 1929, and the repercussions were widespread. Forty years were to pass before the carefree, irreverent, youthful fashion that characterized the 1920s were again in vogue.

This fanciful rendering by Sarah Stilwell
Weber integrates a figure with garden setting.
The natural forms and flowing lines show a
distinct art nouveau influence. (Courtesy of
Harper's Bazaar.)

Soulie regularly illustrates basic fashion
articles for Harper's Bazar [sic]. The vigorous
line technique gives these figures movement
and character. (Courtesy of Harper's Bazaar.)

This typical fashion reporting illustration uses a stylized background to set off the models. (Courtesy of Harper's Bazaar.)

Erté was a regular contributing artist to Harper's Bazaar *after it was purchased by William Randolph Hearst (he changed the spelling of Bazar to the double a). Erté illustrations have spanned sixty years of fashion history. His early fame and exposure peaked during the 1920s. (Courtesy of the Los Angeles County Museum of Art,* Mille Fleurs, *Erté [Romain de Tirtoff].)*

Fashion from the 1930s reflected the Depression mentality of America and the world. Dresses in dull, safe styles and somber colors were the rule. Photography was popular during this period, although illustrations became more common as the decade matured and moved into the 1940s.

American fashion emerged late in the 1930s, and in 1940 *Vogue* covered the American ready-to-wear market for the first time. Design direction still emanated from European couture, however. Motion pictures were popular during the Depression because they offered an inexpensive way to escape the worries of everyday life. Movie fashions were glamorous, and movie stars were widely emulated. Many designers started by costuming stars and developed ready-to-wear businesses after their names had become fashionable on the screen.

Accessories, especially hats, were popular during the thirties and forties. The suit and little fur piece were important trends that developed into the uniform-influenced tailored suit. World War II imposed restrictions on the amount of fabric that could be used in apparel, so until after the war, a slim silhouette prevailed out of necessity.

In 1947 Christian Dior introduced his "New Look," which had a long, bouffant skirt with a nipped-in waistline. Thus began a return to femininity and more exaggerated apparel that was to carry over into the first half of the 1950s. Fashion changes became more rapid from this point.

This was a period of rich fashion illustration inspiration. Look for the work of René Bouché, Marcel Vértès, Carl Erickson (Eric), Ruth Sigrid Grafstrom, Bernard Boutet de Monvel, Dorothy Hood, Christian Berard, and R.B.W. (Count René Bouët–Willaumez).

Vèrtés' quick sketches and fantasy illustrations were popular during the 1930s and 1940s. (Courtesy of Harper's Bazaar.)

The variety of texture and delicate handling of the fluid line of the furs creates a delightful, informal illustration. (Courtesy of Harper's Bazaar.)

The distinctive line carves this silhouette out
of the negative space of the page. (Courtesy of
Harper's Bazaar.)

*The artists interpreted a poster by Toulouse-
Lautrec to advertise fabrics. (Courtesy of
Harper's Bazaar.)*

Bouché was often called upon to illustrate the fashion face during his career. This example captures the elegent, sophisticated model perfectly. (Courtesy Vogue. Copyright © 1959 [renewed 1987] by The Condé Nast Publications, Inc.)

This fresh wash and contrasting line illustration by St. John captures the fluid flow of the fabrics swatched. (Courtesy of Harper's Bazaar.)

The apparel mood in the 1950s in America developed from the bouffant "New Look" to the sack dress, or chemise, late in the decade. The waistline was "lost" for ten years while women wore simple, slim dress silhouettes. The fashion mood then moved from conservative, feminine apparel to the youth revolution that characterized the 1960s.

The American lifestyle was profoundly changed by technological advances that began in the 1950s. Affluence and abundant power allowed the suburbs to grow. Two automobiles and a television set became the symbols of the upwardly mobile, better- educated American middle class. Airplane travel and improved mass communication made the world smaller. Synthetic fiber production was fully implemented, and mass production of inexpensive easy-care textiles greatly enlarged the number of materials available for producing apparel.

VOGUE PATTERN 9485
VOGUE PATTERN 9654

Eva Larson's free, vigorous style suited this full-skirted dress typical of the 1950s. (Courtesy Vogue. *Copyright © 1959 [renewed 1987] by The Condé Nast Publications Inc.)*

This stylish illustration on a toned board uses highlights and line very effectively. (Courtesy of Saks Fifth Avenue.)

The costume blossoms under Sophies tender care — its cling of silk twill coat opening onto a small-waisted duo-print of twill and chiffon, 695.00

Saks Fifth Avenue

René Bouché had an active illustration career spanning several decades. His work was published consistently in Vogue. These exuberant contour drawings were done at the Dublin Horse Show in 1959. The sketches effectively capture the excitement of the spectators and participants as well as the formal evening apparel. (Courtesy Vogue. Copyright © 1959 [renewed 1987] by The Condé Nast Publications Inc.)

J. Hyde Crawford's dramatic charcoal
illustration has a simple elegance. (Courtesy of
Bonwit Teller.)

Kenneth Paul Block is the dean of modern illustrators. His versatile style has illustrated fashion for over two decades. These illustrations capture the youthful sophistication of the mini during the 1960s. (Courtesy of Hoechst-Celanese Corporation.)

The decade of the 1960s was a revolutionary period when change was accelerated by the new passions of the youthful population majority. Fashion responded slowly—the youthquake and fashion from the streets coexisted with the structured space-age dressing designed so well by Courrèges and the typical ladylike look of celebrities such as Jacqueline Kennedy.

The fashion magazines of the 1960s featured a great deal of photographic editorial art. The illustrators of the day flourished in retail store advertisements and trade papers. Newcomers to the fashion illustration scene during these decades included Kenneth Paul Block, Antonio, Dorothy Hood, Eva Larson, Barbara Pearlman, Laslo, and J. Hyde Crawford.

Dorothy Hood's signature style for Lord & Taylor captures the image of their chic yet casual suburban customer of the 1960s. (Courtesy of Lord & Taylor.)

1970 TO THE PRESENT

The "me generation" of the 1970s was clothed with a new conservatism. Fashion for the masses—as opposed to fashion as the privilege of the wealthy—became the rule. In both Europe and American RTW (ready to wear) became the common fashion denominator. European and American designer clothes were the status symbols—available in many price ranges and apparel categories, from jeans to luxe apparel and fine furs.

A fit and active body became the fashion ideal. Cheryl Tiegs' athletic body made her the top model of the early 1970s. There was no longer an easily defined fashion manifesto. Fashions ranging from fantasy costumes to establishment uniforms could hang side by side in the same wardrobe to take a person from a conservative business day through an evening of dining and disco dancing. Modern life created many optional activities that demanded specialized dressing and enlarged the typical wardrobe.

Versatility and variety of apparel offered an opportunity for many styles of fashion illustration to flourish. The illustrator today is supported by trade papers, retail store advertisements, catalogs, manufacturer's ads, and the glossy domestic and foreign fashion publications. These contemporary illustrators are a constant fresh source of inspiration for the fashion student.

Fashion photography displaced the advertising illustrator in the mid-1980s. Gradually, illustration was relegated to the editorial pages of women's magazines in favor of realistic fashion photography.

SONIA RYKIEL
EN RESIDENCE AT
HATTIE INC

555 SOUTH WOODWARD AVENUE, BIRMINGHAM, MICHIGAN 48011 (313) 645-5755

Laslo's distinctive style integrates a subtle blending of tone, wash, and line. (Courtesy of Harper's Bazaar.)

As a beginner, you should clip and save illustrations and photographs that appeal to you. Try to emulate the style and techniques of artists that you admire: Be like the apprentice fine artist copying a masterpiece. Copy to learn how to incorporate the best of another artist's techniques into your own skills. Once you master the techniques, use them to create your own unique images. Follow the style of favorite contemporary illustrators as they evolve into greater and greater proficiency. Emulate and adapt, practice and experiment. In this way you can develop a style that is unique and continuously improving.

The painterly quality of Barbara Pearlman's illustrations creates an interesting interplay of line and texture. (Courtesy of Galey & Lord Ind., Inc.)

Sandra Leichman's drawing has a sophisticated femininity. (Sandra Leichman for Martha. Courtesy of C. J. Herrick Associates.)

The bold line contrasts with the simple border and copy area of this illustration by Sandra Leichman. (Sandra Leichman for Martha. Courtesy of C. J. Herrick Associates.)

"The Tango" by Holly's Harp. Barney's, New York.

*Stavrino's illustrations create a rich pattern of line and
tone interaction. (Courtesy of Barney's New York.)*

STAVRINOS

Lord & Taylor is spirited American fashion

For romantic evenings
– frothy separates in a dance
of point d'esprit

Meant for each other— our airy
white peplum camisole with a light frivolity of organza ruffles,
the slenderest of straps, 80.00
And breath-taking full skirt of navy point d'esprit,
made even fuller by underlayers of organza and taffeta, 130.00
By Jeri in polyester and acetate, 4 to 14.
Evening Collections, Third Floor, Lord & Taylor,
Fifth Avenue at 39th Street—call (212) 391-3300.
Open daily 10 to 6. Thursday 10 to 8. And at Manhasset,
Westchester, Garden City, Millburn, Ridgewood-Paramus and Stamford
Shop Sundays 12 to 5 at our Manhasset,
Westchester, Garden City, Millburn and Stamford stores.

Lord & Taylor artist Fred Greenhill's casually elegent illustrations have a painterly quality. Notice how the shadow area lends drama to the negative space surrounding the figure. The visible brush stroke adds dimension to the fabric. The vigorous line accents the swingy fashion figure. (Courtesy of Lord & Taylor.)

Lord & Taylor is spirited American fashion

Calvin Klein turns your
favorite sweatshirt
into a dress

Our hooded sweatshirt dress is in the pink
(a vibrant dark pink) with all the easy comfort you love—
dropped shoulders, roll up sleeves and roomy pockets
(great to pull over your bikini—or for lazy, lounging days).
All cotton, in sizes 4 to 12, 90.00 The Calvin Klein Shop,
Third Floor, Lord & Taylor, Fifth Avenue at 39th Street—call (212) 391-3300.
Open daily 10 to 6, Thursdays 10 to 8. And at Lord & Taylor, Manhasset,
Westchester, Garden City, Ridgewood-Paramus and Stamford
Shop Sundays 12 to 5 at our Manhasset, Westchester, Garden City and Stamford stores.

This Stavrinos illustration uses a selective light source to highlight and shadow the style of the garment. (Courtesy of Barney's New York.)

FERNANDO SANCHEZ'
NEW QUILT COLLECTION
(TOO BAD THIS PAGE
ISN'T IN COLOR!)

A mischievous mix of vivids; cozy, comfortable quilts...softer and lighter on than a feather.

Fernando has brought home the aura of the Orient and spiced it with the chic delight of moiré satin in nylon, polyester and cotton.

The black kimono spiked with magenta cuff and lining, petite or average, 124.00.
The cummerbund, 13.00.

The red jacket cuffed with magenta, petite or average, 94.00.
The ivory satin top, P-S-M-L, 38.00.
The black roll-up pants with magenta cuffs, P-S-M-L, 56.00.

New York.

DESIGNER LINGERIE/LINGERIE LEVEL **bloomingdale's**

CONTEMPORARY ILLUSTRATORS

*Antonio was a virtuoso draftsman with
superb control of form and technique. His
experience as a fashion photographer
enhances his layout concepts. (Courtesy of
Bloomingdale's, illustration by Antonio, art
direction by John C. Jay.)*

CHRISTMAS: AT THE DAWN OF A DECADE

SANTA CRUISE, OUR HOLIDAY HOT-SHOP OPENS TODAY WITH GOTTEX GALORE

If you're dreaming of a
tan Christmas—have we
got an eyeful for you!
It's Santa Cruise, a torrid
zone of shore-fire
fashion, every scant
thing sun-worshipping
warrants. Come beach-
combing here before
you exchange eggnogs
for tonics.

Here from Gottex:
super shine Lycra®
Textured dots, black-on-
black in a cuffed
bandeau of
nylon/spandex.
8 to 14, 62.00.

Sun cover. Bold
shoulders to the sun in
a Dalmatian-dot jacket.
Black on white
triacetate/nylon, one
size fits all, 104.00.

**Join us in Manhattan
today from 1 to 2 and
tomorrow from noon to
three for informal
modeling of our cruise
collection from Gottex
of Israel. Monday,
Miriam Shir of Gottex
will be here as your
hostess.**

New York and all
fashion stores.

(Talk about elf help...)
Bloomingdale's at
59th Street is open
today, noon to 5.
Don't miss a minute
of the spirit we've
in store.

SANTA CRUISE
SHOP ON 3   **bloomingdale's**

CHRISTMAS: AT THE DAWN OF A DECADE

THE SHORTSUIT: YOU BET WE BELIEVE IN HEIGHTENED POSSIBILITIES

In the tradition of cultivating
long-stemmed American
beauties, may we present
one particular citified linen
that rose to the occasion.
(After our recent introduction
of the American ShortSkirt,
it seemed only fitting
we supply you another
alternative from the
latitude of lengths we
have available.)

Enter the ShortSuit by Bis:
Blazer, 74.00,
CityShorts, 39.00,
in resortful lilac, jade
or raspberry linen.
Sizes 4 to 12.

New York and all
fashion stores.

POSITIVELY Y.E.S. ON 3   **bloomingdale's**

Steve Bieck specializes in illustrating menswear for retail stores and manufacturers. He is challenged by the unlimited potential for growth and interpretation in fashion illustration. (Courtesy of Steve Bieck.)

(Courtesy of Mia Carpenter.)

Mia Carpenter has worked for manufacturers, retailers, and publications for many years. She loves to draw and feels that each time the pen or pencil touches the paper it alters the surface with exciting potential. Carpenter loves fashion, and illustration gives her the ability to exaggerate the form of the clothes and the body in order to heighten the original fashion concepts. See page 285 also. (Courtesy of Mia Carpenter.)

Now you can get into
Studio 54 ... jeans.
You'll find them
exclusively
in our Junior World.

It's the most famous disco
in the world. And you'd love to go there.
Well, we've brought Studio 54 to the west
coast. Their jeans in heavy blue denim
or medium wale corduroy, with a signature
pocket that lets everyone know you're in
touch with New York. Both in waist sizes 26-33.
Denim, **$38.** Corduroy, **$40.**
You'll receive Casablanca's Studio 54
album when you purchase any Studio 54
jean (while supply lasts; limit one
to a customer). Junior World, 236.

We're giving away a Studio 54 trip for two.
Come in and enter our special drawing
for a chance to win. Trip includes: airfare to
and from New York, an evening at Studio 54,
one night paid hotel stay (with dinner and
breakfast), limousine service to and from
Studio 54 and $250 in cash. You must be
18 years or older to be eligible. But no purchase
is necessary to win. Contest runs today
through October 6.

Meet Casablanca recording artists
Love and Kisses at our Century City store
on Saturday, September 29 from 12-3 p.m.
Also in our Junior World.

*David Horii is a versatile illustrator and
superb draftsman. When he is commissioned
to illustrate merchandise that is very basic, he
depends on light and detail to create a
dramatic or romantic effect. He is inspired by
films and photographs from the thirties and
forties. (Courtesy of David Horii.)*

Courtesy of David Horii.

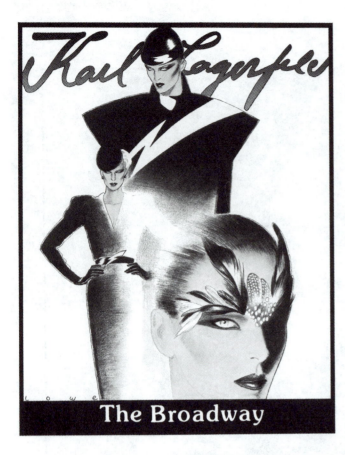

The Broadway

Control of the image and the media characterizes Paul Lowe's versatile style. Lowe uses a light source to focus on the subjects' most dramatic point of view. High-fashion illustration and menswear are Lowe's particular specialities. (Courtesy of Paul Lowe.)

Courtesy of Paul Lowe.

Catherine Clayton Purnell is a staff artist for Women's Wear Daily. Her versatile style and superb control of the human figure enable her to illustrate many categories of fashion. Children are her favorite subject, and she relishes an assignment in children's wear. (Courtesy of Catherine Clayton Purnell.)

Courtesy of Catherine Clayton Purnell.

A designer's control of space and form
characterize Robert Passantino's high-tech
graphic style. He feels an illustrator should
have a strong sense of graphic design,
dynamic use of space, individuality, honesty,
and clarity. Passantino's work is widely seen
in Women's Wear Daily and in ads for fashion-
oriented department stores. (Courtesy of
Robert Passantino.)

This illustrator uses a bold, painterly line to create high-contrast figures. Steven Stipelman works as a teacher and illustrator for fashion-oriented retailers and trade journals. He believes fashion illustration encompasses more than drawing skills. Illustration has to relate the body to clothes. When he plans an illustration, one of two things happens—the clothes dictate the body or the body dictates the clothes. This relationship is the start of a fashion drawing. (Courtesy of Steven Stipelman.)

Courtesy of Steven Stipleman.

Gregory Weir-Quiton is an active and versatile illustrator and teacher. He encourages his students to practice because many will be late bloomers. He heads the local chapter of the Graphic Arts Guild, a national association that helps independent illustrators to market and profit from their commercial graphic work. (Courtesy of Gregory Weir-Quiton.)

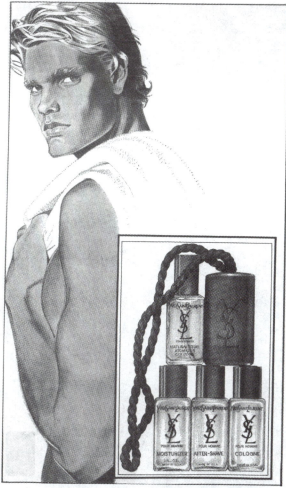

Courtesy of Gregory Weir-Quiton.

Courtesy of Gregory Weir-Quiton.

Courtesy of Gregory Weir-Quiton.

C H A P T E R   10

Drawing Men

The male fashion figure is usully drawn with less exaggerated proportions than the female fashion figure. Realistic facial and apparel details are typical of menswear illustrations. A male figure is drawn eight-and-one-half to nine-heads tall. The torso length is slightly longer than the middle of the body (line 4½). Length is added in the legs, not in the neck.

A man's body is broader than a woman's even though the vertical proportions are similar. Muscle structure has more definition and bulk. The shoulders are broader and the neck is thicker. Hands and feet are broader. A youthful male fashion figure should have a lithe, active, natural look. When an illustration requires a more mature man, slightly more bulk should be added to the torso and shoulders. The features show maturity when they are more boldly defined. A high-

er hairline with a defined widow's peak and a touch of gray hair at the temples adds a final note of distinction for an older male fashion model.

Styles influence fashion types. Fashion sketches of casual, active apparel will usually look best on a more youthful figure with a slim torso and shoulder muscle definition. A European-cut suit will also be more appropriate on a well-developed figure. Fashions that emphasize classic tailoring with natural shoulders and a relaxed fit require a more mature, less muscled figure.

Men's fashions change slowly and subtly. Adept illustrators of male fashions have a keen eye for apparel details and fit. The exact width of a shoulder, lapel, or tie is important when illustrating a man's suit. The silhouette and correct fit of menswear must be very close to reality or the subtle styling will be misinterpreted. Attention to the details and the small variations in style and fabric is essential for successfully illustrating menswear.

Hint: Use simple shapes and shadow and light to create a stylized sketch!

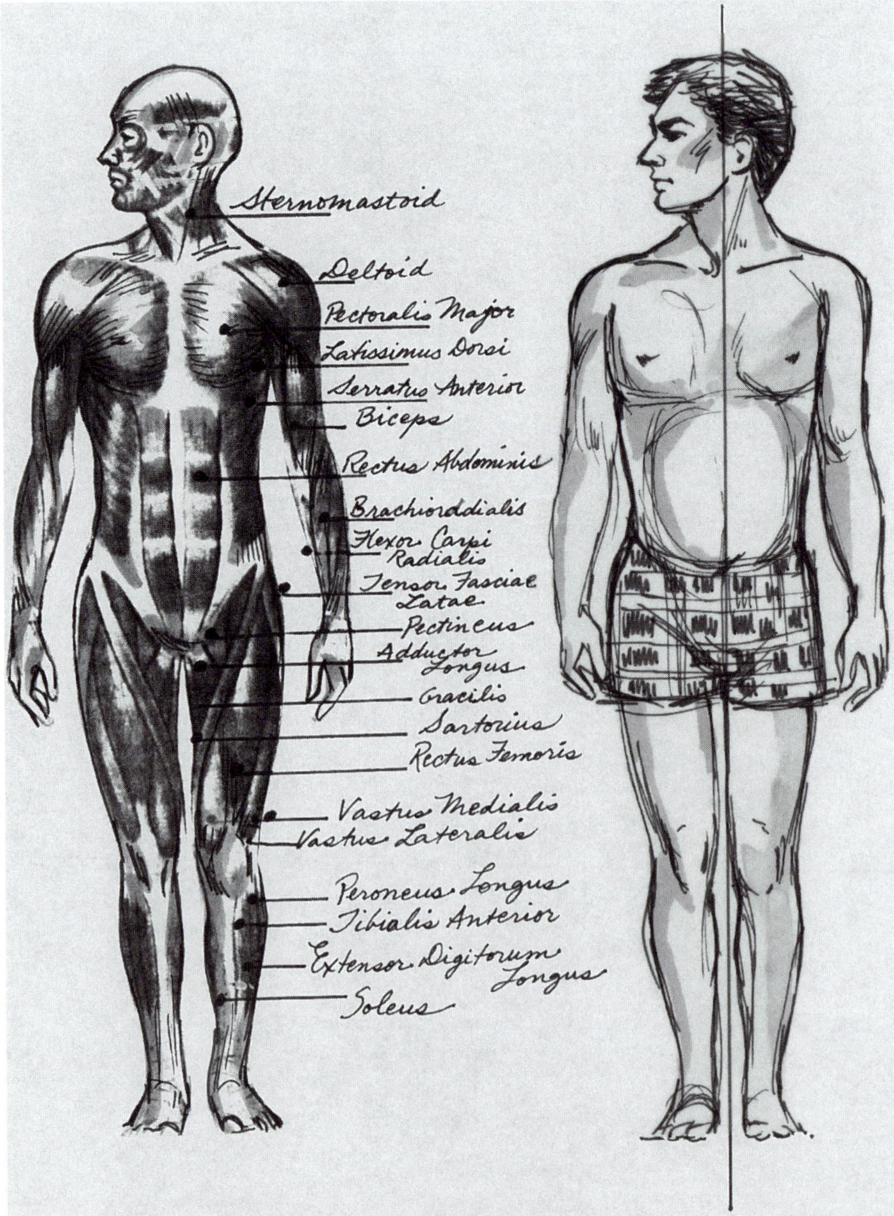

Sternomastoid

Deltoid

Pectoralis Major

Latiosimus Dorsi

Serratus Anterior

Biceps

Rectus Abdominis

Brachiorddialis

Flexor Carpi
Radialis

Tensor Fasciae
Latae

Pectineus

Adductor
Longus

Gracilis

Sartorius

Rectus Femoris

Vastus Medialis

Vastus Lateralis

Peroneus Longus

Tibialis Anterior

Extensor Digitorum
Longus

Soleus

MALE MUSCLE STRUCTURE

Shoulder and neck muscle structure should be well defined in a male fashion model. The torso is slim. Leg and arm muscle structure should be defined but not developed to the point that clothing is distorted.

The axial line determines the weight balance of the male figure just as it does in the female figure. The axial line must drop from the base of the neck to the heel of the support foot when a man stands with the weight primarily on one foot. The balance point falls between the legs when the weight is evenly distributed.

Poses are much more static for illustration of men's suits than for illustration of comparable women's wear. Active clothes are often sketched on men playing an appropriate sport. The same action rules covered in Chapter 4 pertain to movement in both genders.

Sketch the muscle structure of the male figure several times. Label the major muscles. Draw a fleshed-out figure on tracing paper placed over your drawing of the muscles. The following guidelines will help you begin.

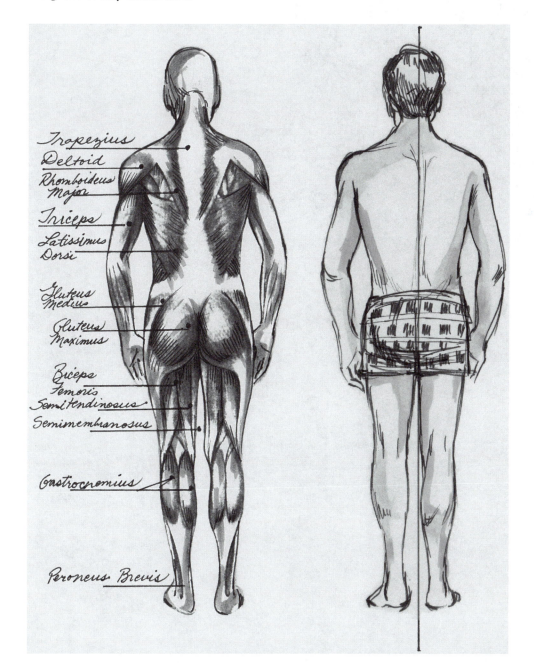

Trapezius
Deltoid
Rhomboideus Major
Triceps
Latissimus Dorsi
Gluteus Medius
Gluteus Maximus
Biceps Femoris
Semitendinosus
Semimembranosus
Gastrocnemius
Peroneus Brevis

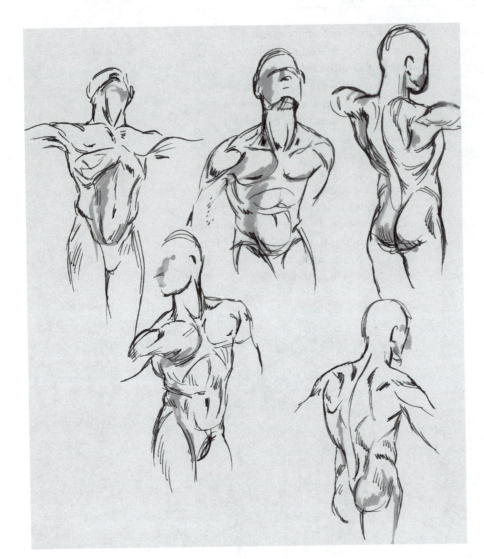

Male form is an inverted triangle—Widest area is shoulder and narrow hips

Female form is a figure-8

Widest area is shoulder and hip—narrow waist

DRAWING MEN, STEP BY STEP

Men's clothes are a series of layers that interact to form a total look. Draw from the example on page 309 for your first effort. Then sketch several outfits from life or detailed photographs. Carefully compare each drawing to its source to correct any missing or inaccurate details.

1. Sketch the body in a relaxed pose.

2. Block in the shirt and neckline details. Draw the lapel line. Draw the silhouette. Be sure the jacket is the correct length. Relate the size of the lapel to the size of the shoulder. Notice that men's jackets and shirts button in the opposite direction from women's, left over right. Draw the trousers. Render the face and hair with a wash or a tone.

3. Paint or tone the sketch with paint, felt pen, or pencils. Interpret the subtle fabric pattern in the jacket, pants, and shirt.

4. Detail the drawing with bold silhouette lines and render the details with a fine-line pen or pencil. Render the features and hair.

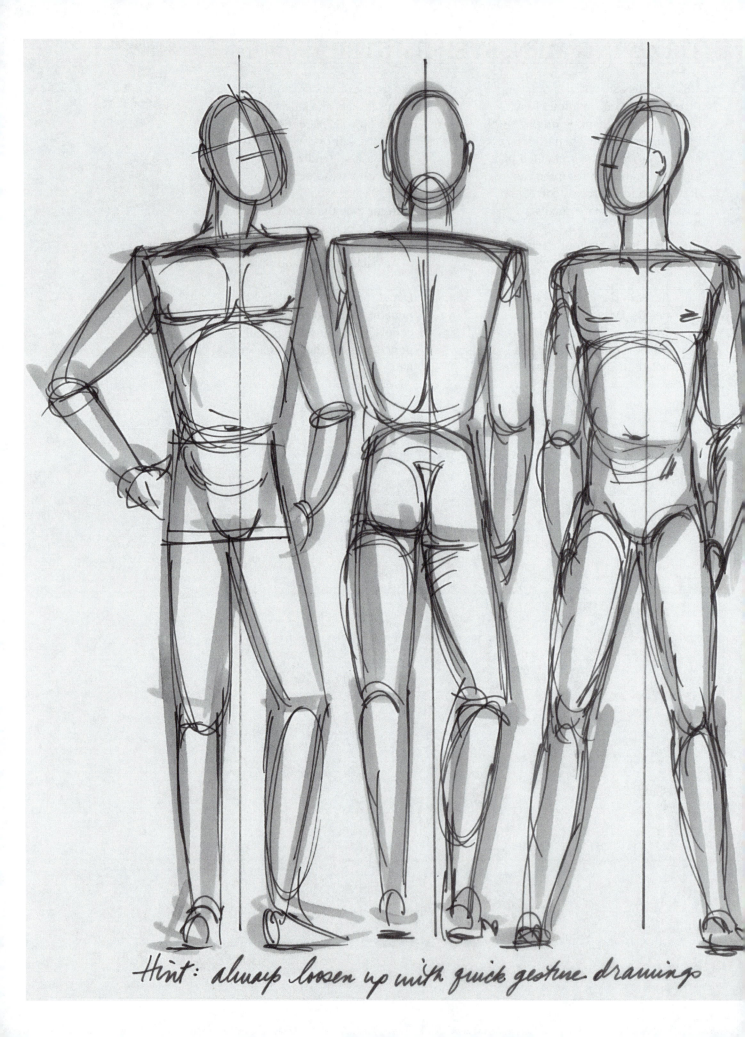

Hint: always loosen up with quick gesture drawings

lock
figure

Lay in
light
wash

Add
detail and
darker
wash—
add
black
last

MEN'S FACES

Feature placement is the same for both men and women. However, a man's face differs in contour and bulk from a woman's. Study the diagrams of the face and the profile head. Notice that the forehead and jawline are fuller. The eyebrows are heavier and well defined. No eye makeup enhances the eyes or emphasizes the lashes. Placement of the eyes is at the horizontal median of the guide rectangle. The length of one eye is the space allowed between the eyes.

The nose is prominent, with a strong bridge and well-defined nostrils. Laugh lines are often drawn. The upper lip is more muscular than a woman's. Do not give special emphasis to the lips because there is no artificial contrast typically created by lipstick. The chin and jaw line are strong.

Draw these diagram faces several times on overlay paper and make corrections by placing your drawings over the drawings in the book. Sketch a number of men from life or photographs.

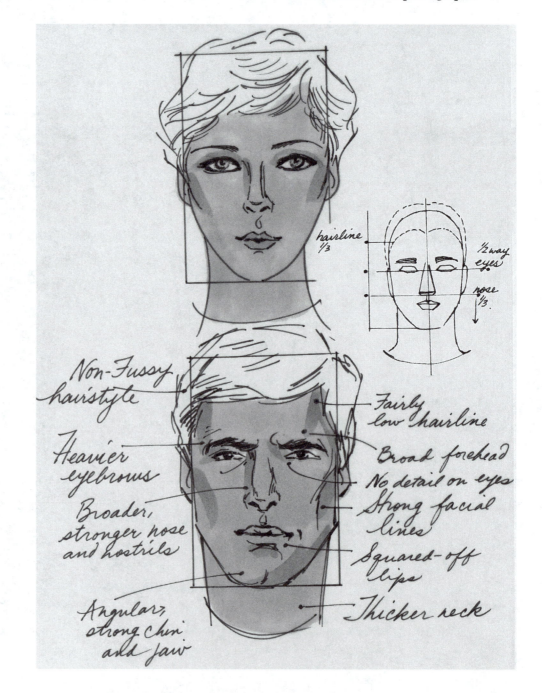

Non-Fussy hairstyle

Heavier eyebrows

Broader, stronger nose and nostrils

Angular, strong chin and jaw

hairline ⅓

½ way eyes

nose ⅓

Fairly low hairline

Broad forehead

No detail on eyes

Strong facial lines

Squared-off lips

Thicker neck

½

¼

higher
hairline

grey at
temples

chiseled
features

prominent
facial lines

heavier
brows

hooded
eyes

MATURE MEN
*Character lines defining the chin, jaw line,
and brow add maturity to a man's face. Raise
the hairline subtly and add gray to the hair at
the temples.*

lower
hairline

lighter
brow

Full
hair

soften
point of
nose

more
open eyes

fuller
lips

YOUTHFUL MEN
Fewer character lines, a lower hairline, and a
thinner face are typical characteristics of the
young male fashion model.

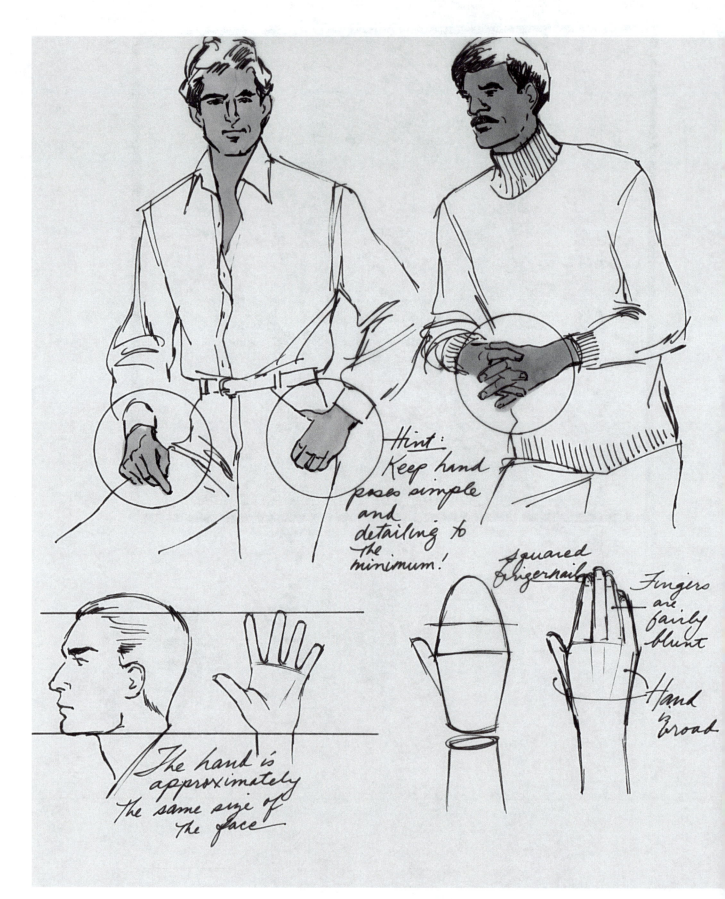

Hint:
Keep hand
poses simple
and
detailing to
the
minimum!

The hand is
approximately
the same size of
the face

squared
fingernails

Fingers
are
fairly
blunt

Hand
is
broad

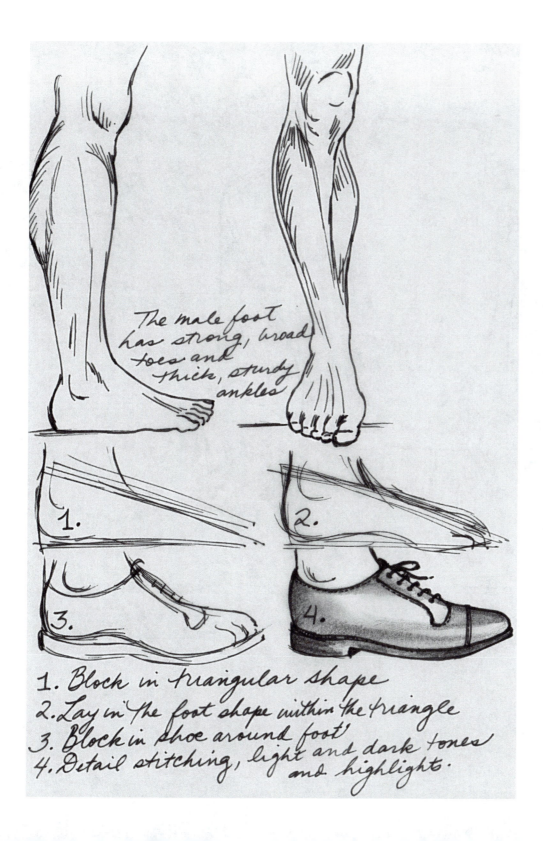

The male foot has strong, broad toes and thick, sturdy ankles

1. Block in triangular shape
2. Lay in the foot shape within the triangle
3. Block in shoe around foot
4. Detail stitching, light and dark tones and highlights.

Double seam

Collar fits snugly around neck

Tie fits tightly under collar

Precise pocket seams

Placket

French cuff has double fold

Back Yoke
and Placket

Novelty
Collar

DRAWING MEN'S SHIRTS

Men's shirts have a typical fit. Dress shirts are designed as underlayers for a suit, and this purpose dictates the styling. The shoulder seam extends slightly beyond the point of shoulder to allow free movement. This style device also makes the shoulders seem wider.

A yoke and one breast pocket are often incorporated into a dress shirt. The collar fits the neck snugly. The size and shape of collars are determined by fashion. The tie knot fits between the collar wings. The placket buttons left over right—the reverse of a woman's garment. Cuffs are designed to show slightly below the jacket sleeve.

DRAWING MEN'S CASUAL TOPS

A casual shirt is designed to be worn alone as well as under a jacket, so more style details are usually added. The collar can be worn open or closed. Double pockets are a styling option. Bold prints and plaids are popular. Sleeves can be long or short. Pleats at the back yoke or shoulders allow additional mobility.

Knit tops are casual alternatives to woven shirts. Rib trim often finishes the sleeves, necklines, and hem. The shoulders are usually extended beyond the point of the shoulder. Raglan sleeves are popular for casual knit tops. Cut-and-sew knits have seams like those of woven shirts. In fully fashioned sweaters, the bodies and sleeves are sewn together with the characteristic pattern illustrated here.

Sweater tops are made in a wide range of styles. Some are designed to be worn under a jacket, and others are heavy enough to be outerwear. The most classic styles are illustrated on these pages. Sweaters can be colored and patterned in a great variety of knits, stitches, and yarns.

Bulky ribbed cardigan

Raglan sleeve pullover

Polo shirt

DRAWING MEN'S SUITS

Men's suits have two main style divisions, the natural shoulder or classic suit, and the European suit. The natural shoulder category has less shoulder definition and a looser, more conservative fit. Traditional fabrics such as tweed, corduroy, plaids, and flannels are popular. Lapels and style details are very subtle and change little from season to season. A more mature model is appropriate in this style, but the natural shoulder suit can also be worn by a younger man.

The European-cut suit is influenced by fashion trends. Italian styling traditionally is more fitted, with a padded, well-defined shoulder line. The body is fitted with several style lines or darts. The lapels are often exaggerated. To emphasize the cut of the suit, fabrics tend to be crisp, hard-woven wool gabardines, linens, and silk blends. A slim, youthful model is appropriate wearing this cut.

A newer trend from European tailors is the loosly fitted suit, popularized by Italian designer, Georgio Armani. Soft, fine fabric is tailored in a looser fit, supported from a well-defined shoulder line. The pants have a fuller fit, and break over the top of the shoe. This style is a contradiction to the more structured Italian look and entered the fashion mainstream during the late 1980s.

Sports coats—jackets meant to be worn with contrasting pants—are styled in all silhouettes. Accessory pieces like vests and pants complement the styling and fabric of suits and are influenced by fashion trends.

European fitted suit

Classic double-breasted jacket

Side vents

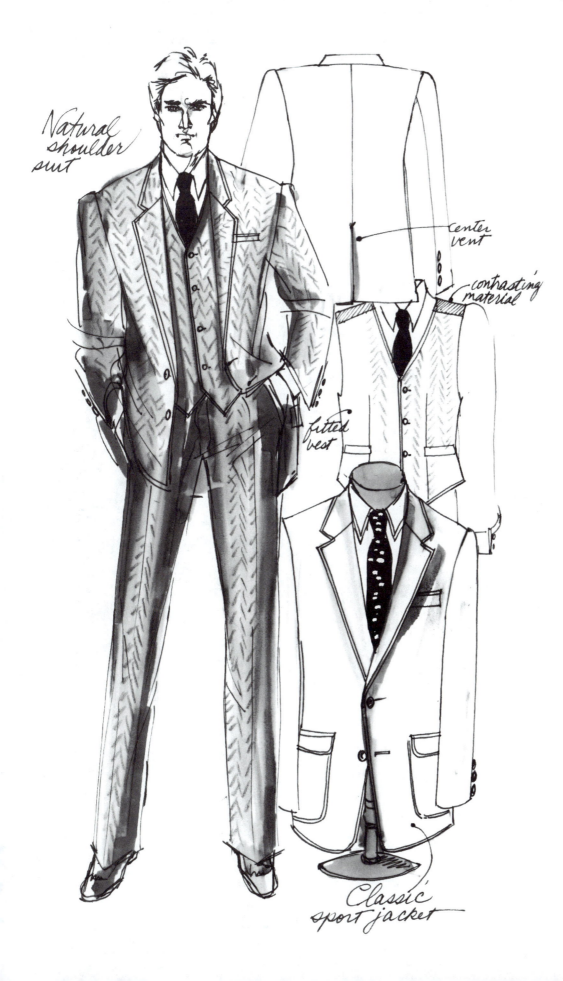

Natural
shoulder
suit

center
vent

contrasting
material

fitted
vest

Classic
sport jacket

DRAWING CASUAL MENSWEAR

Casual apparel is often derived from active sportswear. Styling is influenced by ski wear, western apparel, hunting and fishing gear, swim and surf wear, and tennis apparel. Pieces of active sportswear are often incorporated into spectator day wear.

These styles can be illustrated on vigorous, active men of all ages. Sports props that relate to the specific apparel effectively set the stage for casual wear.

Safari shirt

Bomber or Eisenhower jacket

Walking shorts

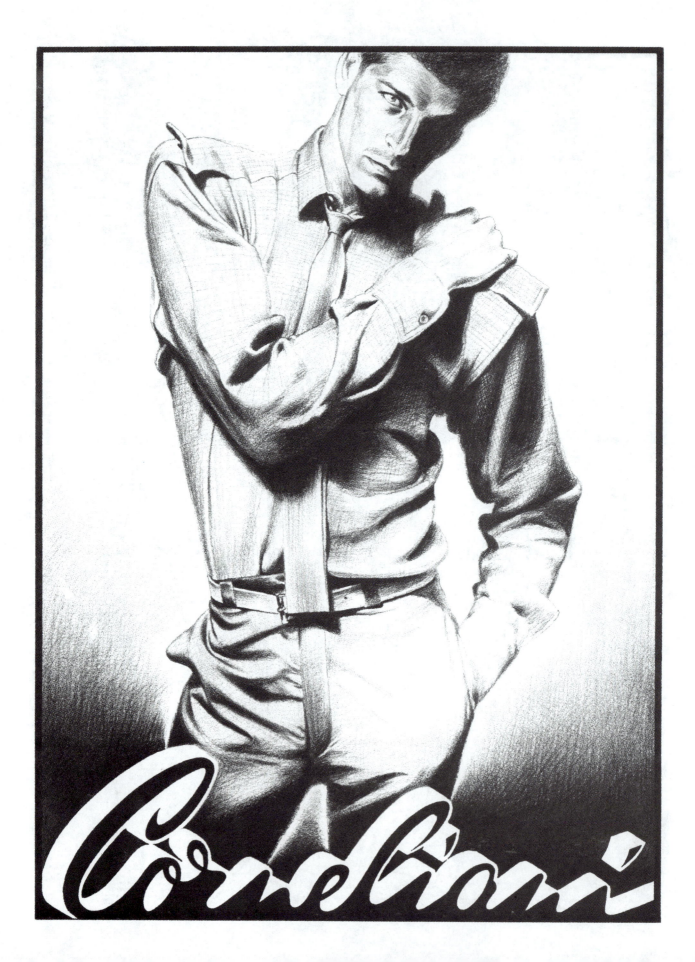

SOURCES OF MENSWEAR INSPIRATION

Menswear is featured in a number of trade, foreign, and consumer publications. Fairchild, publisher of *Women's Wear Daily,* also prints the *Daily News Record (DNR),* which covers menswear. This is a very influential trade journal. Fairchild also publishes *M,* a slick magazine for consumers that reports on style trends and personalities who influence men's dressing. Menswear merchandising is also covered by *Retail Week,* a monthly trade magazine widely read by manufacturers and retailers.

Fashion reports such as *Promostil,* the *Report West Photo Box, The Fashion Service,* and *Pat Tuskey's FOCUS* review European RTW for American designers and retailers. Domestic menswear consumer publications are led by *Gentlemen's Quarterly (GQ),* which offers superior fashion coverage of domestic and foreign menswear and is published monthly. Men's periodicals that often have fashion articles include *Esquire* and *Playboy. Sports Illustrated* covers general sports. Specialized sports, such as surfing, horsemanship (*Equis, Western Horseman, Horse and Rider*), and skiing (*Skiing*) have specialized publications featuring specific apparel for the respective sport.

Menswear catalogs from prestigious menswear stores such as Brooks Brothers, Cable Car Clothiers, Barney's and from fashion-oriented department stores are also important style arbiters. Many sports-oriented catalogs, such as L.L. Bean and Land's End, carry active and spectator sportswear for men.

Casual shirts worn with structured jackets are the "Friday wear" alternative to dressing in a formal suit daily. (Courtesy of Robert Passantino.)

High contrast emphasizes the dramatic, masculine character of this illustration. (Courtesy of Paul Lowe.)

Foreign publications of importance include:

- *Arbiter.* An Italian publication featuring men's suits and formal wear.

- *L'Homme Vogue.* The French fashion magazine covering high-fashion men's wear.

- *L'Uomo Vogue.* Ten issues a year cover general men's fashions in the Italian edition of *Vogue's* specialty publication. Each country has unique issues.

- *Uomo.* Published quarterly by Linia Italia, this glossy features fashion menswear and accessories.

Some foreign consumer magazines focus on a particular sport and contain spot editorials on appropriate clothing for that sport. These include:

- *Uomo Mare.* Published every two months in Italy, this glossy features men's nautical apparel.

- *Linia Italia Sport.* Focuses on sports apparel of all kinds and is published three times per year.

The illustrators and photographers found in these foreign and domestic publications offer the fashion artist a wealth of ideas for illustrating menswear. Painters and illustrators who specilize in sports illustrations for posters often have a style that is easily adapted to fashion. Le Roy Neiman's bold illustrations have influenced menswear fashion illustrations greatly.

A bold, vigorous line quality gives an illustration a masculine tone. The settings should be appropriate to the style and formality of the apparel. Experimentation and observation are the key to developing a definitive menswear illustration style.

Exaggerated proportions dramatize the bulky silhouette of these casual suits. (Courtesy of FOCUS Menswear, *published by Pat Tunsky Inc.)*

C H A P T E R   11

Drawing Children

Children's body proportions differ radically from adult proportions. The toddler's head is about one-fourth of the total body length. As the child grows, the head becomes smaller in proportion to the lengthening body. A young child has a curved spine that is so weak it throws the tummy forward. Limbs are plump, and bone structure is covered with baby fat. The child evolves a mature figure in slow stages.

A toddler (ages 1 to 3) has small features with soft, undefined facial bone structure in the rather large head. The features occupy the lower third of the face. As the child grows and baby fat disappears, the features slowly sharpen and become more defined. When you draw a child's face, you should strive for a natural look. Hairstyles should be simple and uncontrived. Bangs are worn by both boys and girls because the hair tends to grow forward.

Children move differently than adults. Their poses are active and less formal. Children's poses do not follow the same rules of movement and balance line as those of adults.

Each age has inherent figure problems that require special design solutions. Style details such as collars, cuffs, plackets, and trims should be smaller to complement the child's size. Clothing proportions are usually uneven to emphasize height and to create a slender line.

Bringing up baby

Courtesy of Catherine Clayton Purnell.

TODDLER PROPORTIONS

1-YEAR OLDS

The 1-year-old has a body length of four heads. Boys and girls are similar at this age, and fashions are often unisex. Most children do not walk until they are 16 to 18 months old, so at 1 year the baby is usually drawn lying down, sitting, or crawling.

Study the proportion sketch. Notice that the neck is not developed, and the head seems to sit on the shoulders. The shoulders are rounded and have almost no width. The spine is weak and cannot hold the back erect, throwing the tummy forward and

making it a prominent feature of any pose. The buttocks are lower than the crotch.

Dressed, the 1-year-old is well padded with diapers. Shoes are not usually worn, and the feet have a relaxed curve. The foot will flatten out and begin to develop an arch as the child learns to walk.

To establish the baby's proportion in your mind, practice drawing the basic figure in all the views shown here. To increase your mastery, sketch from photographs and life.

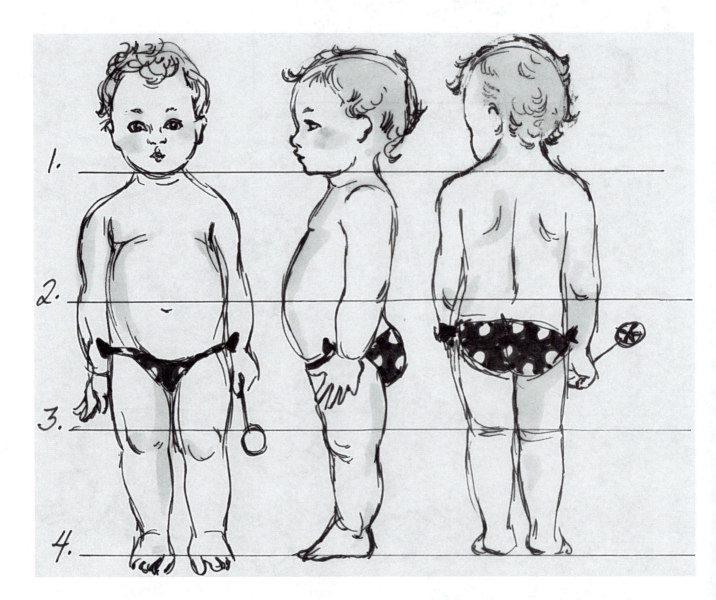

2- TO 3-YEAR-OLDS

A dramatic difference occurs between the ages of 1 and 2. The child begins to walk, which makes the legs stronger and more defined. The typical 2-year-old has a body length of four-and-one-half heads. Most of the length is added in the legs, but the torso is still very long in comparison. Boys and girls have the same body proportions and figures at 2 years of age, but hair and clothing styles are more clearly masculine or feminine. The neck is stronger and now appears to support the head. The shoulders are still narrow. The tummy protrudes because of the natural curve of the spine. Diapers are often worn until 2½ years, so the bottom of the young toddler still has a padded look.

Sketch the proportion drawings several times, then draw both boys and girls from life or photographs.

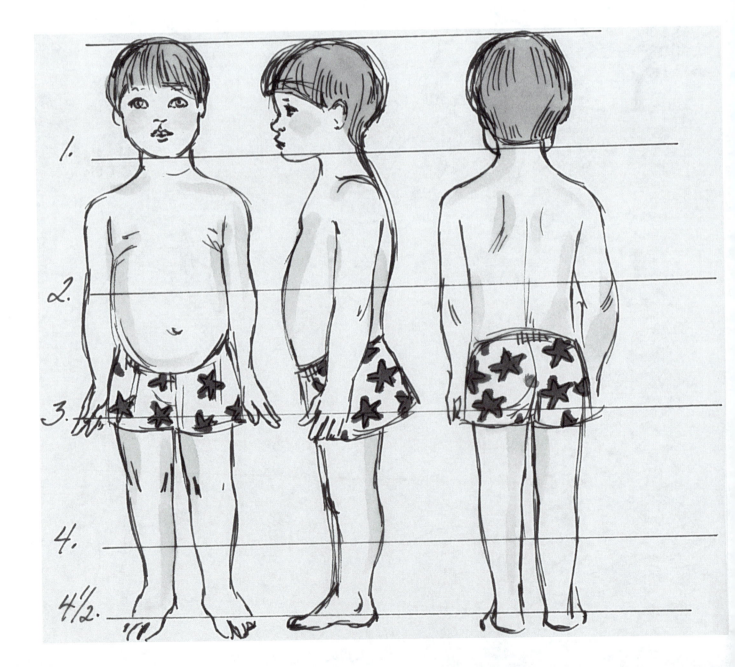

The balance line drops from the base of the neck to the heel of the foot bearing the body weight.

If the feet are equally extended, the balance line drops in the center.

When drawing very young children in action, use the same axial line to keep the figure from tipping off balance that you used when drawing adult figures in action. Block in the proportion and action lines. Draw the body silhouette and then the details. For realistic poses, draw from life.

THE TODDLER'S FACE

The toddler's head is about half the size of the adult head, but most of the size is concentrated in the skull above the forehead. The features are positioned in the lower third of the head. The face does not have a well-developed bone structure and is fleshed out with baby fat. The nose has a soft, rounded shape because the bridge has not developed. The nostrils are small.

A toddler's eyes are often quite large. Place them at equal distances from the median line, with about one-and-one-half eye lengths between. The eyebrows are very light. Because the child is so small, the eyes are often looking up. They should have a wide-eyed, innocent look. The upper eyelid almost disappears when the eyes are wide open.

The lips are soft and small. Because few teeth develop until the second year, the mouth seems narrow. The jaw is undefined and the chin small. The ears are positioned below the level of the eyes and are small and delicate.

Sketch several faces from life or photographs and compare them to the facial proportions shown here. Draw the features and hair with a light line and soft tones, or your drawing will look too heavy and mature. Hairstyles should be soft, natural, and rather short for this age.

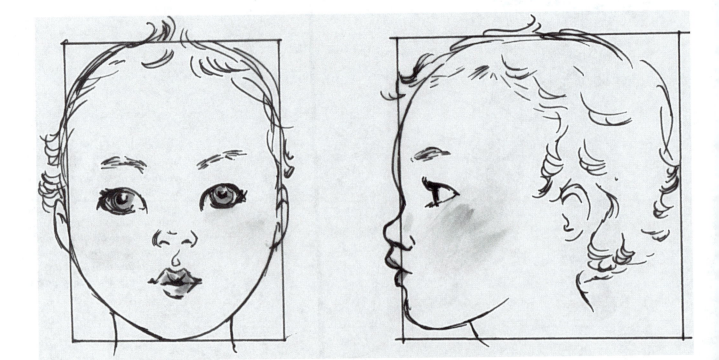

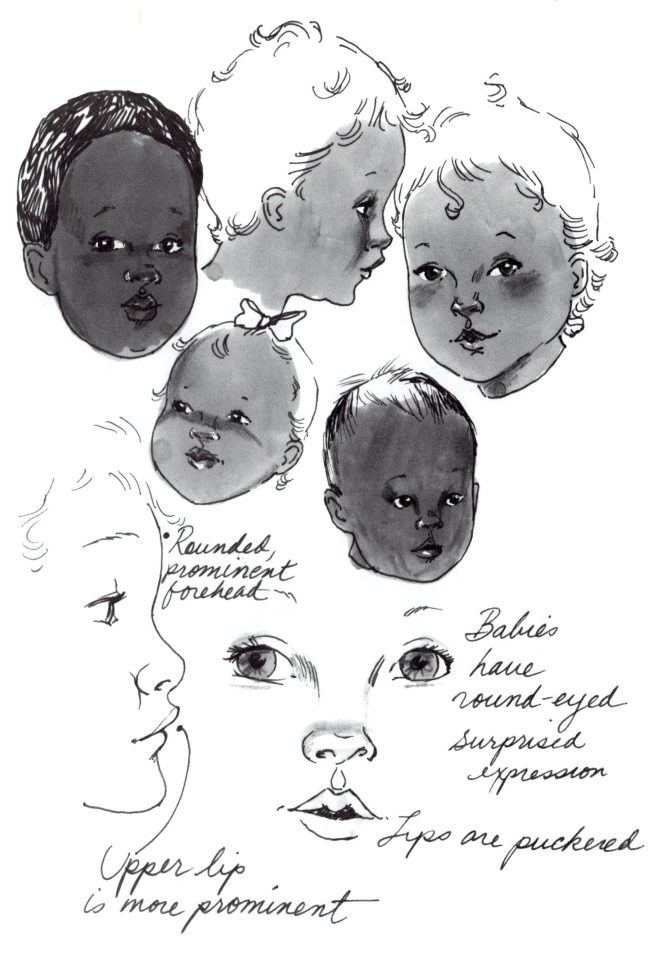

Rounded, prominent forehead

Babies have round-eyed surprised expression

Lips are puckered

Upper lip is more prominent

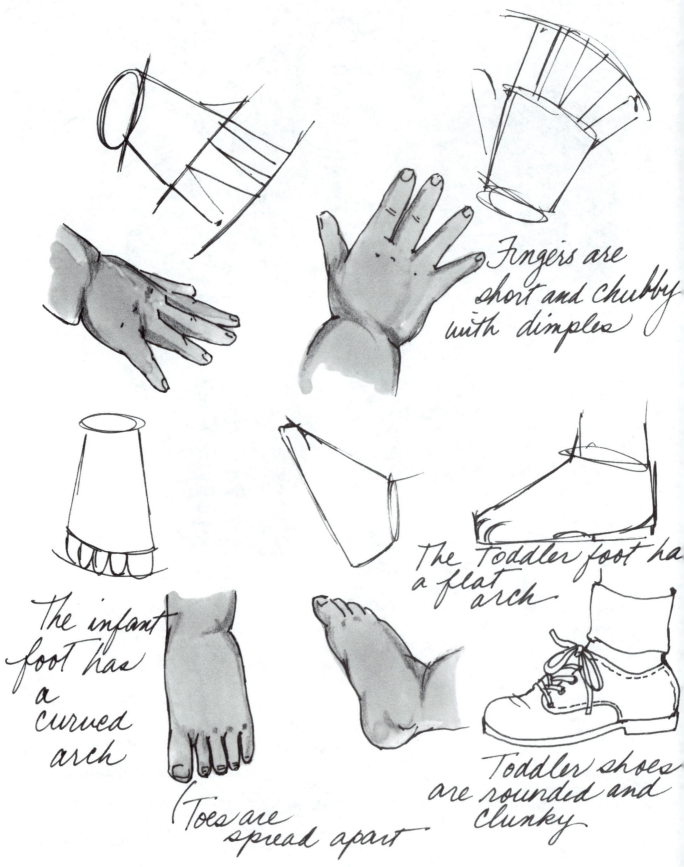

Fingers are short and chubby with dimples

The Toddler foot has a flat arch

The infant foot has a curved arch

Toes are spread apart

Toddler shoes are rounded and clunky

Young children's hands and feet are plump and have a soft silhouette. Practice drawing from these step-by-step sketches.

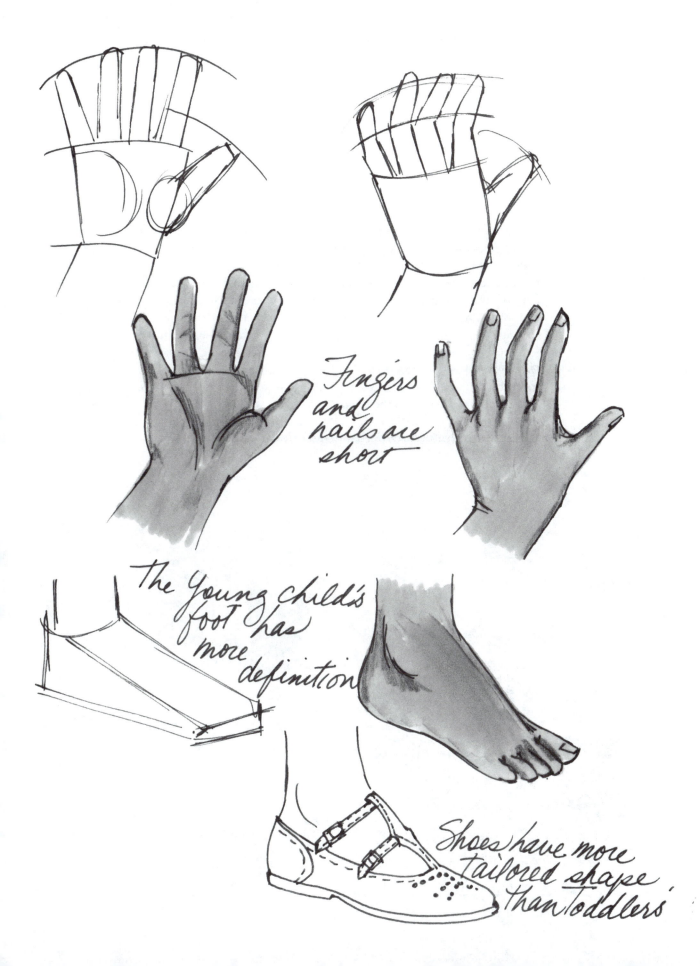

Fingers and nails are short

The Young child's foot has more definition

Shoes have more tailored shape than toddlers'

THE YOUNG CHILD

Children grow rapidly between the ages of 4 and 8. Proportions differ greatly because the torso remains about the same length but the legs grow longer. The body begins to have more definition as the spine strengthens and the stomach is reduced.

Study the comparative proportions of this age group. Boys and girls have very similar figures at this age. The fashion ideal for a child is a slender, active body. Fashion children should have a sleek, well-fed look, but they should not be plump. The waistline has not developed. Dresses often have a high, empire waistline. The uneven proportion makes the girl's figure seem taller and slimmer.

Draw several proportion sketches from the diagrams for each age group. When you have mastered the chang-

ing proportions, begin to sketch quick action sketches from life. For live models, go to a playground or a park where children are playing. Try to capture the personality and movements that are characteristic of each group. Combine the control and accuracy of the proportion exercises with the spontaneity and personality of the action sketches for convincing children's drawings.

Sketch children in a situation or activity. Use simple props such as balls, toys, or sporting equipment. Humor is especially effective when drawing children. Children's books are often illustrated with charming figures and can give a fashion illustrator many ideas for sketching juvenile fashion figures. (Many children's book illustrators are also professional fashion illustrators.)

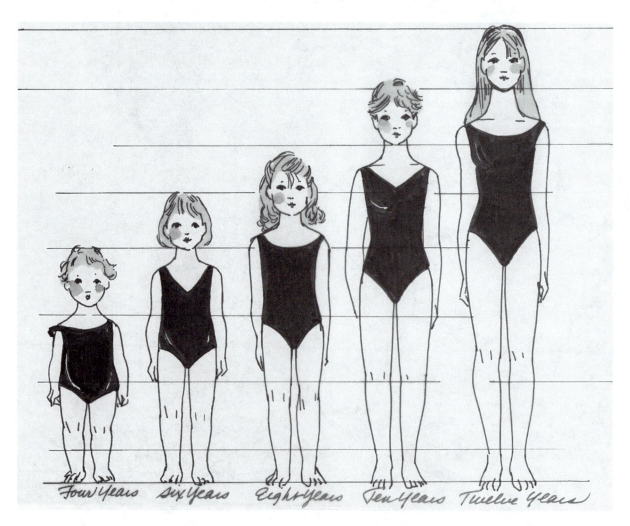

Four Years   Six Years   Eight Years   Ten Years   Twelve Years

Boys and
Girls have
similar
figures and
Proportions
at a Young
age.

THE 4-YEAR-OLD

THE 8-YEAR-OLD

6 years

8 years

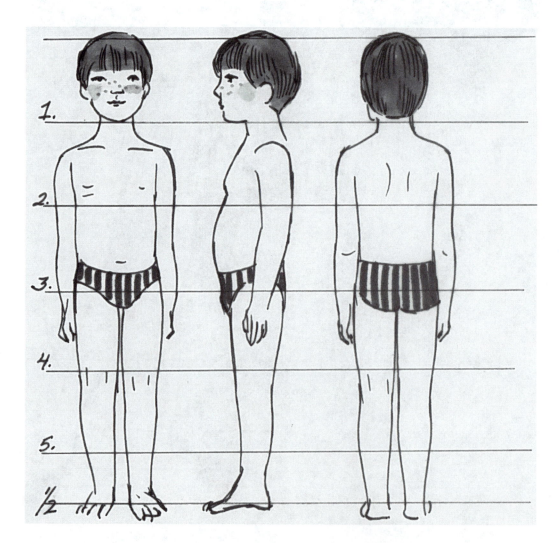

8-YEAR-OLD GIRL

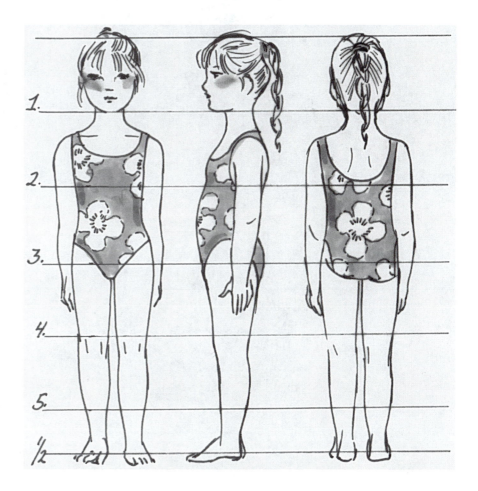

THE YOUNG CHILD'S FACE

The head becomes narrower as the child grows. The features are now concentrated in the lower half of the face. The features have a softer, more natural look than an adult's. Notice that the young child's eyes are smaller in proportion to the face than the toddler's and now have about one eye space between them. The bridge of the nose is more defined, yet the tip still has a rounded, innocent, "pug nose" look. The lips and cheeks are full. The mouth is wider than the toddler's because the teeth are fully developed and the jaw has more definition. A child's expression is often shy or innocent.

Hairstyles should be simple and natural. Curls, braids, and bangs are typical for this age group. Ribbons or hair clips pull the hair off the face.

The proportion and drawing rules for the three-quarter profile follow the same rules given for the adult face. Study photographs and draw from life to develop your skills in drawing the child's face. Keep the lines fine and the shadows light so the face looks young.

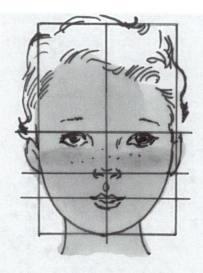
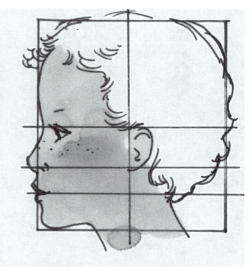

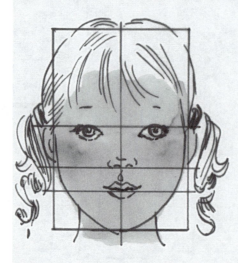
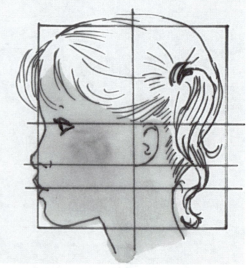

Active, casual clothes featuring groups of teens are a popular way to advertise sportswear.

THE YOUNG TEENAGER

The body proportion is now seven heads long, and the young teenager has developed a specific masculine or feminine body.

GIRLS

Girls have a definite waistline and small bust. Their shoulders have more width, and the leg muscles are more shapely and defined than a child's. The torso is still more than half of the overall length of the body. Hairstyles are definitely feminine, and you should emphasize casual, clean-cut, natural styling when you draw.

Poses can be more formal, with less emphasis on the activities and sponta-neous situations that are appropriate for the younger child or boys of the same age.

Practice sketching the figure. Use a light pencil line and draw from the proportion diagrams. Sketch garments on your lightly drawn figures. Notice how garments ride over the tummy, often emphasizing empire or dropped-torso styles. The uneven proportion makes the figure appear longer.

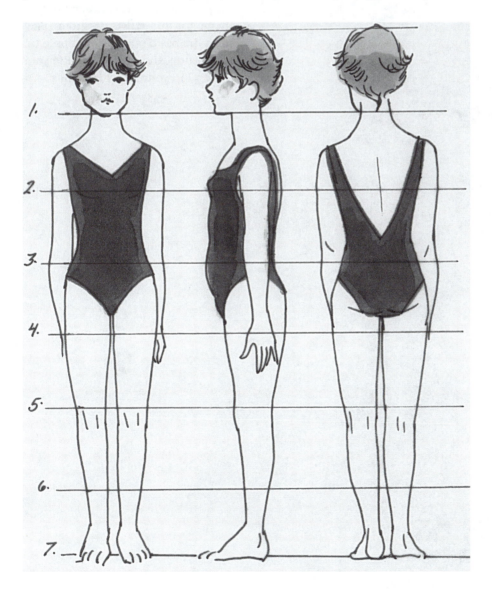

BOYS

Young teenage boys are beginning to develop a masculine silhouette. Their shoulders broaden, and the torso becomes slender. Hands and feet grow and seem large in proportion to body size. Knee and elbow joints also seem too large. Muscles are more developed and give arms and legs a sharper, more defined shape. The crotch is lower for teenage boys than for girls of the same age. As the torso becomes straighter and more slender, the waistline is lowered. Boys tend to wear pants low on their hips. Simple, natural hairstyles are most effective. Features are sharper. The nose is quite well developed, and the mouth is firmer.

Emphasize action sketches and use a simple prop to carry through the theme for this active age group. Sketch from the basic poses to reinforce the proportion, then do several life studies to develop your sketching skills.

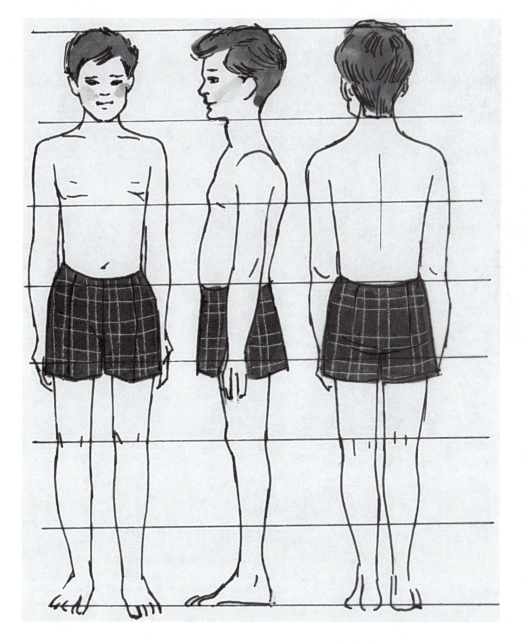

The movements of the body are controlled by the rules of axial-line balance. The axial line falls between the legs when the model's weight is placed equally on both legs. Children's poses should be casual and natural.

THE OLDER TEENAGER

The older teenager has almost adult proportions. Using eight head lengths works well for both boys and girls. Muscle and bone structure is not as developed as an adult's, so the body's curves are smoother and less defined. Girls do not have the extreme emphasis on bone structure that adult models have. The teenage girl has a small, high bust line and slim hips. Her crotch length is almost half the overall body length, but the legs will grow at least half a head longer for adult proportions. The shoulders are narrower, and the length of the neck is not as exaggerated as an adult's.

Teenage boys are beginning to develop the upper torso to adult proportions. The fashion ideal is slender and lithe. The torso proportion is longer for men than for women. More growth occurs in the legs to reach adult proportions.

Facial structure is the same as an adult's, but the features and contours of the face are softer and rounder. A certain wide-eyed innocence and good humor should animate the teenage face as a reminder of childhood expressions.

The Adolescent Attitude.....

STYLIZING OR "CARTOONING" CHILDREN'S ILLUSTRATIONS

Illustrating children's fashions on cartoon figures is an effective design technique. The proportions and action of the figure should be realistic or slightly exaggerated. The features and clothing details can be stylized to give a whimsical, humorous look to the sketch.

Children's book illustrations offer a wealth of ideas for stylization and cartooning the juvenile fashion figure. Look for the illustrations of Hillary Knight (the Eloise series), Maurice Sendak, Gyo, Carl Larsson, and Steven Kellog, among many others, for ideas and inspiration for illustrating children.

Period illustrations of children can also offer illustrators rich insights into styling a drawing. Notice how contemporary many of the styles in these drawings from a 1913 *Harper's Bazaar* are. The artists are Tony Nebb and Grayce Drayton.

Courtesy of Harper's Bazaar.

Using an animal's face on a child's body gives the illustration a whimsical quality.

CHAPTER 12

Drawing Accessories

Accessories are apparel items that are not classified as garments. These include jewelry, hosiery, shoes, handbags, belts, hats, and fabric accessories such as scarves and shawls. Drawing accessories requires accurate rendering of details, a knowledge of simple perspective, and a creative approach to layout and presentation. Accessories must first be drawn by a designer so they can be produced. Handbag buyers often sketch the items they buy so they can be identified when they arrive at the store. Accessories are an important fashion category that is often advertised, and the drawing is usually done by a specialized illustrator, particularly when the accessories are not shown on a figure. More general fashion illustrators often draw accessories on the figure.

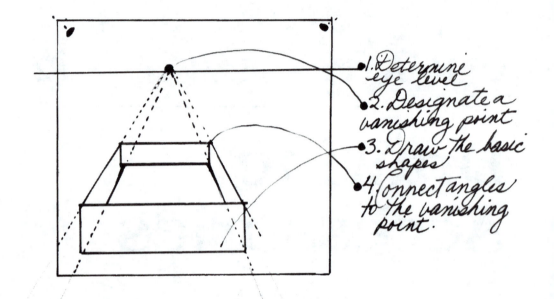

1. Determine eye level

2. Designate a vanishing point

3. Draw the basic shapes

4. Connect angles to the vanishing point.

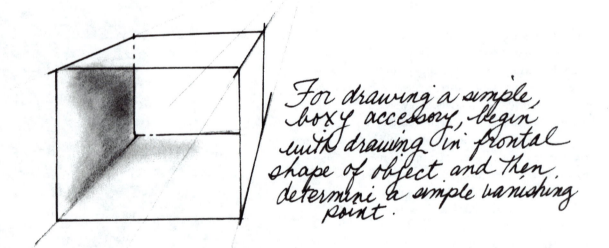

For drawing a simple, boxy accessory, begin with drawing in frontal shape of object and then determine a simple vanishing point.

APPLYING PERSPECTIVE TO FASHION ACCESSORIES

To achieve accuracy of detail and silhouette, you will usually need to make a preliminary drawing. Follow these steps to develop your drawing accuracy:

1. Arrange the object so that you are viewing it from the most advantageous angle. Determine the eye level line and establish your vanishing points. First draw the frontal plane (the area of the object that is closest to you). Use your ruler and the vanishing points to project the sides of the frontal plane into the third dimension.

2. When the silhouette of the object is drawn to your satisfaction, add the details.

3. Study the effects that can be achieved by lightening the composition in various ways. Use a small, intense light to change the setting until the lighting pleases you.

4. Tone the various planes with lead pencils to explore the various surface planes of the object. Practice shading until you can create a smooth, even tone of varying intensities. Notice how different tones add dimension to the object. Let the paper be the lightest value, and shade down from there. You may also highlight your finished rendering with an opaque white paint. The tonal differences will describe the shapes inside the object without a heavy outline around the various planes of the object.

5. Use the pencil-carbon transfer method to draw the accessory on illustration board. Use your tonal sketch as a guide when applying washes. Detail the finished drawing in ink, felt pen, or Prismacolor pencil. Try to keep a fresh, sparkling quality to your finished drawing.

As you become more experienced, you can gradually eliminate step 4 and render the finished drawing from the object.

Lay in basic shapes on vellum

Transfer to illustration board, Lay in type and details

Refine and tone sketch — Paste up copy Detail stitching and hardware

FALL SALE OF HANDBAGS

SETUPS WITH COMPLICATED PERSPECTIVE

Multiple objects in a setting require careful planning before you begin to draw. Arrange the objects until they relate to each other in a logical way. (Review pages 228–229 for layout suggestions on arranging multiple objects.) Try to establish a theme so the accessories tell a story suggested by a setting or figure in the drawing.

Experiment with the lighting so the objects are highlighted and accented appropriately. Many artists use a Polaroid camera to capture a setup so it is not lost before the drawing is complete. The photograph will also validate the setup from various perspective angles so the artist can select the most pleasing one. When you are satisfied with the arrangement and lighting of the objects, begin the preliminary drawing. For more complex drawings, refer to more complete guides to perspective, such as *Perspective Drawing* by Earnest Norling (Tustin: Walter T. Foster, 1985).

You may use a vanishing point off your paper

1. Draw the rectangle of the foreground to establish the angle of placement on your page

2. Draw vanishing point again to establish the top of the item

Draw lines connecting the right angles to the vanishing point

Luggage and handbags are usually drawn from an angle to give a view of the inside or outer edge of item

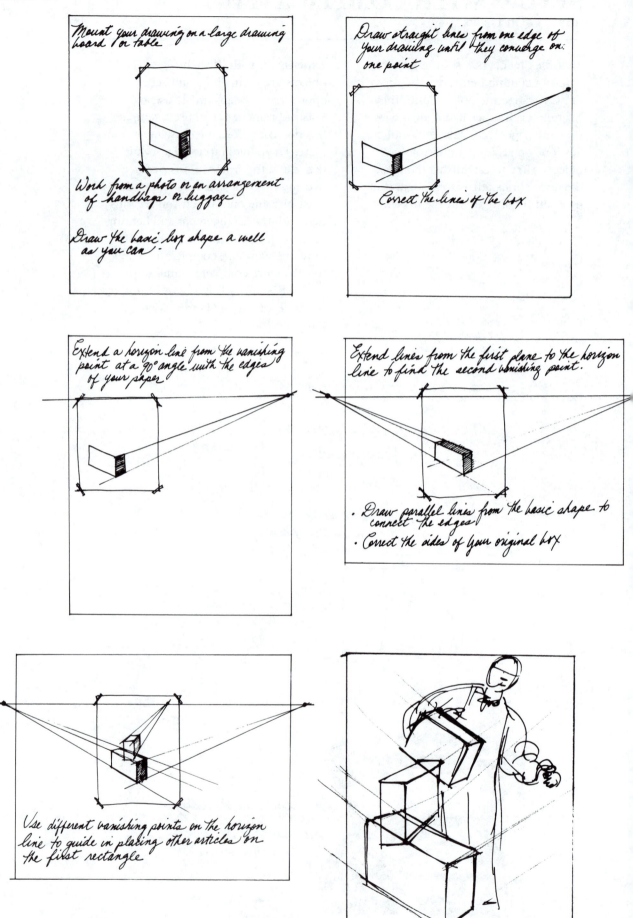

Mount your drawing on a large drawing board or table

Work from a photo or an arrangement of handbags or luggage

Draw the basic box shape a well as you can.

Draw straight lines from one edge of your drawing until they converge on one point

Correct the lines of the box

Extend a horizon line from the vanishing point at a 90° angle with the edges of your paper

Extend lines from the first plane to the horizon line to find the second vanishing point.

• Draw parallel lines from the basic shape to connect the edges
• Correct the sides of your original box

Use different vanishing points on the horizon line to guide in placing other articles on the first rectangle

RENDERING ACCESSORY MATERIALS
Study the pattern of an object and experiment
with wash, pen, and pencil shadowing
techniques to capture the surface of the
material. Detail with a definitive outline and
appropriate highlights.

The linear technique of rendering these
handbags and integrating them into the
foreground gives the illustration visual unity.

1. Divide tufted areas with pencil
2. Lay in wash or light tone marker
3. Shadow with pencil and darker tone marker
4. Add stitching
5. Highlight with white paint or pencil

Tufted leather

Lizard

Polished leather

Woven leather

Suede

SHOES

Illustrating shoes professionally is an exacting, specialized skill. Shoes must look new without looking stiff. Subtle exaggeration on the style lines and cuts are used to enhance the illustration. The heel height establishes the curve of the arch. The sole line should be a straight continuous line, beginning at the toe and gracefully curving into the arch and the back of the heel. The heel is aligned at an angle of 90 degrees with the floor line, though it may be styled to curve into the arch at different angles. Shoes may be illustrated off or on feet.

Study the step-by-step diagram. Draw the foot several times until you have mastered a profile shoe. Select several of your shoes and practice drawing them in different positions. Draw them as if they were new. Review Chapter 6 for help in illustrating shoe leathers correctly.

Begin with a curved line from a right angle.

Draw the shape of the foot in the shoe. Make heel of shoe directly under heel of foot.

Remember to always have the heel and toe lines on the ground!

NO!

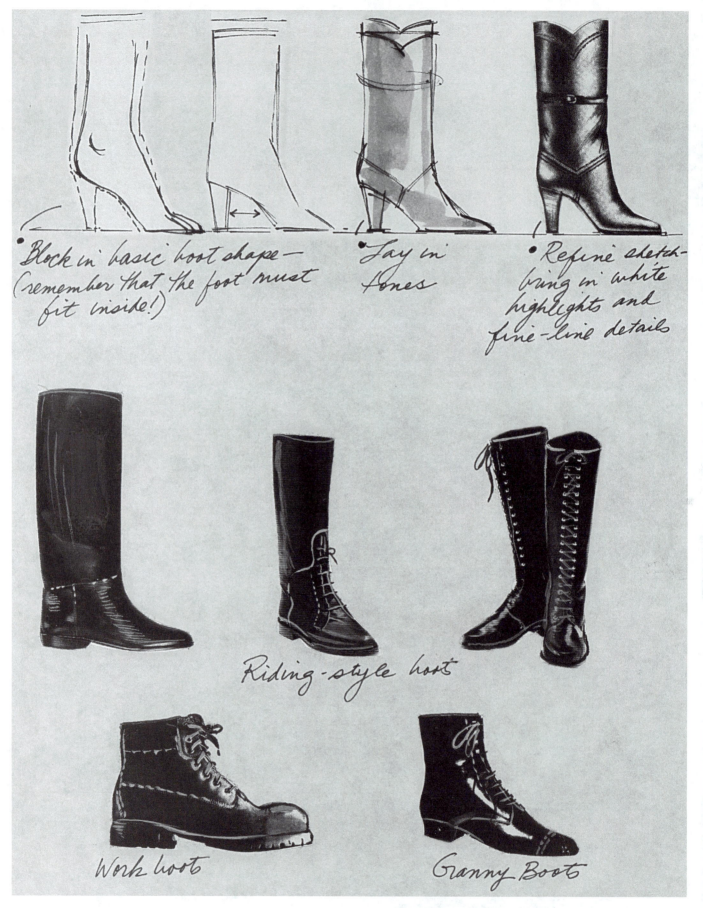

• "Block in" basic boot shape— (remember that the foot must fit inside!)

• Lay in tones

• Refine sketch— bring in white highlights and fine-line details

Riding-style boot

Work boot

Granny Boots

Boots have the same balance as shoes. The heel height determines the contour of the sole line. The top of the boot may have many style variations and details.

SWEATER DRESSING
Eighties n' Easy

Leg Show at
bloomingdale's
1000 THIRD AVENUE, NEW YORK (355-5900). OPEN LATE MONDAY AND THURSDAY EVENINGS.

Legs go to all lengths to be layered.

Something immeasurably wonderful has happened to fall. Skirts are shorter, heels flatter, legs longer—it's a whole new proportion calling for a whole new interaction of interest. Holding the focus in on legs: textures and tiers, colors and crunch. Find it in our consummate collection of tights, leg-warmers, knee-highs and anklets. And although each shape stands on its own, the true fun of it, the real warmth of it, is not achieved until you start layering it on. All in new autumn shadings.

A. Rib tights in Orlon® acrylic/nylon by Hot Sox, S-M-L, 7.00.
B. Leg warmers in Shetland wool/nylon by Hot Sox, 14.00.
C. Anklet in a cashmere-y Orlon® acrylic/nylon by N.Y. Sock Exchange, 2.50.
D. Argyle knee highs in Shetland wool/nylon by Hot Sox, 8.00.
E. Silky tights in Enkalure® nylon, by Hot Sox, A-B, 7.00.
F. Sweater-weight knee-highs in lambswool/nylon by Royce, 5.50.
G. Crochet tights in cotton/nylon by N.Y. Sock Exchange (our own private label), S-M-L, 9.00.

On B'way, New York. Also available at all our fashion stores.

B'way: it's like no other floor in the world.

This illustration by Antonio utilizes a complicated layout, enhanced by line and shadows, to create movement. (Courtesy of Bloomingdale's, illustration by Antonio, art direction by John C. Jay.)

BELTS

Belts are made in a wide variety of styles and materials. They range from neat, functional sport belts to exaggerated cummerbunds and dramatic ties. Belts are most often illustrated on a figure because they are more effective when shown with a garment.

The rules of one-point perspective govern the circular ellipse silhouette of a belt when shown alone. The buckle should be slightly wider than the belt. Tie belts are an inexpensive and popular accessory. Draw a bow or tie with softly curving ties and a full bow so it looks new and fresh. When a belt is used on a loose garment, it creates a soft puff of fabric above and below as it shapes the garment to the body.

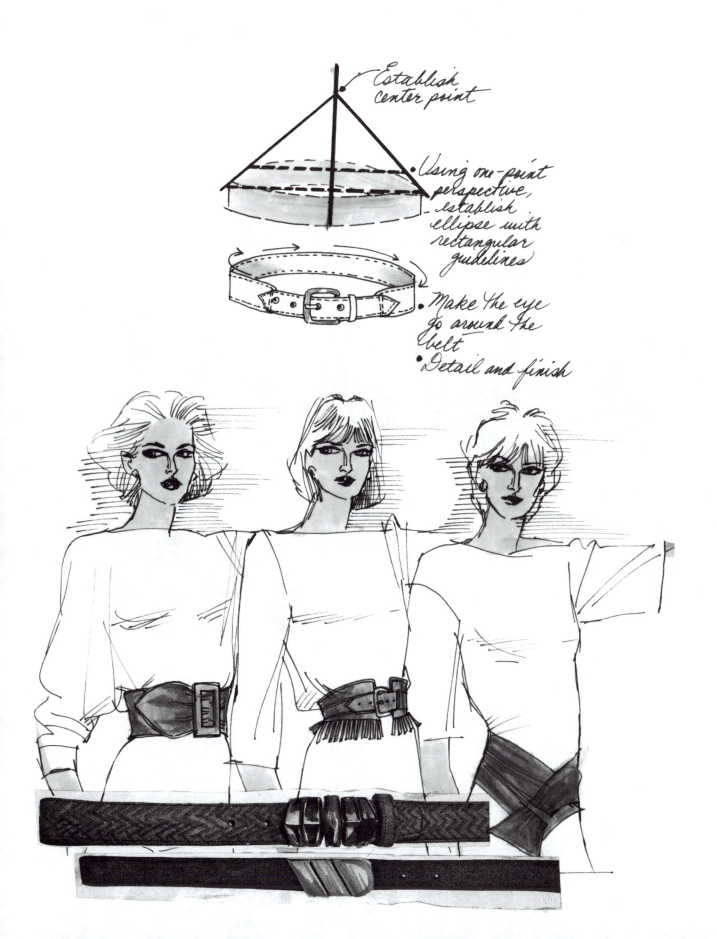

Establish
center point

Using one-point
perspective,
establish
ellipse with
rectangular
guidelines

Make the eye
go around the
belt
Detail and finish

JEWELRY

Rendering jewelry requires precise drawing with accurate details. Study the smooth reflective surfaces of the metal before rendering the piece of jewelry. Notice how the shadows and mid-tones define the planes and details of the design. Control the light source so the highlights are focused in one area of the jewelry, and contrast those with mid- and dark tones. Use opaque gouache or china white paint to accent the highlights.

When you draw diamonds or other faceted precious stones, the sparkle is the most important element. The cut of the stone dictates the shape. Notice how the setting is attached to the stone and accurately render it.

Start a clipping file of examples of jewelry illustration and photography from which to work.

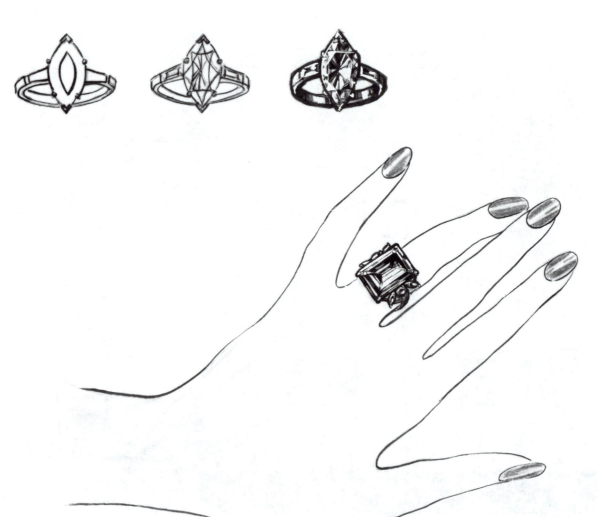

Courtesy of Maria Dawidowicz Shafer.

• Base of fingers
• Knuckle line

Block in hand
within a
Mitten shape.

Block in
tone,
style and
detail
stitching

GLOVES

Gloves are made in leather or fabric and are worn with a great variety of outfits. At one time, every well-dressed woman completed her outfit with sparkling white gloves during the summer and color coordinated leather gloves for fall and winter. Today the functional requirements of sports or cold weather rather than fashion demands dictate the use of gloves.

Gloves follow the contour of the hand and fingers and are shaped with seams that add to the distinctive style of the glove. Elastic insets or crocheted pieces may be added to the fabric or leather to increase the flexibility of the glove.

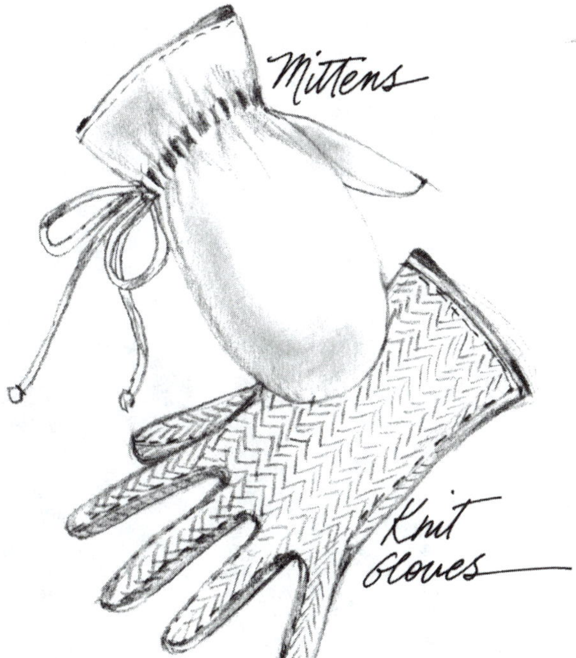

Mittens

Knit Gloves

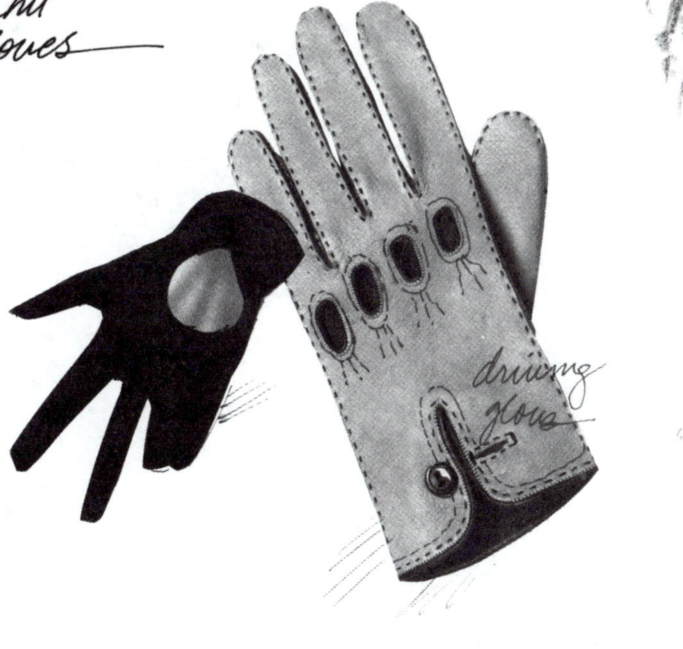

driving glove

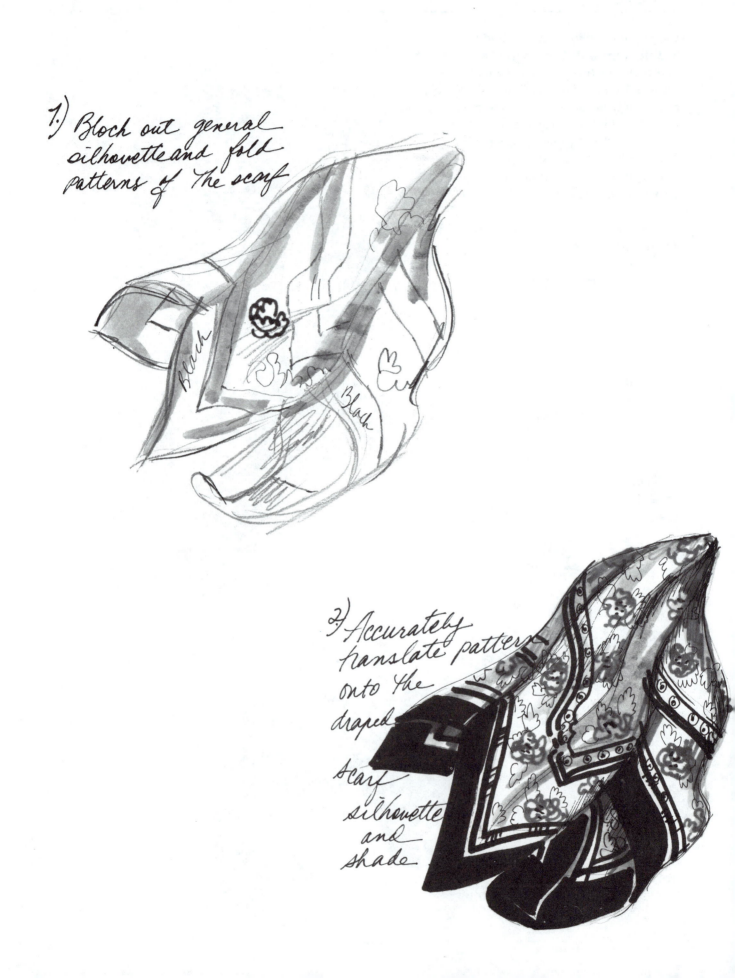

1.) Block out general silhouette and fold patterns of the scarf

Black

Black

2.) Accurately translate pattern onto the draped scarf silhouette and shade

FABRIC ACCESSORIES

Fabric accessories include scarves, shawls, separate collars, and ruffles. They may be illustrated alone or on a figure with other garments. Scarves are often illustrated as floats because the graphics are dramatic.

Before you begin to sketch, drape the scarf without too many folds so the pattern is clearly visible. Focus your light source so the folds are accented. Draw the silhouette and undulations of the fabric. Keep the contours crisp and fresh. Block in the pattern details. Draw the pattern realistically as it is interrupted by the folds of the fabric. Render the floating scarf in halftones and line.

Fabric accessories are effectively illustrated in combination with other garments and add fashion vitality to basic garments. Focus on the accessory in an illustration by cutting down the frame of the picture as if you were cropping a photograph. Make sure the accompanying garment is an appropriate backdrop that enhances the accessory.

Block in the basic shape of head and features. Draw the curve of the hat band, making sure the hat sits firmly on the head.

Block in the crown and brim

Finish and detail sketch

Block in profile and establish the curve of the hat band

Block in the silhouette of the crown and brim

Finish and detail sketch

HATS

Hats are usually professionally drawn by a fashion illustrator because the hat must be worn by an appropriately rendered head. Hats are made in a wide variety of shapes and fabrics and are functional as well as decorative.

Begin your drawing by establishing the band line of the hat as it encircles the head. Be sure to correctly judge the angle or tilt of the hat and how far down it is fitted on the head. Draw the shape and height of the crown. The brim line also encircles the head, but it may have a different contour from the band.

Hats may be shaped and trimmed with many different kinds of accessories. Render these in your final illustration.

Hats are worn as occasional accessories. They should relate to the outfit they are shown with. Style the hair in a simple, complementary way so it does not detract from the shape and style of the hat.

To become familiar with the way a hat enfolds the head, draw the diagrammatic exercises several times. Then begin to draw from life and photographs until you have mastered many hat styles.

Beret

Boater

Cowboy   Fedora   Turban

Index